CMMI^{SM} Distilled

CMMI^{SM} Distilled

A Practical Introduction to Integrated Process Improvement

Dennis M. Ahern
Aaron Clouse
Richard Turner

ADDISON-WESLEY

Boston • San Francisco • New York • Toronto • Montreal
London • Munich • Paris • Madrid
Capetown • Sydney • Tokyo • Singapore • Mexico City

Carnegie Mellon
Software Engineering Institute

The SEI Series in Software Engineering

The publisher offers discounts on this book when ordered in quantity for special sales. For more information, please contact:

Pearson Education Corporate Sales Division
One Lake Street
Upper Saddle River, NJ 07458
(800) 382-3419
corpsales@pearsontechgroup.com

Visit AW on the Web: www.awl.com/cseng/

Library of Congress Cataloging-in-Publication Data

Ahern, Dennis.
    CMMI distilled : a practical introduction to the integrated process improvement /
Dennis Ahern, Aaron Clouse, Richard Turner.
        p. cm. — (The SEI series in software engineering)
    Includes bibliographical references and index.
    ISBN 0-201-73500-8 (alk. paper)
    1. Capability maturity model (Computer software)   I. Clouse, Aaron.   II. Turner,
Richard.   III. Title.   IV. Series.

QA76.758.A397 2001
005.1'068'5—dc21   2001022699

ISBN 0-201-73500-8
Text printed on recycled paper
1 2 3 4 5 6 7 8 9 10—CRS—0504030201
First printing, June 2001

SEI figure list appears on page 286.

Contents

Figure List

Preface

This book is about a new way of approaching process improvement for engineering development. Process improvement is a generally well-understood and accepted means of achieving quality and productivity gains for software development, and the recognition of its importance for other engineering disciplines is growing. The success and wide adoption of the Capability Maturity Model (CMM) for Software have inspired increased development of similar models in disciplines other than software. The resulting proliferation of models in engineering organizations has led to conflicts in process improvement goals and techniques, considerable increases in required training, and confusion on the part of practitioners as to which of the various models applies to their specific needs.

The Capability Maturity Model Integration (CMMI) project, an ongoing effort by industry, the U.S. government, and the Software Engineering Institute (SEI) of Carnegie Mellon University, is attempting to address this situation. Started in 1998, CMMI is an effort to codify the tenets of model-based process improvement and provide a single, integrated framework for improving engineering processes in organizations that span several disciplines. By integrating the tools and techniques used to improve individual engineering disciplines, both the quality and the efficiency of organizational process improvement are enhanced.[1]

---

1. CMMI initially focused on development activities (that is, building things), with a special emphasis on systems and software engineering. Clearly, many aspects of process improvement apply more broadly, to other engineering as well as nonengineering disciplines. As you learn about CMMI, you may gain insight into how its process improvement framework might be extended and applied to other areas. We assume that the majority of readers are interested in the initial CMMI focus on the development of software-intensive systems, and hence we write from that perspective. We also invite readers to think about other potential applications within the engineering development world and beyond.

In the last quarter of 2000, after extensive stakeholder review and piloting, the first official CMMI products were released. These models provide users with a choice of single or integrated disciplines and a choice of a staged or continuous representation. They include a wealth of engineering and process improvement information, such as clear goals and extensive guidance on the best practices to achieve them. Most importantly, a well-defined framework outlines how additional disciplines may be brought into the product suite so as to minimize the development of incompatible models in the future.

Purpose of the Book

This book has a threefold purpose. First, we intend to help organizations understand how an integrated approach to process improvement can help mature their technical and management processes. Second, to support this integrated approach, we present a new set of tools developed by the CMMI project specifically designed for multidiscipline process improvement. Finally, we provide practical guidance in the selection and use of those tools. This guidance is based on lessons learned from organizations that have adopted integrated process improvement, as well as the knowledge and experience gained from the hundreds of professionals who were involved in the development of the CMMI product suite.

Audience for the Book

The intended audience for this book comprises executives, middle managers, team leaders, acquisition specialists, process improvement champions, and the often overlooked and overworked process improvement practitioners. Executives, who may have deferred process improvement in the past because the scope of their business exceeded the boundaries of a single model, will find an approach and tools to mitigate their concerns. Middle managers and team leaders will find information on the effects of process improvement on their responsibilities and the cross-discipline nature of their environments. Process improvement champions will find a means to enlarge their base of support and focus their efforts in a way that heightens the chances of adoption and success. Finally, individuals who are charged with implementing the process improvement will find help in applying models in the real world. It is our hope that when unsuspecting project and program managers are instructed to "implement that CMMI stuff," this book will provide suffi-cient information to save both their careers and their sanity.

While applicable to any organization involved with rigorous, time-crit-ical development of complex systems, this book will hold special inter-est for system developers and systems integrators who supply the U.S. government. The federal government participated in the CMMI devel-opment work, thereby supporting the efforts of its suppliers (both external and internal) to improve process performance. In October 1999, the U.S. Department of Defense established the requirement that its large program development contractors demonstrate full compli-ance with a maturity level 3 as measured by the Software CMM (or equivalent).[2] More recently, it has indicated its intention to have CMMI-SE/SW identified as an equivalent evaluation tool.[3] Given the considerable interest at all levels in adding the acquisition discipline to CMMI, the authors believe that CMMI will likely see application in improving government system acquisition organizations as well.

Organization of the Book

The book is divided into four major parts.

Part I introduces integrated process improvement and provides a ratio-nale for undertaking such an approach. This material is both a primer for the novice and ammunition to gain management support for the process improvement champion. It offers general guidance as well as specific hints on implementation, including pointers to support the migration from legacy process improvement activities and accomplish-ments. Part I also provides case studies and lessons learned from the pioneering organizations that blazed the trail toward integrated process improvement. If you wish to start your reading with the details of CMMI, you could save this first part for review at a later time.

Part II describes the work of the CMMI project. The philosophy, architec-ture, and models of CMMI products are presented, and examples of the models are annotated in detail to provide a better understanding of their

---

2. "Software evaluations for ACAT 1 programs," memorandum from Dr. J. S. Gansler, Under Sec-retary of Defense (Acquisition and Technology), Oct. 26, 1999.

3. "Use of CMMI evaluations by the Department of Defense," memorandum from Dr. Delores M. Etter, Deputy Under Secretary of Defense (Science and Technology), Dec. 11, 2000.

contents. This part also includes much of the rationale for specific CMMI decisions and help in navigating the rather daunting CMMI models.

Part III builds on the first two parts and offers the authors' practical guidance in the use of the CMMI products. It suggests heuristics for choosing models and representations appropriate for a specific organization. It also describes CMMI assessments and explains how to tailor the CMMI products to fit an organization and enhance the probability of success in applying CMMI.

Part IV presents some musings on the future of CMMI. These informed speculations reflect some of the discussions held formally and informally during CMMI development. The ideas included are intended to invite discussion and spark innovation, but not, as the sportswriters say, "as the basis for any actual cash wager."

Like their predecessors, the CMMI models are by necessity large and complex products. This book, while not duplicating all their information, will help you understand the CMMI models and auxiliary materials. It provides a rationale for integrating process improvement, a guide to the structure and contents of the CMMI models, and some practical ideas for using the models effectively in your organization. We strongly encourage you to obtain copies of the models from the CMMI Web site (www.sei.cmu.edu/cmmi) and browse through them as you are reading this book, especially Parts II and III. For readers who would like a flavor of the models, Appendixes A and B presents a concise summary of CMMI/SW/SE/IPPD content in both the continuous and staged representations.

The CMMI project is an ongoing effort, so any project as time-restricted as a book will necessarily be overcome by events. The authors have strived to provide information that is both timely and of lasting value, but understand the reality of the CMMI environment. To that end, the publisher has agreed to support this volume with updates through its Web site (www.awl.com) and, when appropriate, further editions.

Our Intentions

The authors have all been active in process improvement in the real world. We bring considerable practical experience to this effort, together with our ideas on improving the way process improvement is accomplished. Together we struggled through the creation of the CMMI products, benefiting from the wide variety of views brought by the CMMI

Product Development Team. Generally, this book describes the products and positions of the nearly 100 other experienced practitioners and researchers that made up that team. In some places, however, we express our own opinions. In those cases where the text may not reflect the consensus of the team, we have identified our unorthodoxy.

It is our hope that this book reflects the tremendous accomplishments of the entire CMMI Product Development Team. Most of all, we want you to obtain a clearer understanding of the practice and benefits of integrated process improvement based on CMMI products. Through the information in this book, we hope to help make your process improvement initiatives successful.

Acknowledgments

The authors would like to acknowledge the help and support of the CMMI Product Development Team and the CMMI Steering Group. The members of those groups, past and present, may not agree with everything that we say here, but this book would not exist without their devoted efforts over several years on behalf of CMMI. Additionally, several individuals were key to the actual development of this book. They include Karl Arunski, Roger Bate, Denise Cattan, Jeffrey Dutton, Delores Etter, Jack Ferguson, Craig Hollenbach, Linda Ibrahim, Mike Phillips, Sarah Sheard, and Joan Weszka.

Peter Gordon, Asdis Thorsteinsson, and other Addison-Wesley personnel were invaluable in helping us meld the significantly different styles of the three authors into coherent, readable prose. The reviewers engaged by the publisher, including several from the Software Engineering Institute, provided us with many useful improvement suggestions.

Finally, the authors would like to thank our families (and especially Pam, Debbi, and Jo), who put up with crabby spouses and parents, absences from home, and frenetic holidays so that this book could make its production schedule. We love you all.

Dennis, Aaron, and Rich

Baltimore, Dallas, and Washington, D.C., January 2001

The Tower of Babel
Gustave Doré (1832–1883)
© 2000–2001 www.arttoday.com

Part I

Integrated Process Improvement

In the biblical story of the Tower of Babel, God caused this development project to fail by interrupting the communication through the creation of multiple languages. In the modern story of process improvement, we have created multiple languages to serve various development disciplines through the creation of divergent process improvement models. As with the Tower of Babel story, this diversity poses a threat to communication. The Capability Maturity Model Integration project (CMMI) and integrated process improvement in general strive to reverse this situation by providing a single language through which multiple disciplines can share process improvement activities and a unified focus on process improvement objectives.

Part I Contents

1

Chapter 2. Implementing Integrated Process Improvement

In which the authors present valuable guidance concerning the best manner in which such endeavors should be undertaken so as to have the best chance of succeeding. Included are brief histories from industrious and innovative pioneers.

Chapter 1

Why Integrated Process Improvement?

It is not necessary to change. Survival is not mandatory.
W. Edwards Deming (1900–1993)

The complexity of practice has always dwarfed the simplicity of theory.
Robert Britcher, *The Limits of Software* (1999)

The Capability Maturity Model Integration (CMMI) project changes the way in which process improvement is performed. To understand the rationale for change, it's important to look at some shortcomings of traditional process improvement when faced with the engineering paradigm of the twenty-first century. The engineering world has changed in at least three significant areas since the introduction of model-based process improvement.

First, the environment within which engineering is performed has become increasingly complex. Efforts are larger, involve more people, cross corporation boundaries, are distributed far and wide, and must adhere to continually compressing implementation schedules to meet customer needs.

Second, the way in which engineering work is performed has evolved. Cross-discipline teams, concurrent engineering, highly automated processes, and multinational standards have all affected engineering practice.

Third, the success of the Software Engineering Institute's Capability Maturity Model for Software has led to a proliferation of models, each of which addresses process improvement from the aspect of a particular discipline. Organizations have adopted multiple improvement models to address their critical processes.

All of these changes highlight the need to integrate process improvement efforts. The myriad disciplines and processes involved in contemporary engineering are closely intertwined. The overhead and confusion resulting from the application of multiple models are too costly. As a consequence, a means of addressing process improvement across a number of disciplines within a single framework is needed. This chapter discusses how changes in the engineering world have influenced the effectiveness of traditional process improvement strategies and how organizations can benefit from applying an integrated approach.

Model-Based Process Improvement

Model-based process improvement involves the use of a model to guide the improvement of an organization's processes. Process improvement grew out of the quality management work of Deming,[1] Crosby,[2] and Juran[3] and is aimed at increasing the capability of work processes. Essentially, process capability is the inherent ability of a process to produce planned results. As the capability of a process increases, it becomes predictable and measurable, and the most significant causes of poor quality and productivity are controlled or eliminated. By steadily improving its process capability, the organization "matures." Maturity improvement requires

---

1. Deming, W. Edwards. *Out of the Crisis*. Cambridge, MA: MIT Center for Advanced Engineering, 1986.

2. Crosby, P. B. *Quality Is Free*. New York: McGraw-Hill, 1979.

3. Juran, J. M. *Juran on Planning for Quality*. New York: MacMillan, 1988.

strong management support and a consistent long-term focus. In addition, it necessitates fundamental changes in the way managers and practitioners do their jobs.

One means of achieving this focus has been the use of a capability model. Models provide a common set of process requirements that capture best practices and practical knowledge in a format that can be used to guide priorities. By using a model, organizations can modify or create processes using practices that have been proven to increase process capability. They may also employ models to assess process capability for two purposes: to establish a baseline for improvement and to measure progress as improvement activities proceed.

Generally, model-based process improvement begins with management commitment and an assessment. The findings from this assessment, in turn, feed action plans. When these plans have been completed, further assessments are performed and the cycle continues. The goal is for the organization to mature so that it continuously monitors and improves its processes, consistently produces high-quality products, is agile within its marketplace, and adjusts quickly to customer needs.

1.1 The Engineering Environment of the Twenty-First Century

Remember when there was one telephone company and one kind of phone service? When the only telephone-related worry you had was keeping long-distance calls under three minutes? When you understood not only the principles but also (perhaps) the mechanics of how the system worked?[4] Unfortunately (or fortunately in some cases), the era of such relatively simple systems has ended. When you realize that your new telephone contains more software than the lunar landing module,

---

4. If you are too young to remember this time, ask a parent or other elder within your circle of friends. They'll appreciate the time to reminisce. If they begin to talk about the value of hard work, the buying power of the dollar, or walking 20 miles to school barefoot in the snow, however, make your escape quickly!

Dorothy's plaintive "Toto, I don't think we're in Kansas anymore" may all too closely echo your feelings of consternation. Even technology-savvy engineers occasionally profess a sense of awe about the relentless pace of technological change. No one can deny that this change has brought new capabilities, new conveniences, and new complexity.

We are now on the rising edge of the system complexity curve, and there is little chance of moderation in the foreseeable future. The U.S. Department of Defense has estimated that it will soon need to field systems utilizing as many as 20 million lines of software code. In some autonomous military systems, software will provide decision-making functions for reconnaissance and weapon delivery.

Complexity is related to more than purely software components. Many traditionally hardware modules now contain significant micro-code that will inevitably interface in some manner with a software control system housed in yet another hardware device. In increasingly complex systems, the ability to differentiate between hardware and software functions may become nearly impossible, complicating design and maintenance tasks and significantly affecting our ability to calculate expected reliability. This complexity is readily evident in the products and systems being conceived, designed, and manufactured each day; moreover, it is mirrored in the activities of the acquiring and developing organizations, both in industry and government.

As systems grow more complex, the processes used to develop them will follow suit. The complexity of processes inevitably increases to keep pace with the number of individuals who are involved in performance. The theory and concepts of process improvement are elegant and understandable. When we apply them to increasingly complex systems, however, we find that, as Robert Britcher writes, "the complexity of practice has always dwarfed the simplicity of theory."[5] This result is particularly likely when the processes cut across organizational, discipline, corporate, or cultural boundaries.

With large and complex organizations, processes, and systems, process improvement activities can easily become lost in the multiplicity of tasks, agendas, and personalities. Because each office or organization

---

5. Britcher, Robert. *The Limits of Software*. Reading, MA: Addison-Wesley, 1999. This fascinating treatise on the philosophy and practice of software engineering is drawn from the author's work with IBM on the Federal Aviation Administration's (FAA) Advanced Automation System (AAS). AAS was terminated after expenditures of approximately $2 billion, based on the judgment that it could not be accomplished.

has its own responsibilities and diligently strives to improve its own practices, process improvement can evolve into a patchwork of unrelated and uncoordinated activities spread across a variety of organizations. Multiple groups and their executives may vie for process improvement resources. Process groups may select different and sometimes conflicting improvement models. Competition can emerge between groups, and the ownership of process improvement can become hotly debated. In the end, there is often more energy spent in the peripheral activities than in the improvement initiatives.

Lest you think that only large and complex projects lead to process improvement problems, consider the small, entrepreneurial firm racing to meet a rapidly approaching market window. Such an organization finds it difficult, if not impossible, to address process improvement when the time-to-market criterion is so crucial to its survival. Such a firm often has personnel performing multiple engineering functions simultaneously; conceivably, it may have a different process for each individual in the company. As another example, an information technology application services company may be forced to deal with a schizophrenic customer who constantly changes requirements, priorities, and schedules, leaving little alternative except to function in a crisis development environment. Although neither type of organization described here has the financial or schedule resources to pursue traditional process improvement, each could benefit greatly from taking a more disciplined approach to engineering.

1.2 Concurrent Engineering and the Cross-Discipline Team

The organization of engineering and product development work has undergone significant changes in recent years. Much of this change has been aimed at eliminating the inefficiencies associated with stepwise development where intermediate products are handed off to next-phase workers, who may have to do significant rework to correct misunderstandings. Concurrent engineering, cross-discipline teams, cross-functional teams, integrated product teams (IPT), and integrated product and process development (IPPD) all represent ways to address this problem and apply the necessary expertise at the appropriate time throughout the product or service life cycle. In practice, this trend means that designers and customers work with manufacturers, testers, and users to support the manufacturing organization in developing requirements. It has also been described as having "everyone at the table," implying that all critical stakeholders support all phases of product or service development.

Understandably, the concept of concurrency has redefined the nature of organizational structure and development. The general acceptance and rapid deployment of cross-discipline or cross-functional teams in the engineering world has also proved a thorny issue for process improvement. The concept of functional departments, each with its own processes under its own control, strongly clashes with the highly interactive work style associated with cross-discipline teams.

To date, discrete process improvement models have not effectively supported the "mixing bowl" environment of concurrent engineering. If the hardware engineering department is using one improvement model, the software developers a second, and the outsourcing and contracts department yet a third, problems are inevitable. Separate "stovepipe" models offer little chance of improving the processes used by a cross-discipline team, where every member is an actor in most of the processes and the separation between the disciplines has gone the way of the Berlin Wall.

Cross-discipline teams use integrated processes that are matched more closely to the ebb and flow of the life cycle than are the strict stages of classical development. They take advantage of evolutionary development approaches and innovative design techniques. Attempting to apply the discipline-specific models to such processes is analogous to requiring members of a jazz trio to strictly play their individual parts. Of course it's possible—but the outcome is not very satisfying. What is needed is a model that not only integrates the disciplines, but also integrates the processes themselves and supports effective work among various stakeholders, functional personnel, and management.

1.3 A Proliferation of Models and Standards

If imitation is a measure of success, then the Capability Maturity Model (CMM) for Software is exceptionally successful—and for good reason. People in many disciplines were attracted to the elegance of the CMM concept and its close ties to quality management theory and practice. The general response was, "Hey, that's a great idea. Let's build something like that for *our* shop." Table 1-1 shows a number of the better-known

Table 1-1: *CMM-like Models*

Model	Description
CMM for Software	The original CMM developed at the Software Engineering Institute (SEI). In November 1986, the SEI, with assistance from Mitre Corporation, began developing a process maturity framework intended to assist organizations in improving their software processes. In September 1987, the SEI released a brief description of the process maturity framework and a maturity questionnaire (CMU/SEI-87-TR-23). The fully developed model (version 1.1) was released in 1993.
SE-CMM	The Systems Engineering Capability Maturity Model (SE-CMM) describes the elements of an organization's systems engineering process that are essential to good systems engineering. This continuous model was developed by the Enterprise Process Improvement Collaboration (EPIC), which included industry, government, and academic members. It was merged with the INCOSE SECAM to form the Electronics Industry Alliance's EIA/IS 731 in 1998.
Software Acquisition CMM	A collaborative effort among the U.S. Department of Defense, the SEI, industry, and other U.S. government agencies, this model supports benchmarking and improvements of the software acquisition process.
SECAM	The International Council on Systems Engineering (INCOSE) developed the Systems Engineering Capability Assessment Model (SECAM) as a checklist-based model. It has since been merged with the SE-CMM into EIA/IS 731. *(continued)*

Table 1-1: *CMM-like Models (cont.)*

Model	Description
People CMM	This model addresses the ability of software organizations to attract, develop, motivate, organize, and retain talent.
EIA/IS 731	This Systems Engineering Capability Model (SECM) supercedes the SE-CMM and SECAM, and has been issued as an interim EIA standard.
Systems Security Engineering CMM	This model represented an extension and enhancement of the SE-CMM by the U.S. National Security Agency (NSA); it provided additional practices and information concerning security of information systems.
IPD-CMM	The Integrated Product Development CMM (IPD-CMM) was published only in draft form. It was begun under the auspices of EPIC, but was superceded by the establishment of the CMMI project.
FAA-iCMM	The first truly integrated CMM, this model includes all of the material from the SE-CMM, the SA-CMM, and the CMM for Software. Developed at the U.S. FAA, it is being used as a unified means of guiding process improvement across the entire FAA.
IEEE/EIA 12207 (.0, .1, and .2)	The U.S. implementation of the ISO/IEC 12207 standard on software life-cycle processes. (IEEE is the Institute of Electrical and Electronics Engineers.)
ISO/IEC 15288	A draft international standard on system life-cycle processes. (ISO is the International Organization for Standardization. IEC is the International Electrotechnical Commission.)

Model	Description
ISO/IEC 15504	A draft international standard for Software Process Assessment that permits different methods, yet allows assessment results to be obtained in a single form and in sufficient detail to identify places where improvement is needed.
Project Framework	Developed as a proprietary product by ESI International, this model merges the CMM concept with the Project Management Institute's Project Management Body of Knowledge (PMBOK) to produce a management process improvement tool.

CMM-like improvement models in use around the world, together with some relevant international standards.

All of the models described in Table 1-1 were created within an environment of evolving national and international standards and frameworks. As standards become used and accepted, maintaining harmonization between them and the improvement models becomes a continuing challenge, particularly across disciplines. In describing the complexity of this environment, Sarah Sheard of the Software Productivity Consortium has coined the term "the framework quagmire."[6] Figure 1-1 shows her depiction of the proliferation and heritage of the various systems and software engineering standards, life-cycle models, quality awards, and process improvement models. In this diagram, the arrows show where one model or standard contributed to the development of another. As you can see in Figure 1-1, the development of these frameworks bears a striking resemblance to the bloodlines of the European monarchies in the middle centuries of the last millennium. This incestuous nature leaves

---

6. The Software Productivity Consortium is a nonprofit partnership of industry, government, and academia. Its goal is to develop processes, methods, tools, and supporting services to help its members and affiliates build high-quality, component-based systems and continuously advance their systems and software engineering maturity pursuant to the guidelines of the major process and quality frameworks. Membership is open to all U.S.- and Canadian-based companies, government agencies, and academic organizations. Sarah Sheard can be reached at sheard@software. org. Also see www.software.org/quagmire.

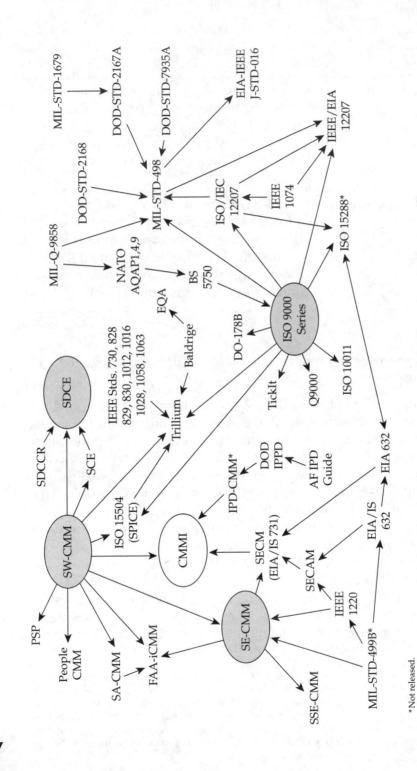

Figure 1-1: *The framework quagmire*

Quagmire Legend:

AF IPD Guide = Air Force Materiel Command Guide on Integrated Product Development: A Guide for Understanding and Implementing IPD Throughout AFMC.

Baldrige = Malcolm Baldrige National Quality Award, administered by the National Institute of Standards and Technology.

BS 5750 = British Standards Institution commercial versions of NATO standards, released 1979. Subsequent to ISO publication, BSI adopted the ISO 9000 text, replacing the 1979 versions.

CMMI = CMM Integration, SEI-facilitated work in progress to integrate SW-CMM, SECM, and IPD-CMM content, CMMI-SE/SW V 1.0 released August 2000; CMMI-SE/SW/IPPD released December 2000.

DO-178B = Software Considerations in Airborne Systems and Equipment Certification, by RTCA, 12/92.

DOD IPPD = DOD Integrated Product and Process Development Guide.

DOD-STD-2167A = Defense System Software Development Standard, 1988.

DOD-STD-2168 = Defense System Software Quality Standard, companion to DOD-STD-2167A.

DOD-STD-7935A = DOD Automated Information System Documentation Standards, 1988.

EIA 632 = Processes for Engineering a System, major modification of MIL STD 499B,1999.

EIA/IEEE J-STD-016 = Release name for interim commercial version of MIL-STD-498, released 1995.

EIA/IS 632 = Systems Engineering, minor modification of MIL STD 499B, to make it more commercial (IS = Interim Standard).

EQA = European Quality Award, European version of Baldrige award.

FAA-iCMM = FAA's internal process improvement model, integrating the SW-CMM, the SE-CMM, and the SA-CMM (i = integrated).

IEEE 1074 = standard for the definition of life-cycle processes.

IEEE 1220 = IEEE Standard for Application and Management of the Systems Engineering Process, IEEE, 1998.

IEEE Stds. 730, 828, 829, 830, 1012, 1016, 1028, 1058, and 1063 = IEEE software engineering standards collection, 1993 Edition.

IEEE/EIA 12207 = U.S. implementation of ISO 12207, 1997.

IPD-CMM = Integrated Product Development CMM. This model will not be issued, but content has been incorporated into the CMMI.

ISO 10011 series = Auditor and Auditor training guidelines, for ISO 9000 auditors.

ISO 15288 = System Life Cycle Processes, Systems Engineering standard being developed by ISC. Due 2001.

ISO 9000 series = Series of quality standards and guidelines for quality systems, including ISO 9000–9004.

ISO 15504 (SPICE) = Software Process Improvement Capability dEtermination, by a subcommittee of ISO.

ISO/IEC 12207 = Information technology—software life-cycle processes, international standard.

MIL-Q-9858 = Quality Management Program military standard, 1959.

MIL-STD-498 = Software Development and Documentation.

MIL-STD-499B = System's Engineering military standard, never released but used as a basis for EIA and IEEE SE standards.

MIL-STD-1679 = Navy standard, Weapon System Software Development, 1970s.

NATO AQAP1, AQAP4, AQAP9 = Allied Quality Assurance Publication; NATO adoption in principle of MIL-Q-9858, 1963.

People CMM = CMM about developing software developers.

PSP = Personal Software Process, software development maturity guidance for individuals, from SEI.

Q9000 = U.S. adaptation of ISO 9000.

SA-CMM = Software Acquisition CMM, acquirer's mirror of SW CMM.

SCE = Evaluation (outside audit) of software capability, using the CMM.

SDCCR = Software Development Capability/Capacity Review, U.S. Air Force original contractor selection vehicle.

SDCE = Software Development Capability Evaluation, evolution of SDCCR and CMM, by the Air Force.

SECAM = Systems Engineering Capability Assessment Model, produced by the Capability Assessment Working Group of the International Council on Systems Engineering (INCOSE).

SECM (EIA 731) = Systems Engineering Capability Model, merger of SECAM and SE-CMM, 1998.

SE-CMM = Systems Engineering Capability Maturity Model, from EPIC.

SSE-CMM = Security Systems Engineering CMM, an adaptation of SE-CMM for the discipline of security engineering.

SW-CMM = SEI's Capability Maturity Model for Software.

TickIT = British Standards Institute's Guide to Software Quality Systems Construction and Certification using ISO 9001:1994.

Trillium = Model for Telecom Product Development and Support Process Capability, merged mode developed by Bell Canada, 1994.

many organizations to ponder the real value of moving from well-established standards to newly evolving ones. The difficulty and complexity of using multiple process improvement models in addition to the appropriate standards for organizations with multidiscipline requirements is a strong rationale for integrating process improvement.

1.4 The Benefits of Integrated Process Improvement

In the preceding sections, we enumerated many factors that complicate process improvement. It is our assertion that many of these obstacles can be overcome by integrating process improvement through a common model. This belief reflects our work on integration and the experiences of the authors and reviewers of the CMMI project. Of course, you may need to be convinced that this endeavor is worthwhile for your organization. At the end of the day, what are the real benefits of integrated process improvement?

Fundamentally, process improvement integration significantly affects four areas: cost, focus, process integration, and flexibility. Some of these changes are more easily quantified than others, but all represent real advantages.

1.4.1 Cost Benefits

Cost improvement is probably the easiest benefit to understand. There is always a cost to integration, but the savings from process improvement integration can be significant. By applying a single model, organizations that would otherwise use multiple models can reduce the cost of

- Training in multiple models and assessment methods
- Performing multiple assessments within the same organizations (and possibly with the same practitioners)
- Maintaining redundant process assets in a repository
- Maintaining or purchasing expertise in multiple models

The better odds of success that arise from integrated process improvement also make it more likely that the organization will achieve cost savings resulting from higher quality, better predictability, and all the other benefits of improved processes.

1.4.2 Clarity of Focus

Within the diverse world of engineering organizations, particularly when projects cut across organizational boundaries, it is difficult to achieve the critical mass necessary to bring about real improvement within individual organizations. This problem can be characterized as stemming from a lack of focus and a need to unify the disparate activities. That is, the pressures from outside the group are too strong, the costs too high, or the resources too thinly applied to both improve local processes and interface them with other organizations or disciplines. Budget changes, the business environment, internal politics, and mergers and acquisitions all take their toll by consuming resources that could be applied to improvement.

An integrated process improvement program can clarify the goals and business objectives of the various initiatives. By integrating process improvement activities across a wider range of disciplines, it becomes easier to rally the troops—both practitioners and executives—to the process improvement banner. Having a single process improvement focus can unify and reinforce vision, efficiently marshal and apply scarce resources, and provide a common language for improvement across various disciplines. In particular, a single model with common terminology and common assessment methods provides this kind of focus.

A word of caution is appropriate at this point. Not every model (such as the CMM for Software) can become the focus for process improvement. If the focus doesn't include all of the disciplines critical to organizational success, it will miss the breadth actually sought by process improvement. An integrated model allows personnel in each discipline to identify with the processes and feel that they have a stake in the now-focused process improvement program.

1.4.3 Process Integration and Lean Organizations

One of the less obvious benefits of integrated process improvement is the "integrating" effect it has on organizations. When processes are defined across organizational and discipline boundaries, new understanding and mutual education often occur, resulting in the streamlining of the critical work flow and the elimination of redundant or unneeded activities.

Stovepipe[7] process improvement often assumes that interfaces between organizations work effectively; rarely is one process aware of closely related or redundant activities in a sister stovepipe. By working on improving processes across the board, the organization essentially obtains a bonus reengineering effort as a by-product of the process improvement initiative. This streamlining supports the lean concept, which strives for increased value to the customer by eliminating waste in the production of products.[8]

1.4.4 Flexibility and Extension into New Disciplines

A final benefit provided by integration is the ability to add disciplines as the business or engineering environment changes. Adding a new individual model results in a great deal of redundancy and often conflicting representations in the common process improvement practices. Adding a discipline within an integrated program simply means a few more process areas and perhaps the reinterpretation of other areas, but the fundamental process improvement structure and terminology remain the same.

1.5 Conclusions

This chapter presented arguments that integrated process improvement is the right, practical, and obvious way to go. It identified changes in the engineering environment, discussed the integration of work process across the product life cycle, and described a cacophony of competing standards—three factors that strongly suggest the need for integrated process improvement. Finally, it defined the benefits of such an approach beyond the simplification of an organization's improvement efforts.

Chapter 2 offers some practical advice on taking the plunge and implementing an integrated process improvement program. By providing some guiding principles and real-life examples of how process improvement integration has worked in large and small organizations, we hope to ease your implementation of this beneficial approach.

---

7. Stovepipe processes are usually organized by discipline and do not include the interfaces between those organizations.

8. Womack, James P., and Daniel Jones. *Lean Thinking*. New York: Simon and Schuster, 1996.

But what if your organization isn't complex or multidisciplinary? Single-model process improvement is better than no process improvement, and it works perfectly well in many organizations. Nevertheless, we invite you to look carefully at the CMMI product suite before returning to your single-model effort. The integration of disciplines in CMMI has produced a better model in a number of ways, even when applied just to a single discipline; you may realize advantages by using the CMMI version. Besides, you'll be a lot better informed if your new CEO starts preaching the benefits of cross-discipline teams.

Chapter 2

Implementing Integrated Process Improvement

Do what you can, with what you have, where you are.
Theodore Roosevelt (1858–1919)

We find by experience (our own or another's) what is hurtful or helpful.
Giovanni Battista Lamperti, *Vocal Wisdom,* (1895)

I have but one lamp by which my feet are guided,
and that is the lamp of experience.
Patrick Henry, Speech before the Virginia Convention (1775)

The two questions most frequently raised at integrated process seminars and presentations are

> *How do I pull it all together?*

and

> *What do I do with my existing process improvement investments?*

Both old hands and novices may be overwhelmed by what they see as the complexity of integrating their often disparate process improvement activities. This chapter presents some practical advice for implementing integrated process improvement. The advice is based on the experience of some of the Capability Maturity Model Integration (CMMI) authors and others who have used a variety of methods to integrate their process improvement activities. The chapter doesn't attempt to summarize or repeat the information found in the wealth of process improvement and change management books now available. Rather, it points out critical strategies that can facilitate process improvement integration.

The first section of this chapter addresses the issues of starting a new process improvement initiative in an integrated way. It is intended for organizations that have not yet implemented formal process improvement and hence will be starting out with a clean slate. Building the needed support systems, networks, and sponsors, and the way in which this activity differs from single discipline process improvement, is addressed in the second section. The third section is intended for organizations that are currently pursuing process improvement. It suggests ways to incorporate legacy processes and current process improvement initiatives into an integrated process improvement structure, without losing the organization's existing investments. The fourth section focuses on the use of appraisals to provide encouragement and energy to the improvement process, without leading to a "checklist mentality." Finally, the fifth section presents a number of case studies— mini-summaries of integrated process improvement initiatives and the lessons learned by several organizations.

2.1 Starting Integrated Process Improvement

You have successfully convinced your organization to initiate a new integrated process improvement program. Or perhaps your organization has informed you that your raise or bonus now depends on such an event. In either case, you need to understand a few key principles about starting process improvement. Although these principles apply to any process improvement effort, they are especially valuable when embarking on an integrated process improvement path.

Integrated Process Improvement Principles

1. *Maintain executive support.* Strong consistent support is crucial.
2. *Pick your targets carefully.* Don't underestimate the effort needed, because process improvement is hard work.
3. *Leverage best practices.* Use what is available and "steal with pride."
4. *Align process improvement with your business objectives.* Leverage existing objectives or create new ones to support process improvement.

2.1.1 Principle 1—Maintain Executive Support

One of the most critical factors for all process improvement is the strength of executive support. The organization's leadership must be strong, consistent, and visible to build a consensus among practitioners that the endeavor is not merely the management approach du jour. (Whatever happened to total quality management?) Executive support is critical to obtain the resources for process improvement activities and to ensure the rewards for the innovation and additional hard work that are fundamental parts of any change strategy. Particularly when initiatives cut across organizations, executives need to bridge the organizational gaps and soothe the damaged egos that inevitably arise in multidisciplinary endeavors. Leadership must achieve consensus among both middle management and the practitioners; otherwise, process improvement will become a paper exercise that produces hollow artifacts and lackluster performance.

For these reasons, it is essential to get commitment from executives early and often. Help them construct the "elevator speech" they need to counter the push back from middle management.[1] Executives should understand that if they take actions that run counter to process improvement tenets, the message will be heard just as loudly as public denigration of the program. Help them to develop achievable goals and

---

1. By an "elevator speech," we mean a two- or three-minute summary of the goals, costs, and benefits of your project. This sales pitch should be short enough to give effectively in the space of an elevator ride.

good metrics for their own performance plans that can trickle down to their direct reports. Above all, make sure that upper management is notified of early successes, which they can use to defend the program when the first wave of cash-flow issues, schedule adjustments, or other similar crises that can impact organizational priorities appear.

In short, concentrate on keeping your executives aware, involved, and excited. You will then be well on your way to a successful integrated process improvement program.

2.1.2 Principle 2—Pick Your Targets Carefully

Many process improvement programs fail because they make poor estimates of what they can reasonably accomplish in a given amount of time.[2] Process improvement can be difficult work, especially across organizations with strong personalities and well-defined cultures (a description that fits most organizations we know). For this reason, carefully consider your initial process improvement goals. Select achievable objectives that can immediately show a benefit to the organization. This point may seem obvious, but it is less widely recognized that progress in a difficult area may be readily achievable; indeed, the greatest value for a new improvement program can often be achieved by attacking a tough problem first. Consider an initial goal of improving at least one cross-discipline or cross-organizational process—you not only bring more of the stakeholders into the early planning, but often find significant reengineering gains that can pay for some of the later process improvement work.

One important task that often becomes lost in the early excitement—and, if not addressed, nearly always comes back to haunt process improvement teams—is the early design and use of a measurement program. Make sure that you establish a baseline against which to compare your process improvement activities. You don't want a year to pass and have only anecdotal data to defend your successes against any naysayers left in power. No matter how good your persuasive skills, you must have convincing data that process improvement is affecting the organization's bottom line (or at least someone's bottom line). Otherwise, your program

---

2. For an analysis of the reasons why process improvement efforts may fail, see the following: Hayes, W., and D. Zubrow. *Moving On Up: Data and Experience Doing CMM-Based Process Improvement.* CMU/SEI-95-TR-008; and Goldenson, D., and J. Herbsleb. *After the Appraisal: A Systematic Survey of Process Improvement, Its Benefits, and Factors That Influence Success.* CMU/SEI-95-TR-009.

may soon find itself below the budget cut-off threshold, with resume writing being the only process improved.

2.1.3 Principle 3—Leverage Best Practices

For some reason, process improvement champions are often creative types. Don't let your creativity blind you to the fact that many solid, proven process assets are available.[3] Suzanne Garcia, a self-professed process improvement guerrilla, cajoled the students in her Software Engineering Institute (SEI) classes to "steal with pride!" This instruction doesn't mean stooping to industrial espionage or illegal acts. Rather, it entails searching for what's working and then building on those methods.

If your company has organizational process assets that could be applied to your new process improvement program, use them. Network with process improvement groups that operate at both national and local levels.[4] Sometimes consultants can provide assets that have been developed for similar organizations and domains at a fraction of the cost of custom development. Of course, just as with commercial-off-the-shelf (COTS) products, you must ensure that anything you obtain will meet your requirements or else be willing to change your requirements to fit the product.

SEI books, reports, conferences, and classes can all provide a wealth of good ideas. Read the journals and surf the Web. Somewhere among the naughty ads, shopping invitations, and stock come-ons, you may find a process description that eliminates a considerable chunk of your process development work. You'll never find it, however, if you don't refocus that creative energy.

---

3. Appendix D lists some of these resources. One especially useful resource is the Software Engineering Information Repository (SEIR), which provides a forum for the contribution and exchange of information concerning software engineering improvement activities. Registered members of SEIR can ask questions, provide tips, and contribute (deposit) experiences or examples to assist one another with their implementation efforts. As part of this process, SEIR members are building a knowledge base in this repository for their future use. The Web site for SEIR is http://seir.sei.cmu.edu/.

4. One important process improvement group for systems engineering is the International Council on Systems Engineering (INCOSE), which operates both at the national level and through local chapters. Another is the Software Process Improvement Network (SPIN), made up of individuals who want to improve software engineering practices. These individuals are organized into regional "SPINs" that meet and share their experiences in initiating and sustaining software process improvement programs.

2.1.4 Principle 4—Align Process Improvement with Business Objectives

No step is more critical than closely coupling your process improvement activities with corporate or organizational goals. In the long run, if process improvement will not affect the bottom line, then it will not be seen as valuable by practitioners or management. When you develop your plan, look for existing goals and objectives to support and bring focus to your activities. Efficiency and quality goals are often good candidates, for example.

If you cannot identify clearly related business goals, determine how corporate objectives are developed. Then get your team or your sponsor involved in creating a specific objective that will support process improvement.

2.2 Building an Integrated Improvement Infrastructure

It is critical to establish roles and responsibilities for those individuals who will lead, carry out training, and perform the process improvement activities. This infrastructure becomes even more critical when the organization is approaching process improvement in an integrated fashion. Generally, a cadre of process champions will provide the core energy, experience, and the initial sweat and blood to get process improvement off the ground. These people, however, may not represent all the stakeholders or power centers that will have an important role in the fully integrated environment.

It is almost always necessary to convene a steering group of interested or "volunteered" parties to handle issues that may arise during the process improvement activities. In many cases, this group may simply represent an extension of the software engineering process group (SEPG) concept into an engineering process group (EPG) (or just a process group [PG] if the effort extends beyond engineering development), with membership that spans the broadened process improvement landscape.[5]

---

5. SEPGs are a fundamental part of software process improvement, and the SEI has developed considerable literature describing their activities. The SEI and a regional SPIN co-sponsor an annual Software Engineering Process Group (SEPG) Conference. Check the SEI Web site, www.sei.cmu.edu, for more information on SEPGs and SPINs.

Be aware of the political ramifications of integrating your process improvement activities when forming your process group. Make sure that all of the organizations involved have a place at the table; their participation will help counter the idea that the initiative is "something being done to them" against their wishes. Hold open meetings and advertise the outcomes. Also, keep a sense of equity throughout the effort—everyone should share in the rewards as well as the work.

The steering group should not be limited to practitioners and process improvement specialists. It will prove much more effective if middle management is included and if executive management is represented or chairs the group. In this way, the process group can adequately deal with resource and other management issues.

A process group that comprises mostly managers probably will not get the nitty-gritty work done. To achieve its goals, it will need subgroups, committees, or work teams to coordinate the training, build better processes, maintain process assets, and perform all the other crafts involved in process improvement. Make sure that sufficient resources and guidance are available to allow these groups to function reasonably autonomously. Otherwise, you'll end up with your steering group micromanaging process improvement and chaos waiting at the doorstep.

Training is probably the most expensive—and most important—aspect of the infrastructure. With integrated process improvement, the required training goes beyond simple process definition, facilitation, and model comprehension courses, reaching into the various disciplines involved. Software and systems engineers may need to be cross-trained. They certainly need to understand the fundamentals of one another's discipline to define effective processes that involve both. Although most organizations have internal resources that can provide much of this training, others may need to look into local university courses or professional training resources. Whatever way you acquire it, the quality, timeliness, and relevance of the training can have enormous implications for the success of your program.

2.3 Integrating Legacy Processes and Initiatives

Many organizations have already spent a great deal of time, effort, and money in establishing process improvement programs using one or more of the legacy models. How do you leverage that investment when moving to CMMI? Organizations that already have successful process improvement programs may have an easier task than those creating one from scratch, for three fundamental reasons. First, they probably have the entire improvement infrastructure in place and merely need to extend it to include the new disciplines or organizations. Second, they may have existing leadership support for this type of improvement and a fundamental appreciation of process improvement. Third, and most importantly, members of the initiative should have real success stories that they can use in promoting process improvement in those areas of the company not involved with the legacy efforts. This good news may not convince everyone, but it should at least win a hearing and will certainly provide executives with some of the support they need to pursue the program.

While establishing objectives is key to novice process improvement champions, identifying the barriers to achieving desired objectives may be the equivalent challenge in moving from a legacy model(s) to an integrated approach. You should have a good feel for the location of the pockets of resistance in your organization. Work carefully to provide these skeptics with the first benefits, if possible. Be sure to include them when setting goals and identifying initial processes.

To win over doubters, you may need to return to the early days of your process improvement experience and actively market the new integrated approach. Although this book will provide some of the raw material for that marketing, ultimately it is your responsibility to show how integrating processes and process improvement will benefit the organizations involved. Be upbeat about the opportunity. Have meetings between the "new member" organizations and some of your process improvement leads in which you give concrete examples of how process improvement works and its effects on the rank and file. Be honest about risks and barriers and proud of your achievements. After all, if you hadn't been successful, you wouldn't be considering an integrated approach.

One danger arises when you assume that disciplines new to the process improvement effort will be able, in a relatively short time, to achieve the same level of process maturity as the disciplines that have been using the legacy models for many years. While the use of the legacy models will facilitate the efforts to bring new disciplines into the integrated approach, a multiyear adoption schedule will likely still be needed.

Another risk (or possible benefit) relates to the program's effects on your customers and suppliers (or, more generally, your business partners). In some instances, your partner may be considering the same type of integrated process improvement. If so, you can cooperate in the experience, share lessons learned, and work together in defining processes that are common to both organizations or that span the partnership interface. In other instances, you will need to let your partners know how your process changes will affect them. Although the impact may be negative, it is more likely that your partners will also reap benefits as your organization performs better.

Most of the organizations that have been pilots for the CMMI Product Suite have developed a mapping between their existing process improvement assets and the CMMI. This mapping provides a good sense of the "delta" between where you are and where integration will take you. It can be used to monitor progress and to market integration by showing how little additional work is necessary to gain the benefits of integrated process improvement.

2.4 Using Assessments

Assessments are the Dr. Jekyl and Mr. Hyde of process improvement. On the one hand, they provide diagnostic support and document hard-earned progress. On the other hand, they can be used as a weapon to force compliance, support preformed management opinions, or limit access to contract opportunities. Obtaining a specific process area capability level or maturity level by a particular date is often used as a goal. While this tactic can be very effective when applied rationally, it can also lead to the dreaded scourge of all true process improvement advocates—the checklist mentality. Integrated process improvement broadens the range of potential victims of this syndrome, especially for processes across organizational boundaries. Fortunately, some good ways exist to prevent organizations from falling into this trap.

One way to prevent the emergence of a checklist mentality is to make sure everyone understands that assessments are intended to support process improvement and are temporal in nature. Unlike your grades in high school, they don't necessarily end up on your "permanent record." Rather, they highlight strengths that will help you succeed and identify weaknesses that could damage your business.

Another strategy is to ensure that assessments are timed so that they are not "big bang" events but rather represent the culmination of a methodical improvement plan. To prevent the assessment from being viewed as a "final exam," some organizations have implemented a series of mini-assessments along the way, each of which supports the improvements needed before the milestone assessment occurs. In this way, assessment is seen as a way of helping achieve the goals, rather than a goal in and of itself.

2.5 Integrated Process Improvement Examples

In this section we pay homage to some of the pioneers in the integrated process improvement movement. These organizations identified and responded to a business need to bring together the various process improvement initiatives.

- The U.S. Federal Aviation Administration (FAA) was spending considerable energy on separate, uncoordinated process improvement activities, so it developed and deployed an integrated model.

- Litton PRC's approach to integrating its software and systems engineering process improvement could provide a road map for organizations in their transition from the Software Engineering CMM to CMMI-SE/SW.

- Lockheed Martin responded to an unmet need for better assessment efficiency by developing a creative appraisal method.

- An integrated enterprise-wide process was created at Northrop Grumman to build upon its successful experiences with the Software CMM.

- Raytheon was smothering under several feet of engineering processes and standards, so it integrated its product development process.

- Sverdrup Technology took a chance on beginning its process improvement journey with an integrated model that was still very much a work in progress.

- THALES (formerly Thomson CSF), like Northrop Grumman, wanted to leverage software process improvement successes and found that it needed to include surrounding processes and disciplines.

These organizational stories provide the reader with insight into how integrated process improvement works in real companies. Each of the descriptions is organized into three sections: the *problem*, the *solution*, and *pearls of wisdom* that may help you and your organization. Note that the results mentioned and opinions expressed here are those of the organizations cited and not necessarily those of this book's authors or the larger CMMI team. The approaches may or may not be appropriate to your particular needs—only you can determine that. Where you feel it is appropriate, use the ideas and draw on their experiences as you plan your own program.

2.5.1 Federal Aviation Administration: The First Integrated Model

The Problem. The FAA was using three separate models to guide process improvement in various parts of the organization. Although some progress was being made, the organization clearly needed better coordination and a tighter focus on process improvement goals.

The Solution. The FAA developed a single CMM to guide process improvement within its diverse organizations—the first major integrated CMM in existence.[6] The FAA-iCMM, released in 1997, faithfully and robustly captures and integrates all principles, concepts, and practices of the Systems Engineering CMM, the Software Acquisition CMM, and the CMM for Software. It is now guiding the improvement of the FAA-wide processes to manage, acquire, and engineer systems, products, and services. In addition, the FAA developed a companion appraisal method that integrates a variety of approaches for measuring improvement progress against the model.

The FAA-iCMM rapidly became the single framework for improvement across the FAA. In 1997, the Associate Administrator for Research and Acquisition designated selected major acquisition programs as being targeted to achieve FAA-iCMM maturity level 2 by December 1999. Soon several additional programs and organizations across the FAA life cycle began applying the FAA-iCMM. By 1999, the acquisition and operational organizations, representing the majority of FAA personnel, committed to a common improvement goal: to realize high-quality

---

6. The information in this section is based on Ibrahim, Linda. *Using an Integrated Capability Maturity Model—The FAA Experience.* Proceedings of the Tenth Annual International Symposium of the International Council on Systems Engineering (INCOSE), MN, July 2000, pp. 643–648.

solutions to agency and user needs, predictable cost and schedule, and increasing productivity. As of early 2001, FAA was using the iCMM to support its evolutionary restructuring into a more service-based organization. As each service team is launched, the processes are defined in accordance with the iCMM.

Initial anecdotal data indicate that the FAA-iCMM efforts have led to many benefits: better predictability; improved communication; improved teamwork; increased quality; greater consistency; cost reductions; time savings; greater clarity of roles, responsibilities, and processes; a more streamlined work effort; easier training of new hires; and more appreciation and attention to the roles of different disciplines and processes.

The FAA intends to enhance the FAA-iCMM to include additional disciplines so as to address broader agency needs. Possible new targets include strategic planning, investment management, security, safety, and specialized technical and operational processes. The FAA-iCMM, the appraisal method, training materials, and enthusiastic support are all available to the general public.

Because the FAA believes in standardized improvement models, it has pledged to adopt CMMI when it believes that CMMI will meet the agency's needs.[7] Until that time, the FAA will continue to support the CMMI effort by sharing its ongoing, leading-edge experience in developing and using the FAA-iCMM.

Pearls of Wisdom

- The integrated approach identifies many cross-organizational issues and provides a unique opportunity to address them.

- It has proved useful to adopt an integrated model to prevent sub-optimization of processes in a cross-discipline environment.

- Explicitly identifying, recognizing, and mapping legacy process improvement investments to the integrated effort decreases the chance that these investments will be marginalized or duplicated.

- The FAA-iCMM's architecture of continuous representation with staging provides a well-balanced combination of guidance and flexibility that is ideal for the FAA's integrated organizational environment.

---

7. For example, current formal releases of CMMI do not include Acquisition as a discipline; it is a central component of the FAA-iCMM.

2.5.2 Litton PRC: Core Business Processes Guide Integration

The Problem. When Litton PRC made the decision in 1996 to adopt a systems engineering capability model to complement its adoption of a software engineering model, the process improvement staff was struck by the considerable overlap present in the two models. Furthermore, most of the process areas where general overlap occurred also described the process requirements from perspectives that were unique to either software or systems engineering.[8]

The Solution. Two pivotal events followed quickly upon the decision to deal with the overlap. The first was a product of the continuous improvement legacy of the Litton PRC organization. Rather than spawn a totally separate group that might duplicate processes with a slightly different perspective, the systems engineering group approached the Litton PRC Software Engineering Process Group (SEPG) with a request. They asked the SEPG to take responsibility for the common process areas it was already supporting for software engineering and to upgrade those areas to accommodate the requirements of the systems engineering model. The Systems Engineering Lead Team offered to author, control, and maintain the process areas specific to systems engineering. Justification was based on a simple business case: it was less expensive to control and maintain a common set of process areas that met the needs of both models than to control and maintain two divergent sets. Within weeks, the SEPG proposed that the systems engineering team join the SEPG to become an Engineering Process Group (EPG). This move involved more than a name change—it was the first major step in changing Litton PRC from a two-discipline culture to a multidiscipline culture.

The second event occurred when SEI and INCOSE agreed with EIA to develop a single Systems Engineering Capability Model that eventually became EIA/IS 731. Faced with the challenge of the SE-CMM disappearing and morphing into a new model, Litton PRC studied what would have to change in its company processes. Personnel found that the firm's processes, when combined into a complete and unified engineering process, didn't really match any model exactly. Where the company used Litton PRC-wide processes, it had not been necessary to train the process executors in any model, but rather in adherence to the company processes. Therefore, the processes themselves were the core element of the business, not the model. Indeed, as models changed, the

---

8. This section is based on material provided by Hal Wilson and Craig Hollenbach of Litton PRC.

core processes were merely slightly amended to cover gaps when improvements were suggested. From then on, the Litton PRC processes no longer attempted to match the terminology or the structure of the model du jour—they simply attempted to be the most complete and effective processes in support of Litton PRC's business.

Litton PRC has never required that its software engineers become literate in the CMM for Software. Instead, these software engineers must become literate in and execute the corporate processes. Therefore, any model change has far less impact on ongoing projects because workers understand what they must do and take the necessary steps. The task of mapping functions to the model is left to a central Litton PRC organization, the Systems and Process Engineer Group, which also provides the assessment resources for Litton PRC and the process definition core talent within the company.

Litton PRC is pleased that it undertook the integration of software and systems engineering processes when they did, because this move enabled the firm to achieve an advanced position on CMMI implementation. On the downside, the company might have saved $1 to $2 million by waiting for the CMMI's completion. One PRC vice president recently said, "At least it gives those that come after us a pretty good measure of what the CMMI is really worth to them."

Pearls of Wisdom

- An integrated process improvement group is essential to success.
- It is useful to focus on core business processes and use models to look for gaps and areas to improve.
- If you train to the processes, rather than the model, then model changes will have smaller effects on the organization.
- Processes work better when they directly match the needs of the organization in which they are applied than when they match a generic model to which the organization must adapt.

2.5.3 Lockheed Martin: A Continuous Assessment Method

The Problem. Assessments are a difficult but necessary component of process improvement. Although Lockheed Martin realized the benefits of process improvement, as the company began to apply it in an integrated fashion involving more organizations and disciplines, the cost and logistics of performing assessments became extremely burdensome.

The Solution. Lockheed Martin's Continuous Appraisal Method (CAM)[9] is a "build-a-little, test-a-little" approach to process assessment that is effective in minimizing the burden imposed by assessments while maximizing their benefits. Developed jointly by Lockheed Martin Information Systems and Lockheed Martin Mission Systems–Systems and Software Resource Center, CAM represents a significant departure from the CMM-Based Assessment for Internal Process Improvement (CBA IPI) method. It provides a high-value-added, nonadversarial process maturity appraisal method at reduced cost.

A CAM assessment involves three phases. In the first phase, the organization develops a standard process that complies with the target maturity level. An independent team appraises this process and identifies deficiencies. Once those deficiencies have been addressed, the independent team reappraises the process. Once certified, the standard process is subjected to a pilot project to ensure its usability and, if successful, deployed to all projects.

The second phase involves the selection and appraisal of a few programs to the target maturity level. Deficiencies are identified, addressed, and reappraised until the processes associated with each process area are compliant.

In the third phase, the organization institutionalizes the process by repeating the phase II activities for the remaining projects (Figure 2-1). Maintenance reviews are periodically conducted on all projects to ensure continuing compliance.

A team consisting of at least two people—an Independent Appraisal Team Lead and the Organization's Process Owner—conducts an appraisal. The lack of preparation time for the projects means that there is no objective evidence library to build, no "studying for the test," and no practice interviews. Project personnel receive incentives to participate as additional critical reviewers. The appraisals are nonadversarial,

---

9. The information presented in this section is based on the following paper: Carr, Marvin, and W. Neil Crowder. *Continuous Appraisal Method (CAM): A New Paradigm for Benchmarking Process Maturity.* Presented at INCOSE 2000.

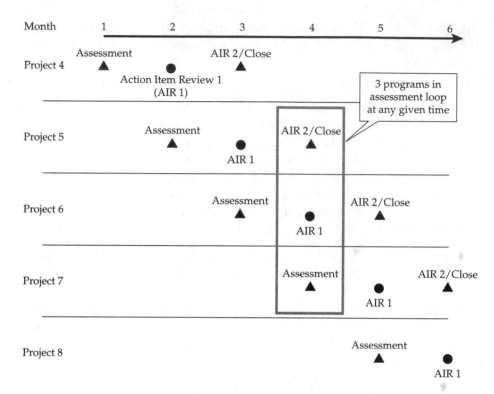

Figure 2-1: *Typical CAM phase III schedule*

because the only way to fail is to not correct identified deficiencies. When the projects in an organization meet all practices for a level, the organization is declared to be functioning at that level.

Pearls of Wisdom

- More effective process improvement results from the continuous appraisal of projects.
- Emphasizing proactive process improvement replaces the audit philosophy and decreases the fear factor involved in appraisals.
- There is value in focusing on *continuous process improvement* as opposed to "snapshot" audits.
- It is advisable to maintain a consistent appraisal team for consistent findings.

2.5.4 Northrop Grumman ESSS: An Integrated Enterprise Process

The Problem. The Northrop Grumman Electronic Sensors and Systems Sector (ESSS) had successfully improved its processes for software using the Software CMM. Because most large projects in the Sector were run with integrated product teams, however, the interfaces linking software with other processes became an issue. Management desired to build on the benefits of improved process definition within software and extend them across the enterprise.

The Solution. The ESSS developed and deployed an Integrated Enterprise Process (IEP).[10] The IEP addresses all disciplines associated with project development, and it includes program management, systems engineering, software engineering, hardware engineering, manufacturing, program operations, quality assurance, and support engineering. Key elements of the IEP include an infrastructure to support Integrated Product Team (IPT) development, common and closely integrated processes across disciplines, a process time management system to record and measure performance, and tailored procedures for projects. In large part it is based on the proven successes of the Northrop Grumman ESSS Software Engineering Process Organization.

An essential prerequisite to the success of this endeavor was the commitment of Northrop Grumman's senior management. Given the cultural issues and differences between and within the various organizational levels and components, the changes needed for the IEP effort would have posed insurmountable challenges without this commitment. Senior management established an Engineering Process Organization, consisting of a process group, a users group, and a process change control board (PCCB). This organization is sponsored by and reports to the ESSS Vice President of Engineering and Manufacturing.

The Engineering Process Organization is responsible for defining, maintaining, and improving processes; developing or acquiring training courses; transitioning projects to the processes; and maintaining process assets (which include a metrics database and a training database). The users group, which represents the process users, is

---

10. The information in this section is based in part on the following paper: Freeman, Don, Michael Hinkey, and Jesse Martak. *Integrated Engineering Process Covering All Engineering Disciplines*. Presented at the SEPG 99 Conference.

staffed with personnel from engineering, manufacturing, and other business areas. It reviews and approves new processes and provides feedback based on practical project experience. The PCCB uses a formal process to release updates to the standard processes and ensures appropriate stakeholder review.

Prior to full-scale deployment of new processes, pilot projects are chosen to test, fine-tune, and measure the effectiveness of the process change. This approach facilitates the broad adoption of the processes.

Wherever possible, the engineering process organization sought to define common processes that could be used for all of the company's engineering. A large core group of common processes was viewed as essential to the success of integrated process engineering. Where complete commonality was not possible, closely interrelated processes were identified. Although some discipline-unique processes are inevitable, the effort was made to keep them to a minimum.

As no existing process model covered the desired scope, the Engineering Process Organization created an Integrated Capability Model (I-CM), making maximum use of existing models. Its sources included the Software CMM, EIA/IS 731, ISO 9000, CMMI draft materials, and "best value process requirements" from disciplines not explicitly addressed in the existing models. The I-CM specifies that projects must use integrated product teams (IPT), hold formal work-product inspections of key system development products prior to use outside of the IPT that developed them, and have a requirements manager oversee the critical area of requirements.

The process time management system is based on standard process activities that are mapped to the integrated engineering process. This mapping facilitates the comparison of measurement data across projects. The system records the activity, life-cycle phase, and product being addressed. All work must be identified as either original effort, work-product inspection effort, or rework effort.

Tailoring of the standard engineering process on projects ensures that the enterprise as a whole can operate at "maturity level 3" in all areas; individual disciplines may achieve higher maturity levels. Data are being collected to lay the foundation for enterprise-wide activities that reach higher maturity levels in the future. Indeed, projects must create a comprehensive program plan that goes beyond collecting stovepipe documents to explicitly address all common, interrelated, and discipline-unique processes. Thus Northrop Grumman no longer needs documents such as a traditional software development plan, systems engineering management plan, and stand-alone SQA plan. Through the IEP and the associated comprehensive program plan, activities are fully integrated and redundant information is eliminated. To date, the company has achieved an order-of-magnitude reduction in the amount of required documentation.

Pearls of Wisdom

- It is important to form an integrated team staffed with real process users that is empowered to steer process improvement effort. Team members can force the process definitions to be user-friendly and address multidiscipline concerns in the real world.

- A well-designed cost accounting system can greatly facilitate the collection of useful process metrics data, particularly for cross-functional activities.

- To integrate processes across disciplines, the organization must make a focused, continuing effort to identify common process opportunities.

2.5.5 Raytheon—Integrated Product Development Process

The Problem. Large programs are difficult to manage; keeping them on schedule and budget may seem an impossible task. At Raytheon, this task was complicated by a nearly 2½-foot-high stack of separate, over-lapping, and sometimes contradictory standards, processes, and documentation requirements designed as a "one-size-fits-all" standard.

The Solution. The Integrated Product Development Process (IPDP)[11] is a comprehensive process engineered for the defense industry. It includes the concurrent engineering tasks for the program-capture phase of a program through production and disposal (Figure 2-2).

A fundamental concept in the IPDP is that of the "nominal program"—that is, the program life cycle as described by government documentation, standards, and so on. The nominal program is the basis for the

---

11. The information in this section is based on Clouse, Aaron, and Richard Shaw. *An Integrated Product Development Process Case Study.* Proceedings of the Sixth Annual International Symposium of the International Council on Systems Engineering (INCOSE), Boston, MA, July 7–11, 1996, vol. I, pp. 541–546.

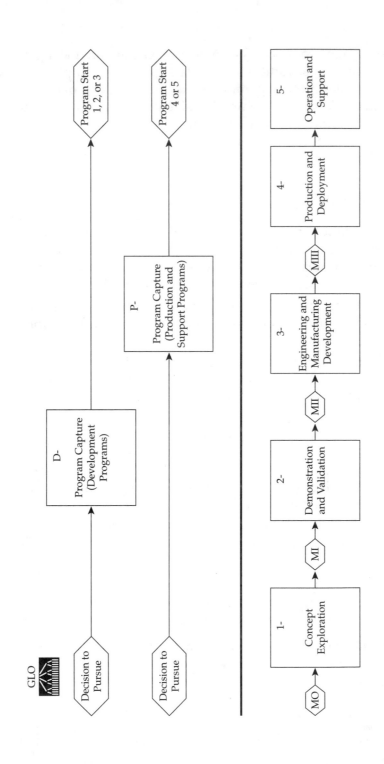

Figure 2-2: *IPDP flowchart*

full IPDP, and all of the flowcharts and task descriptors are based on it. Of course, virtually all real programs are unique in some way and therefore don't match exactly (or, in some cases, even roughly) the nominal program. Thus, before its application to a specific program, the IPDP must be tailored. This tailoring ensures that only the steps necessary for the program are implemented, and it eliminates the specter of multiple-foot stacks of standards.

The IPDP is deployed to programs through a series of training workshops. The first workshop helps organize the program and plans the process for tailoring the IPDP by creating a program plan. Once the program is staffed with the lead engineers, these workers further tailor the process in a two-day workshop facilitated by a trained moderator, aided by an IPDP champion and clerical assistance to document the results. Key components of this workshop are brainstorming sessions to determine assumptions about the program. Once everyone involved agrees to them, those assumptions drive the tailoring of the IPDP for the program. Because an important element of the tailoring session is the drive to keep the program focused on customer needs, ideally customer representatives will attend as well.

Pearls of Wisdom

- A single, tailorable, integrated process for a large organization has large payback.
- Integrated process improvement yields more accurate project planning and reduced cycle time.
- An integrated approach increases buy-in from all affected organizations.

2.5.6 Sverdrup Technology: Starting from Scratch with CMMI

The Problem. The Sverdrup Advanced Systems Group (ASG), which supports diverse technical domains and customer cultures and is physically distributed in 10 office locations across eight states, had no formal process foundation. The group needed to develop and institutionalize an integrated engineering process for systems and software engineering.[12]

---

12. This section is based on material provided by Jeffrey Dutton of Sverdrup.

The Solution. The Sverdrup strategy for success was developed around five major themes: distributed process infrastructure, process and product engineering cost reduction, focus on the internal customer, consistent tailoring mechanisms, and extendibility of resulting processes.

The ASG had to develop both the infrastructure and CMMI process culture from scratch. Its first attempt centered on experienced and motivated process engineering representatives from each field office, who collaborated through a single Web site. Unfortunately, this initial group did not meet its scheduled objectives, primarily due to its failure to pay enough attention to motivating intermediate management. Sufficient buy-in was achieved only after a mini-assessment with the CMMI-SE/SW and the realization that the integrated model would affect nearly all functions of the organization. Eventually, the initial group was disbanded in favor of an Engineering Performance Improvement Group (EPIC), which is currently developing an advanced distributed work environment that will be used to support both process engineering and project management.

Minimizing the cost of process and product engineering was critical to maintaining Sverdrup's corporate profit goals and directly supported the generation of new business. To reduce process engineering costs, the company decided to implement both system and software engineering in a single integrated process, saving an estimated 40% over the cost involved in adopting each type of engineering separately. Other cost reduction activities included the following:

- Minimizing the size of the full-time staff
- "Workshopping" all technical and management meetings
- Relying on the contributions of some of the best engineers in the organization as process designers and domain experts
- Implementing the distributed work environment
- Using pilot projects to finalize the details of the standard process and testing its veracity
- Adopting a knowledge management approach to training

The development of the Standard Integrated Engineering Process was the goal of the cost reduction work. The all-inclusive *Integrated Engineering Handbook* focuses directly on the needs of the project manager, engineers, and engineering support personnel, as well as intermediate and senior management (Figure 2-3).

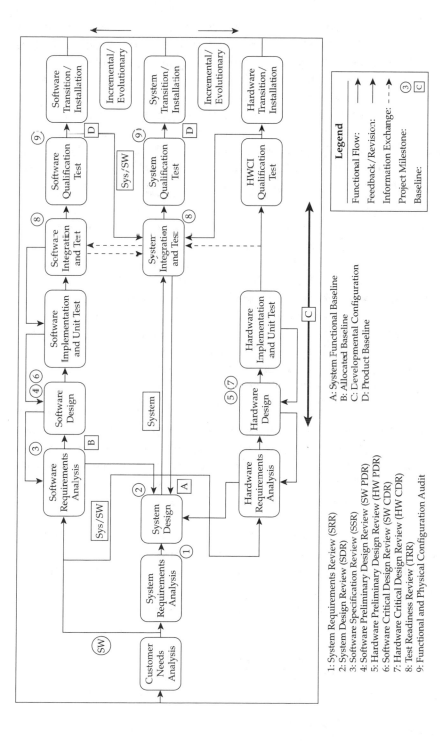

Legend

Functional Flow:
Feedback/Revision:
Information Exchange: – – –
Project Milestone: ③
Baseline: [C]

A: System Functional Baseline
B: Allocated Baseline
C: Developmental Configuration
D: Product Baseline

1: System Requirements Review (SRR)
2: System Design Review (SDR)
3: Software Specification Review (SSR)
4: Software Preliminary Design Review (SW PDR)
5: Hardware Preliminary Design Review (HW PDR)
6: Software Critical Design Review (SW CDR)
7: Hardware Critical Design Review (HW CDR)
8: Test Readiness Review (TRR)
9: Functional and Physical Configuration Audit

Figure 2-3: *EPIC integrated engineering life cycle*

The process engineering group worked hard to put itself in the shoes of its customers. The Standard Integrated Engineering Process and its work products were designed for clarity and ease of use from the point of view of the project manager first, the engineering and engineering support personnel second, and intermediate and senior management third—a focus greatly appreciated when the company began to test its process in pilot projects. An Engineering Management Council, chaired by the General Manager and composed of the organization's business managers, was established to operate as the "owner" of the Standard Integrated Engineering Process and to provide oversight and direction to the EPIC.

Because Sverdrup's engineering projects, products, and services were so diverse, a straightforward, repeatable, tailoring mechanism was crucial to ASG success. A Project Attribute Form was developed that describes the essential characteristics of each project; the form is complete enough to differentiate projects on the important points. From these attributes a tailoring guidance factor—a function of the number of developmental items, architecture complexity, integration complexity, and the number of project technical personnel—is calculated for each project and applied consistently in decisions regarding project planning, monitoring, and engineering.

Not surprisingly, concerns arose regarding the rapid evolution of process standards and practices. First, an integrated process architecture was developed to insulate core processes from all but the most drastic changes in the CMMI-SE/SW. Twelve core processes, including six processes focused specifically on product engineering and engineering support, were fashioned around the ISO/IEC 12207 life-cycle framework. This effort proved very successful. Second, Sverdrup joined the CMMI Product Development Team. Through that collaboration, it has gained a much greater appreciation of the underpinnings of the model and a clearer understanding of the potential direction of its evolution.

Pearls of Wisdom

- It is important to focus on the development of a straightforward (if not simple) and consistent method for tailoring standard processes, especially for organizations that include highly diverse project domains.

- Cross-discipline meetings can be contentious and time-consuming. The "workshop" approach to process engineering meetings can result in a tenfold increase in productivity for typical meetings.

- Adoption of distributed work technology can improve process engineering efficiency and reduce training costs substantially, especially when the organization is applying integrated process improvement.

- The (early) use of pilot projects with a draft integrated process allows for fine-tuning of the process. A good cross-section of projects gives early feedback on where improvements are needed.

2.5.7 THALES: An Integrated Improvement Process

The Problem. During the period 1992–1996, THALES made a significant effort in the domain of software process improvement, using the Capability Maturity Model for Software (CMM) to improve its software process to maturity level 3. For the company to obtain the maximum return on its investment, however, the surrounding processes needed to be improved as well. As a consequence, other THALES departments began developing models for their specific disciplines. This abundance of models led to incompatible activities and separate ownership of the practices and related knowledge.[13]

The first process that was directly linked with the software process was the systems engineering process. Systems engineers are the "customers" for software developers. As a result, the firm's concern about process evaluation, improvement, and management was extended to systems engineering, and Systems Engineering Process Improvement was established as a top management priority for the years 1996–2000. This effort became known as the System Engineering Process Improvement (SEPI) initiative. The first model was derived from the SE-CMM for the purpose of improving systems engineering practices. THALES' main objective was to provide explicit direction for process improvement that was consistent with the software approach.

The Solution. Ultimately, THALES decided to join the CMMI project. This project offers the opportunity to examine and consolidate the tentative approaches arising from various disciplines as distinct as

---

13. This section is based on material provided by Denise Cattan of THALES Corporation.

purchasing, logistic support, and bid and proposal, where each discipline has specific, unique needs. The combination of engineering systems and software with the CMMI ensures consistency between disciplines and use of a common language, and it reduces the interface misinterpretation. Use of the model is facilitated by appropriate training and communication and by a significant effort in language adaptation. The model serves as a reference when developing checklists in the languages of the disciplines; practitioners can then use these checklists in their day-to-day work for process audits. Thus the checklists represent good practices that are shared throughout the THALES group based on the CMMI model (Figure 2-4). A set of metrics has been identified and a measurement program is being developed to collect the results.

Pearls of Wisdom

- Simultaneous improvement is important; no value-added arises from improving processes for a discipline that interacts with another discipline for which the maturity level difference is two or higher.

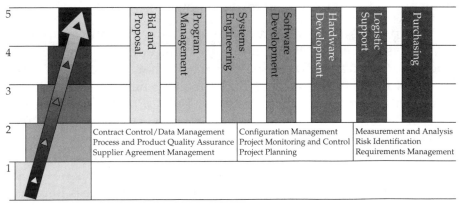

CMMI taken as reference: level 2 requirements are applicable to all disciplines (management and engineering).

Approach:
- CMMI assessment by BU with TTM follow-up
- Campus qualifying training
- Consistency with ISO 9000-2000/CMMI

Figure 2-4: *THALES CMMI initiative*

- The "not invented here" culture should be opposed. The goal is to reuse other units' know-how and to disseminate good practices from one discipline to another.

- You are never alone. Whenever you change something, another area will be affected. Consequently, the organization should ensure that its communications lines among the disciplines involved are strong and used frequently.

Chesapeake Bay Area
LandSat 5 Thematic Mapper (1998)
NASA—Goddard Space Flight Center
Scientific Visualization Studio

Part II

The CMMI Models

The Chesapeake Bay is a highly productive economic engine. It is also a fragile ecosystem. Its best use and long-term prospects depend on an understanding of the complex relationships that exist between nature and humans.

Similarly, CMMI products are complex structures containing multiple layers of information. To achieve the highest benefit, users need to be aware of sometimes subtle relationships. In Part II, we discuss the CMMI architecture and components. The goal is to help the reader more clearly understand how they relate to each other and to process improvement as a whole.

Part II Contents

Chapter 3. The CMMI Concept

In which the reader is introduced to the CMMI project, its goals, limitations, accomplishments, and history.

Chapter 4. CMMI Content

In which we describe the various elements and materials found in the CMMI models. Their relative importance is discussed to some extent, and the locations of the materials are elucidated.

Chapter 5. CMMI Representations

In which the authors describe the two model representations—staged and continuous—and explain how they were accomplished within the CMMI project. A discussion of how the continuous representation can approximate the staged representation is presented.

Chapter 6. CMMI Dimensions for Measuring Improvement

In which the authors explain the manner by which the CMMI models—in both representations—guide and measure the improvement of processes. Both the capability and maturity dimensions are addressed. The concept of generic practices is introduced and their role in CMMI explained.

Chapter 7. CMMI Process Areas

In which the CMMI process dimension is described in detail, so that the practitioner may understand the relationship between the goals, practices, and improvement dimensions.

Chapter 3

The CMMI Concept

It must be remembered that there is nothing more difficult to plan, more uncertain of success, nor more dangerous to manage than the creation of a new order of things. For the initiator has the enmity of all who would profit by the preservation of the old institutions, and merely lukewarm defenders in those who would gain by the new order.
Machiavelli, *The Prince* (1513)

In this age, which believes that there is a short cut to everything, the greatest lesson to be learned is that the most difficult way is, in the long run, the easiest.
Henry Miller, *The Books in My Life* (1957)

The implementation of integrated process improvement in an organization is possible using two or more single-discipline models. There are many advantages, however, in having just one model that covers multiple disciplines. For this reason, the U.S. Department of Defense—specifically, the Deputy Under Secretary of Defense (Science and Technology)—teamed up with the Software Engineering Institute (SEI) at Carnegie Mellon University and the National Defense Industrial Association (NDIA) to jointly sponsor the development of Capability Maturity Model Integration (CMMI). In 2000, this effort produced the first integrated CMMI models, together with associated assessment and training materials.

This chapter provides information on the CMMI project, its objectives and scope, the source models on which it drew, and the concept it developed.

3.1 CMMI Project Organization

During the development phase that led to the initial CMMI materials, the project was organized with a Steering Group, a Product Development Team, and a Stakeholder Group. In all, it involved the efforts of approximately 175 people over a period of more than two years. The three groups comprised representatives from industry, government, and the SEI. Representatives of the disciplines whose models were to be integrated into CMMI were included in all three groups.

The Steering Group produced a list of requirements for CMMI, which was reviewed by the Stakeholder Group and subsequently used by the Product Development Team to guide its creation of the CMMI products. The Product Development Team was a cross-discipline group created for the initial development work; it was charged with ensuring that the viewpoints and interests of each discipline were adequately considered in the integration process. The Stakeholder Group reviewed the initial draft CMMI materials, with its work being followed by a public review of a second round of draft materials, prior to the version 1.0 release in late 2000.

The CMMI Team

The following organizations supplied members to the CMMI Product Development Team: ADP Inc., AT&T Labs, BAE, Boeing, Computer Sciences Corporation, EER Systems, Ericsson Canada, Ernst and Young, General Dynamics, Harris Corporation, Honeywell, KPMG, Litton PRC, Lockheed Martin, Motorola, Northrop Grumman, Pacific Bell, Q-Labs, Raytheon, Rockwell Collins, Software Engineering Institute, Sverdrup Corporation, Thomson CSF, TRW, U.S. Federal Aviation Administration, U.S. Institute for Defense Analyses, U.S. National Security Agency, U.S. Air Force, U.S. Army, and U.S. Navy.

The cross-discipline team that produced the initial CMMI models included members with backgrounds in software engineering, systems engineering, and integrated product and process development. Most engineering organizations maintain these skills, but the manner in which they are aligned and interact varies across organizations. Thus the CMMI team not only had to resolve differences between the three source models, but also had to bridge the cultural, linguistic, and professional differences separating engineering specialties and organizations. The bridges that had to be built in constructing the CMMI models serve as precursors of those that users of the models will need to construct to successfully support integrated process improvement and process assessment.

During the CMMI development effort, the team actively sought to keep balanced membership across the three disciplines. This move was supported by the strong interest espoused by the software and systems engineering communities. Thanks to the wide acceptance of the Software CMM, strong advocacy was provided by the SEI and organizations that had used the model, understood its value, and wanted to see that value preserved in the integrated CMMI models. Likewise, in the systems engineering world, the International Council on Systems Engineering (INCOSE) advocated inclusion of systems engineering practices. Even the integrated product and process development community was represented on the Product Development Team, albeit with members voicing a somewhat wider range of views on how integrated product and process development should be handled than did the more established discipline representatives. In the end, this team of experienced and active people, each of whom brought his or her specific expertise and preferences to the table, came together to create version 1.0 of the CMMI product suite.

Once the development phase of the initial CMMI product suite was complete, a new organizational structure was established. That is, the CMMI Product Development Team evolved into the CMMI Product Team. This team has access to expert groups for software, systems engineering, integrated product and process development, acquisition, assessment, and the core CMMI components. A configuration control board was established to guide CMMI evolution, and the SEI was named as the Steward of the CMMI product suite. In its role as Steward, SEI is responsible for maintenance and support of CMMI. As time goes on, new cross-functional teams of experts will be required to

Figure 3-1: *Phase II CMMI project organization*

handle revisions of existing products and the subsequent work of adding more disciplines to the CMMI framework.

Figure 3-1 shows a recent (January 2001) CMMI project organization.

3.2 CMMI Objectives

The CMMI project had both initial and longer-term objectives. The initial objective (which was achieved in 2000 with the release of version 1.0 of the CMMI-SE/SW and CMMI-SE/SW/IPPD models) was to integrate three specific process improvement models: software, systems engineering, and integrated product and process development.[1] This integration was intended to reduce the cost of implementing multi-discipline model-based process improvement by

---

1. CMMI-SE/SW designates the CMMI model that contains the disciplines of systems engineering and software; CMMI-SE/SW/IPPD indicates the model that adds materials for integrated product and process development to CMMI-SE/SW.

- Eliminating inconsistencies
- Reducing duplication
- Increasing clarity and understanding
- Providing common terminology
- Providing consistent style
- Establishing uniform construction rules
- Maintaining common components
- Assuring consistency with ISO 15504
- Being sensitive to the implications for legacy efforts

The longer-term objective was to lay a foundation for the later addition of other disciplines (such as acquisition and security) to CMMI. Figure 3-2 illustrates these objectives. To facilitate both current and future model integration, the CMMI Product Development Team created an automated, extensible framework that can house model components, training material components, and assessment materials. Defined rules govern the potential addition of more disciplines into this framework.

From the start, the CMMI project had to find an acceptable balance between competing requirements relating to change. The task of integration, which by its very nature requires change from each of the original single-discipline models, meant that all model users could expect new ways of thinking about process improvement to be needed in a CMMI environment. At the same time, an equally strong requirement called for protecting the investments in process improvement made by

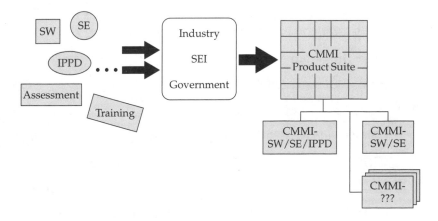

Figure 3-2: *The CMMI concept*

former users of those models, which meant controlling the introduction of new materials for each discipline. In the end, CMMI users will determine whether the CMMI project has achieved an appropriate balance between old and new for the initial effort, and whether in the future the project demonstrates the needed sensitivity in this area as other disciplines are added.

One pleasant surprise of the CMMI project was the extent of the integration achieved between software and systems engineering. To their amazement, members of the CMMI Product Development Team found that the integration of software and systems engineering produced a truly common set of process areas, with the only differences being relegated to "discipline amplifications," which are included in the

---

CMMI Milestones

1997 CMMI initiated by U.S. Department of Defense and NDIA

1998 First team meeting held

First A-Spec (1.1) released

Steering Group charter released

Model version 0.1 released

1999 Revised A-Spec (1.4) released

Custodian plan released

Concept of operations released

Model version 0.2 released

Transition plan released

First pilot completed

2000 Additional pilots completed

CMMI-SE/SW/IPPD/A to stakeholders released for review

CMMI-SE/SW version 1.0 released for initial use

CMMI-SE/SW/IPPD version 1.0 released for initial use

CMMI-SE/SW/IPPD/A released for initial piloting

informative model material. At the outset of the project, CMMI was envisioned as including distinct software and systems models, reflecting significant differences in the way in which the source models had been inspired, designed, developed, and implemented. In hindsight, the commonality is perfectly understandable. The fundamentals of process management and project management can be applied to any discipline. If one writes the engineering process areas in a very general manner, they can be applied directly to any form of engineering—including software. In the same way, the practices of the support processes such as configuration management and training may be implemented differently for different disciplines, but the goals and practices remain the same.

3.3 The Three Source Models

To truly appreciate the significance of the CMMI accomplishments, you need to understand a bit of the history that led up to the development of the CMMI product suite. Of primary importance are the stories of the source models. Table 3-1 summarizes the three source models for CMMI-SE/SW/IPPD.

3.3.1 The CMM for Software

The character of software development sometimes seems closer to mathematics and art than it does to most other engineering disciplines. Software is inherently an intangible, intellectual development medium. No laws of physics govern its behavior; it is both marvelously and dangerously malleable. For this reason, it is critical that mature disciplines and processes be applied when working with software.

Table 3-1: *Source Models for CMMI-SE/SW/IPPD*

Model Discipline	Source Model
Software	SW-CMM, draft version 2(c)
Systems engineering	EIA/IS 731
Integrated product and process development	IPD CMM, version 0.98

Software engineering and process management have been intimately associated since the pioneering work of Ron Radice and Richard Phillips at IBM in the 1980s.[2] Basing their work on the tenets of the quality movement, Radice and Phillips led the way in crafting a way to capture the best practices of successful software developers and then organize those best practices in a way that helped struggling organizations get a handle on their processes and improve them. Given the nature of software development, it was not surprising that the large majority of the practices related to management discipline and processes.

Software Engineering

As defined in IEEE Standard 610.12, *software engineering* is the application of a systematic, disciplined, quantifiable approach to the development, operation, and maintenance of software—that is, the application of engineering to software.[3]

In 1986, Watts Humphrey, the SEI, and the Mitre Corporation responded to a request by the U.S. federal government to create a way of assessing the software capability of its contractors. The group used IBM's concepts to create a software maturity framework, a questionnaire, and two assessment methods. Over the next few years, this work was continued and refined.

In 1991, the SEI published the CMM for Software version 1.0, a model that describes the principles and practices underlying software process maturity. The CMM is organized to help software organizations improve along an evolutionary path, growing from an ad hoc, chaotic environment toward mature, disciplined software processes. The CMM was used and evaluated for two years, then revised and released as version 1.1 in 1993.[4] A similar revision was planned for 1997 as

---

2. Radice, R. A., J. T. Harding, P. E. Munnis, and R. W. Philips. "A Programming Process Study." *IBM System Journals,* 2/3, 1999. Radice, R. A., and R. W. Phillips. *Software Engineering, an Industrial Approach, vol. 1.* Englewood Cliffs, NJ: Prentice Hall, 1988.

3. *IEEE Standard Glossary of Software Engineering Terminology.* IEEE Standard 610.12–1990. New York: Institute of Electrical and Electronics Engineers, 1990.

4. Paulk, Mark C., et al. *Capability Maturity Model for Software, Version 1.1.* CMU/SEI-93-TR-24; also ESC-TR-93-177. Pittsburgh, PA: Software Engineering Institute, Carnegie Mellon University, Feb. 1993.

version 2.0;[5] this version was developed but never released as an independent model, however. The good work did not go to waste: the proposed revision was used as the source for the CMMI integration effort. In addition, two documents regarding software assessments were used: the CMM Appraisal Framework, version 1.0,[6] and the CMM-Based Appraisal for Internal Process Improvement (CBA IPI): Method Description.[7]

The IEEE definition of software engineering extends software engineering's scope beyond the primary material contained in the CMM for Software to include software-related topics such as requirements elicitation, installation, operation, and maintenance. The CMMI model covers these areas in more detail through inclusion of appropriate material from EIA/IS 731.

3.3.2 The Systems Engineering Capability Model

Systems engineering integrates all of the system-related disciplines so that systems meet business and technical needs in the most effective way, while striving to minimize local optimization and maximize return on investment. Another way of envisioning systems engineering is as the application of a set of rigorous engineering techniques to the solution of a complex technical problem.

Systems Engineering

INCOSE defines *systems engineering* as "an interdisciplinary approach and means to enable the realization of successful systems."[8]

---

5. For more on the history of the CMM for Software, see Paulk, Mark C. "The Evolution of the SEI's Capability Maturity Model for Software." *Software Process—Improvement and Practice*, 1995, pp. 3–15.

6. Masters, S., and C. Bothwell. *CMM Appraisal Framework (CMU/SEI-95-TR-001)*. Pittsburgh, PA: Software Engineering Institute, Carnegie Mellon University, Feb. 1995.

7. Dunaway, D., and S. Masters. *CMM-Based Appraisal for Internal Process Improvement (CBA IPI): Method Description (CMU/SEI-96-TR-007)*. Pittsburgh, PA: Software Engineering Institute, Carnegie Mellon University, April 1996.

8. INCOSE Winter Workshop 1996, January 1996.

It is difficult to fully understand the scope of systems engineering without looking at the various specialty disciplines associated with it. In *Essentials of Project and Systems Engineering Management*, Howard Eisner lists 30 key elements of systems engineering. These elements include such diverse areas as mission engineering, architectural design, life-cycle costing, alternatives analysis, technical data management, operations and maintenance, integrated logistics support, and reengineering.[9]

The systems engineering material in the CMMI has a complex history. In a modern-day "Tale of Two Capability Models," two organizations undertook to model systems engineering practices. In August 1995, the Enterprise Process Improvement Collaboration (EPIC), a group of industry, academic, and government organizations, released the Systems Engineering Capability Maturity Model (SE-CMM). EPIC enlisted the SEI and architect Roger Bate to lead the development. The team pulled its systems engineering expertise primarily from aerospace and defense industry corporations and from the Software Productivity Consortium. The result was a model based on the assessment model architecture contained in draft versions of ISO/IEC 15504 that addressed engineering, project, process, and organization practices.[10]

Around the same time that the SE-CMM was under development, INCOSE created a checklist for evaluating the capabilities of systems engineering organizations based on various engineering standards. Over time, this checklist evolved into a full-blown capability model known as the Systems Engineering Capability Assessment Model (SECAM). SECAM extended the SPICE concepts of a continuous model but focused more specifically on systems engineering practices than the SE-CMM, using EIA 632, "Processes for Engineering a Model," as the fundamental reference.

Needless to say, an environment with two models developed by two reputable organizations that purported to address the same issues was ripe for a model war. Which model would emerge as the "standard" by which organizations could be evaluated? After a year of heated

---

9. Eisner, Howard. *Essentials of Project and Systems Engineering Management*. New York: Wiley Interscience, 1997.

10. In January 1993, an international working group (WG 10) was formed as part of subcommittee 7 (SC7) of the ISO/IEC Joint Technical Committee 1 (JTC1) to create a standard for software process assessment. Piloting of working drafts was accomplished through a project called SPICE (Software Process Improvement and Capability dEtermination). The combined effort of WG 10 and the SPICE project resulted in the development of ISO/IEC 15504 as a draft standard.

discussions, in 1996 EPIC and INCOSE agreed to work together under the auspices of the Government Electronic and Information Technology Association (GEIA) of the Electronic Industries Alliance (EIA), with the goal of merging the two models into a single EIA standard. The result was an interim standard EIA/IS 731, "Systems Engineering Capability Model" (SECM).[11] By issuing the interim standard, the systems engineering community could apply a single, common description of systems engineering processes to the CMMI project.

Systems engineering in CMMI remains heavily influenced by EIA/IS 731. While echoes of the controversy between SECM and SE-CMM found voice in CMMI discussions, the resulting systems engineering content reflects an even stronger evolution of the original concepts. It preserves some of the innovations of EIA/IS 731 while providing a more consistent underlying architecture compatible with the emerging ISO standards.[12] The interim standard includes both the SECM model (Part 1) and an appraisal method (Part 2).

3.3.3 The Integrated Product Development CMM

The source model for integrated product and process development was a draft of the Integrated Product Development CMM, known as IPD CMM version 0.98. This model had been developed almost to the point of its initial formal release when the CMMI project began in 1998.

From the outset, the CMMI Steering Group wanted to include the concept of integrated product and process development (IPPD) in the CMMI product suite. This concept was fundamental to many of the large member corporations of NDIA, and it was strongly supported by the Department of Defense (DOD).[13] Unfortunately, the definition of IPPD used in the CMMI requirements document was derived from the DOD's experience with integrated operation of government system acquisition programs—and acquisition was not an initial discipline for CMMI. This discrepancy led to some difficulty in addressing the IPPD tenets within the CMMI scope. Adding to the confusion was a lack of consensus in the industry (and among members of the development team) regarding the fundamental concepts and best practices of

---

11. *EIA Interim Standard, Systems Engineering Capability*. EIA/IS 731, (Part 1: Model, EIA/IS 731–1, version 1.0; Part 2: Appraisal Method, EIA/IS 731–2, version 1.0), 1999.

12. For example, see ISO/IEC 15504 and ISO/IEC 15288.

13. The U.S. Air Force played a significant role in the development of the IPD CMM.

integrated product development. Because it represented a relatively new means of organizing and accomplishing engineering work, there were nearly as many definitions as there were organizations.

This problem was not unique to CMMI. Indeed, the team established by EPIC to develop the IPD CMM, which was supported by many of the same members of the SE-CMM team, struggled with IPPD concepts for more than two years before being subsumed into the CMMI effort. The final draft IPD-CMM was established as a source document for CMMI, but the draft never achieved the status of a finished product.

Integrated Product and Process Development

CMMI defines *integrated product and process development* as a systematic approach to product development which increases customer satisfaction through a timely collaboration of necessary disciplines throughout the product life cycle.

IPPD emphasizes the involvement of stakeholders from all technical and business functions throughout the life cycle—customers, suppliers, and developers of both the product and product-related processes, such as testing and evaluation, manufacturing, support, training, marketing, purchasing, financial, contracting, and disposal processes. Clearly, implementing IPPD affects more than an organization's engineering processes and practices. Because it is essentially a way of doing business, it may radically change organizational structure and modify leadership behavior.

3.4 Process Areas

A fundamental concept of all CMMI models is the "process area." Not everything related to processes and process improvement is included in a process improvement model. Like its predecessor models, CMMI selects only the most important topics for process improvement and then groups those topics into "areas." This classification results in a small set of process areas: 22 in CMMI-SE/SW version 1.0, and 24 in CMMI-SE/SW/IPPD version 1.0. For a comparison with the source models, see Table 3-2.

Table 3-2: *Number of Areas in the CMMI Source Models*

Model	Areas
SW-CMM version 2(c)	19
EIA/IS 731	19
IPD-CMM version 0.98	23
CMMI-SE/SW version 1.0	22
CMMI-SE/SW/IPPD version 1.0	24

We will discuss the CMMI process areas in detail in Chapter 7. For now, to introduce the concept of a process area, let's look at one and see what it covers. For our example, we'll use Requirements Management.

Within both systems and software engineering, it is widely believed that the management of the product requirements is a central area of concern during any development effort. Experience has demonstrated that a failure to adequately identify the requirements and manage changes to them is a major cause of projects not meeting their cost, schedule, or quality objectives. This experience justifies collecting information related to the management of requirements into a major model component—that is, a process area. Users of the model should, therefore, focus on this process area to establish process area capability relating to the management of requirements.

As stated in the model, the purpose of the Requirements Management process area is "to manage the requirements of the project's products and product components and to identify inconsistencies between those requirements and the project's plans and work products." In addition to this purpose, the process area has goals that describe the results of a successful requirements management process and practices that can help achieve these goals. There is also a great deal of explanatory and "how to" material meant to provide some concrete help with managing requirements. That's pretty much a process area in a nutshell.

While the source models all had concepts similar to what CMMI includes as a process area, they (of course) used different names for them as illustrated in Table 3-3. Obviously, the first task was to define the set of process areas for the integrated model—that is, which to pick, which to merge, which to drop? On the surface, this endeavor might

Table 3-3: *Major Components in CMMI Source Models*

Model	Term for Major Model Component
CMMI	Process area
SW-CMM version 2(c)	Key process area
EIA/IS 731	Focus area
IPD CMM version 0.98	Process area

seem straightforward. In reality, the subtleties of the interactions within and among process areas made this definition one of the most perplexing challenges faced by the CMMI Product Development Team. One significant contributor to this challenge was the way in which engineering development was treated in the source models.

The Software CMM focused primarily on process management. Among the key process areas in the model, only one specifically targets the core engineering tasks, which range from the analysis of software requirements at the front end of development, to software integration and testing at the concluding end. This key process area was called Software Product Engineering in the Software CMM, and it dealt with tasks specific to software development. All of the other SW-CMM key process areas were written such that they could easily be applied to development work other than software. Along with the success of the Software CMM in improving software development, this flexibility may explain the interest in applying the CMM concepts to disciplines beyond software; much of what was believed to be good with the Software CMM had a utility that was not restricted to just the software area.

For systems engineers, a more detailed examination of the engineering development steps was deemed necessary to apply these modeling concepts to their broader scope of responsibility. In the Systems Engineering Capability Model (EIA/IS 731), 7 of the 19 focus areas (more than one-third of the focus areas) fall within the systems engineering technical category. Clearly, for the team of systems engineers who created this model, the capability of an organization in the technical areas deserved equal footing with its capability in process management and support areas.

To achieve an integrated model that addressed both systems engineering and software concerns, compromise and change would clearly be necessary. The CMMI team decided to include six engineering process areas that applied to both systems and software in the initial CMMI release. This choice was made to preserve the value of past efforts to improve systems engineering realized through each source model, and it reflected the judgment that many in the software community would, in fact, welcome more attention on the engineering tasks. The result might expand the scope of concern for past users of the software model, but it should in no way reduce or undercut the value of prior process improvement efforts for software.

Due to this and other decisions to keep the valued parts of each of the source models, the resulting integrated model was larger than any one of its sources. This expanded scope will certainly be of value in providing additional guidance for process improvement. Nevertheless, it increases the challenge in providing process assessment methods that are accurate and reliable, yet not overly time-consuming, expensive, and intrusive. We will say more about this assessment issue (and others) in Chapter 10.

3.5 An Extensible Framework

When you review a CMMI model (available from the SEI's Web site (http://www.sei.cmu.edu/cmmi/), you might say that it looks like a traditional document. In reality, each model is produced by assembling materials from a database that contains thousands of small parts. This construction approach facilitates using the same materials across different representations (continuous and staged) of the same model, and across different selected disciplines that share common parts.[14] Both the model and the training materials are stored in this database, which improves the consistency and commonality between the model and the training materials, and across different course offerings.

The database architecture also provides a means to easily integrate new disciplines into the model with this framework approach. The

---

14. Of the 24 process areas in the CMMI-SE/SW/IPPD model, 21 are exactly the same as, and one is a modification of, the 22 process areas in the CMMI-SE/SW model. See Section 7.5 for details.

Acquisition discipline is the first "new" discipline to test this mechanism. Its development has led to the identification of several new architectural issues and lessons learned that should be resolved prior to the release of version 1.1. For example,

- Can existing process areas be modified, other than through the addition of amplifications, with the addition of a discipline?
- Can new generic practices be added?
- Can specific practices in the new process areas overlap with existing practices?

The significance of these questions will become clear as you learn more about CMMI in the chapters that follow.

Chapter 4

CMMI Content

All that is gold does not glitter,
Not all who wander are lost.
J. R. R. Tolkien, *The Fellowship of the Ring* (1954)

I have gathered a posie of other men's flowers, and nothing
but the thread that binds them is mine own.
John Bartlett, Preface to *Familiar Quotations* (1901)

What's in a Capability Maturity Model Integration (CMMI) model, and how can your organization use it? At several hundred pages in length, the CMMI models seem formidable even to the most experienced process improvement champion. With just a little understanding of how the models are put together and what kind of material is presented, however, you can begin to navigate the depths of CMMI with confidence. This chapter describes the types of information you can find in the CMMI models and notes the location where you can find it. You will also learn to interpret the importance of the various types of information.

From the discussions in previous chapters, you can surmise that the models contain process areas. They also include background material, architectural descriptions, and a glossary that is critical for comprehension and interpretation of the model material. To use the models effectively, it's best to know where to look for the really important material.

4.1 Content Classification

Any process improvement model must, of necessity, include a scale relating to the importance and role of the materials contained in the model. In the CMMI models, a distinction is drawn between the terms "required," "expected," and "informative." The most important material is *required*; these items are essential to the model and to an understanding of what is needed for process improvement and demonstrations of conformance to the model. Second in importance is the *expected* material; these items may not be fully essential, and in some instances they may not be present in an organization that successfully uses the model. Nevertheless, expected material is presumed to play a central role in process improvement; such items are a strong indicator that the required components are being achieved. Third in importance (and largest in quantity) is *informative* material; these items constitute the majority of the model. The informative materials provide useful guidance for process improvement, and in many instances they may offer clarification regarding the intended meaning of the required and expected components.

If you are seeking only a quick overview of a CMMI model, one recommended approach is to review all of the required material. This strategy may be thought of as an "executive overview" level. For a still high-level but slightly more detailed review, you could focus on the combined required and expected materials. This approach may be considered a "manager overview" level. With either type of review, the best place to look is Appendix D (Required and Expected Model Elements) of the CMMI-SE/SW/IPPD, version 1.0, model, or Appendixes A and B of this book. Here the first two categories of model components are joined (with a very minimal amount of informative material) to present only the most essential elements of the model.

4.2 Required Materials

The sole required component of the CMMI models is the "goal." A goal represents a desirable end state, the achievement of which indicates that a certain degree of project and process control has been achieved. When a goal is unique to a single process area, it is called a "specific goal." In contrast, when a goal may apply across all of the process areas, it is called a "generic goal." Table 4-1 lists four examples of specific goals.

Table 4-1: *Specific Goals for Four Process Areas*

Process Area	Specific Goal
Requirements Management	REQM SG 1: Requirements are managed and inconsistencies with project plans and work products are identified.
Project Monitoring and Control	PMC SG 2: Corrective actions are managed to closure when the project's performance or results deviate significantly from the plan.
Organizational Process Performance	OPP SG 1: Baselines and models that characterize the expected process performance of the organization's set of standard processes are established and maintained.
Causal Analysis and Resolution	CAR SG 2: Root causes of defects and other problems are systematically addressed to prevent their future occurrence.

Each process area has between one and four specific goals; the entire CMMI-SE/SW/IPPD version 1.0 model includes a total of 54 specific goals. Table 4-2 compares CMMI specific goals with the three source models.

Table 4-2: *Goals and Themes for CMMI Source Models*

Model	Goals/Themes
SW-CMM version 2(c)	43
EIA/IS 731[1]	77
IPD-CMM version 0.98	60
CMMI-SE/SW version 1.0	48
CMMI-SE/SW/IPPD version 1.0	54

1. Themes are informative in EIA/IS 731 and are used to categorize the specific practices within a focus area.

As is evident from the four examples in Table 4-1, a goal statement is fairly succinct. In each case we should inquire what it might mean in practical terms by looking into the model in greater depth. This effort does not (either explicitly or implicitly) increase the amount of required material in the process area, but it may provide for a better understanding of the specific goal statements.

In contrast to a specific goal, a generic goal has a scope that crosses all of the process areas. Because their application is so broad, the wording of generic goals tends to be somewhat more abstract than the wording of specific goals. Consider, for example, GG 2: "The process is institutionalized as a managed process." To better understand what this statement means, let's start with the CMMI Glossary (CMMI-SE/SW/IPPD, version 1.0, Appendix C). There we find two definitions of special relevance to GG 2, as shown in Table 4-3.

Taken together, the two definitions in Table 4-3 provide much more detail than the short statement of the generic goal itself. Nevertheless, even with these definitions, questions about practical meaning may linger. What are the key features of an "ongoing way of doing business"? How is a process "evaluated for adherence to requirements"?

Although the goal is the only required element in a CMMI model, no statement of any goal—specific or generic—can be fully understood

Table 4-3: *Definitions Related to CMMI Generic Goal 2*

CMMI Glossary Term	CMMI Definition
Institutionalization	The building and reinforcement and corporate culture that support methods, practices, and procedures so that they are the ongoing way of doing business, even after those who originally defined them are gone.
Managed process	A performed process that is planned and executed in accordance with policy, employs skilled people having adequate resources to produce controlled outputs, involves stakeholders, and is reviewed and evaluated for adherence to requirements.

without exploring more of the model. The first expansion of that understanding comes by looking at the expected components.

4.3 Expected Materials

The only expected component of the CMMI models is the statement of a "practice." A practice represents the "expected" means of achieving a goal. Every practice in the CMMI models is mapped to exactly one goal. A practice is not a required component, however; a specific organization may possess demonstrated means of achieving a goal that do not rely on the performance of all the practices that are mapped to that goal. That is, "alternative" practices may provide an equally useful way of reaching the goal. With the models that preceded CMMI, the use of alternative practices was rare. Whether that will hold true in the future with the CMMI integrated models remains to be seen. While CMMI practices (as a class) are not required, they act as strong indicators that the goals to which they are mapped are being met. However, alternative practices are acceptable when organizations need adequate flexibility in special or unusual situations.

When a practice is unique to a single process area, it is called a "specific practice." When a practice may apply across all of the process areas, it is called a "generic practice."

Table 4-4 details several examples of specific practices, together with the goal to which they are mapped. Note that a goal, which represents an end state, is always written in the passive voice, whereas a practice, as a means to achieve the goal, is always written in the active voice.

Between two and seven specific practices are mapped to each specific goal; the entire CMMI-SE/SW/IPPD version 1.0 model includes a total of 186 specific practices, which are mapped to the 54 specific goals.[2] Table 4-5 compares CMMI specific practices for the three source models. It points out the difference between a staged and continuous model and the number of specific practices or activities. To make a better comparison, examine the SW-CMM version 2(c) relative to the staged count in CMMI-SE/SW (146 to 162).

---

2. The continuous representation includes 186 specific practices; the staged representation includes 181. The discrepancy arises because, when the continuous representation includes both a "base" practice and an "advanced" practice on the same topic, only the advanced practice appears in the staged representation. See Section 7.3 on the Engineering process areas for further information.

Table 4-4: *Specific Practices Associated with Specific Goals*

Specific Goal	Specific Practice
REQM SG 1: Requirements are managed and inconsistencies with project plans and work products are identified.	REQM SP 1.1–1[3]: Develop an understanding with the require-ments providers on the meaning of the requirements.
PMC SG 2: Corrective actions are managed to closure when the project's performance or results deviate significantly from the plan.	PMC SP 2.1–1: Collect and analyze the issues and deter-mine the corrective actions necessary to address the issues.
OPP SG 1: Baselines and models that characterize the expected process performance of the organization's set of standard processes are established and maintained.	OPP SP 1.2–1: Establish and maintain definitions of the measures that are to be included in the organization's process performance analyses.
CAR SG 2: Root causes of defects and other problems are systematically addressed to prevent their future occurrence.	CAR SP 2.2–1: Evaluate the effect of changes on process performance.

When the specific practices mapped to a specific goal are taken as a unit, they provide additional insight into how the goal should be under-stood. Table 4-6 shows one goal together with its full complement of practices. In this example, establishing and maintaining work-product baselines involves identifying configuration items, implementing a con-figuration and change management system, and establishing baselines for both internal and external use.

In contrast to a specific practice, a generic practice has a scope that crosses all of the process areas. For example, one generic practice that is

3. The numbering for this practice is SP 1.1-1 in the continuous representation, and SP 1.1 in the staged representation. The addition of "-1" in the continuous representation indicates a capability level, which is not used in the staged representation. Chapter 6 describes the two representations and the concept of capability level.

Table 4-5: *Specific Practices for CMMI Source Models*

Model	Staged/Continuous Specific Practices or Activities
SW-CMM version 2(c)	146/X
EIA/IS 731	X/383
IPD-CMM version 0.98	X/106
CMMI-SE/SW version 1.0	162/167
CMMI-SE/SW/IPPD version 1.0	181/186

mapped to the generic goal to institutionalize a managed process (GG 2) addresses the training of people. Consider GP 2.5: "Train the people performing or supporting the process as needed." In other words, a project is expected to provide the training that is needed when it follows a managed process in such a way that the process becomes institutionalized. For each process area in a CMMI model, needed training is expected, based on the application of this generic practice.

Table 4-6: *Specific Goal and Specific Practices for Configuration Management*

Specific Goal	Specific Practices
Configuration Management (CM) SG 1: Baselines of identified work products are established and maintained.	CM SP 1.1-1: Identify the configuration items, components, and related work products that will be placed under configuration management.
	CM SP 1.2-1: Establish and maintain a configuration management and change management system for controlling work products.
	CM SP 1.3-1: Create or release baselines for internal use and for delivery to the customer.

4.4 Informative Materials

CMMI models contain 10 types of informative components.

1. Purpose. Each process area begins with a brief statement of purpose for the process area. Generally, a purpose statement consists of one or two sentences that summarize or draw together the specific goals of the process area.

Consider the purpose statement from Risk Management:

> *The purpose of Risk Management is to identify potential problems before they occur, so that risk-handling activities may be planned and invoked as needed across the life cycle to mitigate adverse impacts on achieving objectives.*

The three specific goals in Risk Management address preparations, identification and analysis of risk, and mitigation as needed. In this way, the purpose statement provides a quick, high-level orientation for the entire process area.

2. Introductory Note. The purpose is followed by a section including multiple introductory notes that apply to the entire process area. Typically, these notes present information on the scope of the process area, its importance, the way in which it reflects recognized best practices, unique terminology used in it, and the interaction of it with other process areas.

3. Reference. Explicit pointing from one process area to all or part of another process area is accomplished with a reference. In CMMI, a reference is simply an indicator noting that, to obtain more information on some topic, one should look in another process area.

4. Names. In CMMI, all required and expected components (goals and practices) are given a name, which provides a convenient handle for referring to the component. Table 4-7 lists examples of names from the Measurement and Analysis (MA) process area. Thus, in training classes or in discussion, we can refer to the "align activities" goal or the "specify measures" practice in Measurement and Analysis. Although this name provides a convenient shorthand, do not confuse the name of the model component with the component itself. The components form the basis for process improvement and process assessment—not the names.

Table 4-7: *Names from the Measurement and Analysis Process Area*

Component	Name	Required or Expected Material
MA SG 1	Align Measurement and Analysis Activities	Measurement objectives and practices are aligned with identified information needs and objectives.
MA SP 1.2-1	Specify Measures	Specify measures to address the measurement objectives.

5. *Practice-to-Goal Relationship Table.* Using the names for goals and practices, this item in each process area maps each specific and generic practice to its related specific or generic goal, respectively.

6. *Notes.* Whereas the general notes at the beginning of a process area are labeled as "introductory notes," there are also (plain) notes attached to other model components, such as goals, practices, and sub-practices. They represent a rich source of information that should prove valuable in planning and conducting process improvement efforts.

7. *Typical Work Products.* When a practice is performed, there will often be outputs in the form of work products. The CMMI Glossary (Appendix C) defines a work product (in part) as follows:

> *Any artifact produced by a process. This may include files, documents, parts of the product, services, processes, specifications, and invoices.*

The items identified in a list of typical work products are examples; they should not be considered essential to the performance of the process, and the list should not be thought of as exhaustive. The intention is merely to provide initial guidance regarding the type of work products that may be produced by a practice. During an assessment, however, you will be required to produce evidence proving that your process produces outputs and to show examples of those outputs to get credit for institutionalization of the process area.

8. *Subpractices.* For many practices in the CMMI models, subpractices provide a decomposition of their meaning and the activities that they might entail as well as an elaboration of their use. Unlike practices,

which are expected model components, subpractices appear in the model for information purposes only.

9. *Discipline Amplifications.* One of the most distinctive aspects of CMMI as compared with prior source models is the fact that the CMMI model components are discipline-independent. The advantage of this approach derives from the ability of different disciplines to use the same components, which promotes common terminology and understanding across various disciplines. The limitation on discipline-independent components becomes apparent, however, when one considers that generalization can entail the removal of content. For example, the Software CMM included a practice that made explicit reference to developing estimates of software size. In contrast, CMMI speaks more generally about producing estimates for the attributes of work products and tasks (see Project Planning, SP 1.2–1).

To maintain the usefulness of the discipline-specific material found in its source models, CMMI provides discipline amplifications that are introduced with phrases such as "For Software Engineering," or "For Systems Engineering." For example, in the Project Planning process area, the specific practice on establishing estimates of project attributes has a discipline amplification for software that mentions software size and examples of size measures. It also has a discipline amplification for systems engineering that mentions the number of functions and the number of interfaces as important attributes to include in the estimate. Amplifications are informative material, so they are not required in an assessment. Nevertheless, the assessors may use them as guidance on how to interpret the practice for specific disciplines and to gain a better idea of how the practice will affect the process improvement activities.

10. *Generic Practice Elaborations.* Whereas discipline amplifications provide details for each specific discipline, generic practice elaborations provide details regarding the application of a generic practice in a given process area. For example, in the Product Integration process area, the generic practice on establishing an organizational policy is elaborated with these words:

> *This policy establishes organizational expectations for developing a product integration strategy and environment, ensuring interface compatibility among product components, assembling the product components, and delivering the product and product components.*

Sometimes, in a given process area, a generic practice and a specific practice may seem to address a similar topic. For example, the generic practice may deal with planning the process, and a specific practice may focus on planning a particular aspect of the process. In such a circumstance, a generic practice elaboration is used to comment on the distinction intended between the generic and specific practices.

4.5 Document Map

Figures 4-1 and 4-2 show where to find the various types of information described in the continuous and stages representations, respectively.

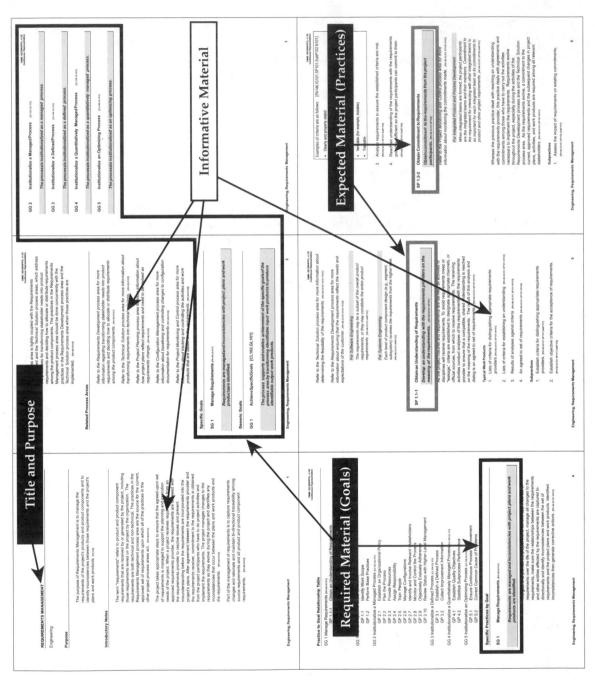

Figure 4-1: *Document map for continuous representation*

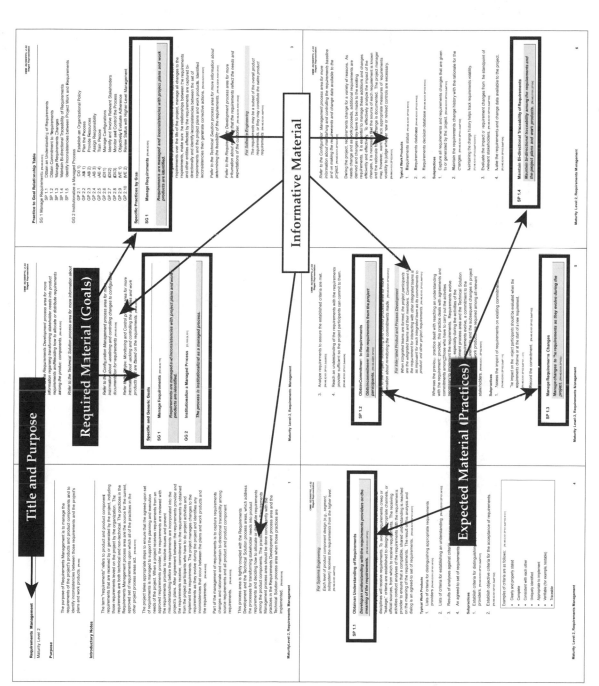

Figure 4-2: *Document map for staged representation*

Chapter 5

CMMI Representations

*If we cannot now end our differences,
at least we can help make the world safe for diversity.*
John Fitzgerald Kennedy (1963)

*We tend to see our own experiences as the normal process,
so we are often amazed that anyone could have taken a different path.
But when we do meet up, it's always fascinating to compare
notes about the different ways to get there.*
Daniel Gilly, *Unix in a Nutshell* (1992)

A fundamental choice faces the user of a Capability Maturity Model Integration (CMMI) model today: Do you use the continuous or staged representation? The question relates to the architectural structure of the model. One source model for CMMI, the Software Capability Maturity Model (CMM), was a "staged" model. Another source model, the Systems Engineering Capability Model, was a "continuous" model. The third source, the Integrated Product Development (IPD) CMM, was a "hybrid" that combined features of both the staged and continuous.

One way to think about the architectural options is to focus on process improvement. An organization may choose to approach process improvement from the perspective of either process area capability or organizational maturity. Simply put, a process area capability perspective focuses on baselining and measuring improvement results in each area individually. This approach is supported in a continuous representation, with its use of the key term "capability." In contrast, an organizational maturity perspective emphasizes sets of process areas that are intended to define proven stages of process maturity across an organization. This approach is employed in a staged representation, with its use of the key term "maturity."

While many may have wished that the CMMI team had selected a single architectural representation for its integration task, that decision was judged to be premature and "too hard" for the initial integration effort. The fundamental problem related to the lack of consensus regarding which approach to process improvement would be better, and hence which architecture would be preferable.[1] Each side had many strong proponents, so the CMMI team made the judgment that the risk of losing support for CMMI would be too great if it summarily eliminated either representation or tried to find a single "hybrid" solution. Hence the CMMI models (version 1.0) for each combination of disciplines are presented with two representations, continuous and staged. Note, however, that the CMMI Product Development Team put a great deal of effort into ensuring the logical equivalence of the two representations.

5.1 Staged Models

A staged model provides a predefined road map for organizational improvement based on proven grouping and ordering of processes and associated organizational relationships. The term "staged" comes from the way that the model describes this road map as a series of "stages" that are called "maturity levels." Each maturity level has a set of process areas that indicate where an organization should focus to improve its organizational process. Each process area is described in terms of the

---

1. The phrase "religious war" comes to mind. This disagreement is unfortunate, as both approaches have positive aspects.

practices that contribute to satisfying its goals. The practices describe the infrastructure and activities that contribute most to the effective implementation and institutionalization of the process areas. Progress occurs by satisfying the goals of all process areas in a particular maturity level.[2]

The CMM for Software is the primary example of a staged model. Figure 5-1 shows the CMM for Software and its five stages, and Table 5-1 shows the key process areas within each stage.

The key process areas at level 2 of the Software CMM focus on the software project's concerns related to establishing basic project management controls. Level 3 addresses both project and organizational issues, as the organization establishes an infrastructure that institutionalizes effective software engineering and management processes across all projects. The key process areas at level 4 focus on establishing a quantitative understanding of both the software process and the software work products being built. Level 5 covers the issues that both the organization and the projects must address to implement continual, measurable software process improvement.

Assessments against a staged model evaluate the organization as a whole by determining how many of the process areas have been achieved—that is, how many goals have been met. Based on the satisfied

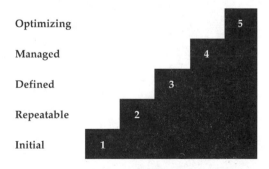

Figure 5-1: *The Software CMM stages*

---

2. The concept of five stages or maturity levels goes back to Crosby in *Quality Is Free,* which described a five-level scale with "world-class" as level 5. Actually, Crosby's proposed scale is closer to capability levels in a continuous model than to maturity levels in a staged model, because he applied a similar scale across many areas. Section 5.2 describes the capability levels in a continuous model.

Table 5-1: *The Software CMM Version 2(c) Key Process Areas*

Level	Focus	Key Process Areas
Optimizing	Continuous process improvement	Organization Improvement Deployment
		Organization Process & Technology Innovation
		Defect Prevention
Managed	Quantitative management	Statistical Process Management
		Organization Process Performance
		Organization Software Asset Commonality
Defined	Process standardization	Peer Reviews
		Project Interface Coordination
		Software Product Engineering
		Integrated Software Management
		Organization Training Program
		Organization Process Definition
		Organization Process Focus
Repeatable	Basic project management	Software Configuration Management
		Software Quality Assurance

Level	Focus	Key Process Areas
		Software Acquisition Management
		Software Project Control
		Software Project Planning
		Requirements Management
Initial	Competent people and heroics	None

key process areas, the organization may be assigned a single maturity level. When you hear that a corporation "is at level 3," for example, it means that the organization has been assessed to have satisfied all goals associated with the process areas included in levels 2 and 3 of a staged model.

5.2 Continuous Models

Continuous models provide less specific guidance on the order in which improvement should be accomplished. They are called continuous because no discrete stages are associated with organizational maturity. EIA/IS 731 is an example of a continuous model.

Like the staged models, continuous models have process areas that contain practices. Unlike in staged models, however, the practices of a process area in a continuous model are organized in a manner that supports individual process area growth and improvement. Most of the practices associated with process improvement are generic; they are external to the individual process areas and apply to all process areas.[3] The generic practices are grouped into capability levels, each of which

---

3. EIA/IS 731 introduced the concept of advanced practices. These technical practices within a process area (called a focus area in 731) are associated with higher capability levels and so augment the generic practices. CMMI models include a version of the advanced practice mechanism.

has a definition that is roughly equivalent to the definition of the maturity levels in a staged model. Process areas are improved and institutionalized by implementing the generic practices in those process areas. In a continuous model such as EIA/IS 731, goals are not specifically stated, which puts even more emphasis on practices. The collective capability levels of all process areas determine organizational improvement, and an organization can tailor a continuous model and target only certain process areas for improvement.

In a continuous assessment, each process area is rated at its own capability level. An organization will most likely have different process areas rated at different capability levels. The results can be reported as a capability profile, like that shown in Figure 5-2.

The capability profile may include just the level number ratings, as in Figure 5-2, or it may also contain detailed information at the goal or practice levels. The latter option provides more specific information in graphical form by highlighting the findings (weaknesses and strengths) with different colors. Profiles have generally been implemented via a spreadsheet.

Capability profiles can also be used to define a target for process improvement activities in an organization. Because a target profile

Figure 5-2: *Capability level profile (simple)*

shows the desired capability profile at a specific point in time, it can be used to show progress on the process improvement journey.

Another way to use capability profiles is to organize the process dimension so that it represents the staged maturity levels. For example, a series of profiles may be used to set goals for the organization or to evaluate the results of an assessment using equivalent staging (Section 5.3.3 describes the application of this concept to CMMI). In addition, capability profiles can be defined for subsets of process areas when different parts of the organization own the processes related to them. Alternatively, the same process areas may be included in multiple owners' target profiles. When the entire organization is assessed, the process areas are rated as a whole.

5.3 CMMI Model Representations

The CMMI Product Development Team was given an unprecedented challenge: create a single model that could be viewed from two distinct perspectives, continuous and staged. This mandate meant that each representation should include the same basic information for process improvement: a CMMI process assessment that addressed the same scope should result in the same findings, no matter which model representation was used during the assessment.

5.3.1 Selection of Process Areas

As described in Chapter 3, a major challenge centered on the selection of the process areas for CMMI.[4] A second, even thornier issue was whether the process areas in the two representations would need to be (or should be) identical.[5] The team employed a well-defined set of criteria in identifying process areas. That is, a process area was defined as

---

4. The CMMI Product Development Team did not start with a blank slate. Its task was not to create a new model from scratch, but rather to integrate (initially) three existing models. Each of these models already had process areas identified, and these areas made up the initial set of candidates, with team members considering the hopes or expectations among users of the CMMI source models that process areas to which they were accustomed would continue in CMMI.

5. In this section we invite the reader to enter (briefly) this "briar patch"—not to share the pain (well, maybe a little), but to provide some insight. You can, of course, decline the invitation. The bottom line (which you need to know) is that the two CMMI representations have the same process areas.

containing a related set of activities that, if performed, would result in a high probability of significant improvement in the area and thus aid in the achievement of business objectives for the organization.[6]

For example, the inadequate definition or management of project requirements is frequently mentioned in trying to understand what went wrong in a given program. Furthermore, a set of recognized activities exists that, if performed, would go a long way toward correcting what might have gone wrong with requirements. As a consequence, it should come as no surprise that CMMI includes two process areas related to this topic: Requirements Development and Requirements Management. No debate occurs regarding whether process areas such as Requirements Development and Requirements Management would be appropriate in both a staged representation and a continuous representation. Whichever architectural representation was to be adopted for the model, both areas would be of critical importance.

Suppose, however, that the CMMI Product Development Team had been asked to proceed differently. That is, suppose it had been asked not to develop one model with two representations, but rather a single model representation (for example, continuous, staged, or some hybrid). It is not clear that the resultant list of process areas would have been exactly identical for each of the various possible single model representations. In other words, the process areas needed in a staged representation and the process areas needed in a continuous representation are not necessarily the same.

For example, in a staged model the process areas exist at a single maturity level only; they do not span levels. In the Software CMM, for instance, Requirements Management is a process area staged at maturity level 2 (as it is in the CMMI staged representation); no parts of the Requirements Management process area exist at higher maturity levels. Thus, as an organization works to achieve maturity levels 3, 4, or 5, it need not tackle additional tasks that come from the Requirements Management process area. Of course, the organization should not ignore the maturity level 2 process areas as it moves ahead to higher maturity levels. To be an organization at maturity level 3 means (in

---

6. A variety of other criteria for what makes a good process area exist, including the following: A process area tells you what to do, not how to do it or who should do it; it can be implemented in multiple organizational and product contexts; and it has sufficient cohesion and granularity to be separately implemented, rated, and improved.

general) that the processes used on projects are tailored from the organization's standard set of processes. This approach includes the management of requirements; a standard set of processes should exist for doing requirements management across the organization, and individual projects should derive their specific processes for requirements management from that standard set.

In CMMI, the Integrated Project Management (IPM) process area, which is staged at maturity level 3, requires an organization to return to the process areas from maturity level 2 (such as Requirements Management) and perform them in a manner consistent with maturity level 3 requirements. In IPM, a goal for a project is to use a defined process that is tailored from the organization's set of standard processes.

Moving from the staged to the continuous representation, a generic practice at capability level 3 (GP 3.1) also sets the expectation for a defined process. In Requirements Management, for example, GP 3.1 reads: "Establish and maintain the description of a defined requirements management process." By performing that practice, and the comparable generic practice in other process areas staged at maturity level 2, the organization may raise each process area to capability level 3 when viewed from the perspective of the continuous representation. The continuous representation does not require an independent mechanism such as the first goal in IPM to raise maturity level 2 process areas to the corresponding maturity level 3 defined level.

Also, if you look at IPM from a continuous viewpoint, some practices may look like they really belong (perhaps as "advanced" practices) in the Project Planning or Project Monitoring and Control process areas.

We will not explore in detail all of the architectural nuances that might distinguish the two representations. Rather, we will simply note that the CMMI team had a choice: allow the process areas to be different in the two representations, or keep them the same. The former option (different process areas) would have allowed for the construction of "better" or "purer" staged or continuous representations, but at the cost of potential confusion to those who might need to deal with two representations having different process areas. The latter option (same process areas) would enhance the sense that the two representations are really just one CMMI model with two views, but at the cost of potentially confusing duplication or positioning of material in the model, which would be needed to allow both representations to work. The decision was made to have the same process areas in both representations for CMMI version 1.0.

Although the CMMI product team decided not to have a single CMMI representation in the initial release, the decision to have the same process areas in the two representations will support any future movement toward hybridization. This merger, of course, could be accomplished only with some degree of inelegance and duplication, as exemplified by the IPM requirement for use of a defined process described both by a goal and a generic practice.

5.3.2 Organization of Process Areas

The 24 process areas of CMMI-SE/SW/IPPD are divided into four maturity levels in the staged representation and four process categories in the continuous representation. Tables 5-2 and 5-3 show these two structures, respectively.

Table 5-2: *Staged Groupings*

Staged Grouping	Acronyms	Process Areas
Maturity level 2	REQM	Requirements Management
	PP	Project Planning
	PMC	Project Monitoring and Control
	SAM	Supplier Agreement Management
	MA	Measurement and Analysis
	PPQA	Process and Product Quality Assurance
	CM	Configuration Management
Maturity level 3	RD	Requirements Development
	TS	Technical Solution
	PI	Product Integration
	VER	Verification
	VAL	Validation
	OPF	Organizational Process Focus

Staged Grouping	Acronyms	Process Areas
	OPD	Organizational Process Definition
	OT	Organizational Training
	IPM	Integrated Project Management
	RSKM	Risk Management
	IT	Integrated Teaming
	DAR	Decision Analysis and Resolution
	OEI	Organizational Environment for Integration
Maturity level 4	OPP	Organizational Process Performance
	QPM	Quantitative Project Management
Maturity level 5	OID	Organizational Innovation and Deployment
	CAR	Causal Analysis and Resolution

Table 5-3: *Continuous Groupings*

Continuous Grouping	Acronyms	Process Areas
Process Management	OPF	Organizational Process Focus
	OPD	Organizational Process Definition
	OT	Organizational Training
	OPP	Organizational Process Performance
	OID	Organizational Innovation and Deployment

(continued)

Table 5-3: *Continuous Groupings (cont.)*

Continuous Grouping	Acronyms	Process Areas
Project Management	PP	Project Planning
	PMC	Project Monitoring and Control
	SAM	Supplier Agreement Management
	IPM	Integrated Project Management
	RSKM	Risk Management
	IT	Integrated Teaming
	QPM	Quantitative Project Management
Engineering	REQM	Requirements Management
	RD	Requirements Development
	TS	Technical Solution
	PI	Product Integration
	VER	Verification
	VAL	Validation
Support	CM	Configuration Management
	PPQA	Process and Product Quality Assurance
	MA	Measurement and Analysis
	DAR	Decision Analysis and Resolution
	OEI	Organizational Environment for Integration
	CAR	Causal Analysis and Resolution

5.3.3 Equivalent Staging

To reinforce the concept of one model with two views or representations, CMMI provides a mapping to move from the continuous to the staged perspective. For maturity levels 2 and 3, the concept is straightforward and easy to understand. If an organization using the continuous representation has achieved capability level 2 in the seven process areas that make up maturity level 2 (in the staged representation), then it can be said to have achieved maturity level 2 (Figure 5-3).

Similarly, if an organization using the continuous representation has achieved capability level 3 in the seven process areas that make up maturity level 2 and the 13 process areas that make up maturity level 3 (a total of 20 process areas), then it can be said to have achieved maturity level 3 (Figure 5-4).

For maturity levels 4 and 5, a similar mechanism is not available to define an equivalent staging. For example, maturity level 4 in the staged representation does not require that level 4 kinds of activities go on in each and every process area. Nor is quantitative management of processes or subprocesses required for any given process area. One organization that achieves maturity level 4 may do quantitative management in one set of areas, and another organization may handle quantitative management in another set of areas; there may be

	CL1	CL2	CL3	CL4	CL5
Maturity Level 2 Process Areas	Target Profile 2				
Maturity Level 3 Process Areas					
Maturity Level 4 Process Areas					
Maturity Level 5 Process Areas					

Figure 5-3: *Target profile 2*

	CL1	CL2	CL3	CL4	CL5
Maturity Level 2 Process Areas	Target Profile 3				
Maturity Level 3 Process Areas					
Maturity Level 4 Process Areas					
Maturity Level 5 Process Areas					

Figure 5-4: *Target profile 3*

no overlap between the two sets, and yet both organizations may operate at maturity level 4. Thus, in Figure 5-5, we cannot highlight any particular process area as being capability level 4 and claim that it is required for an equivalent staging to maturity level 4.

Instead, to obtain an equivalent staging for maturity level 4, we require that an organization meet the goals up through capability level 3 in the process areas that are staged at maturity level 4. This idea may sound confusing, but it is correct. Table 5-4 details the three goals of the two maturity level 4 process areas. To achieve capability level 3 in these two process areas means two things:

1. The three specific goals in Table 5-4 are met: the project is quantitatively managed, subprocesses are statistically managed to meet quality and process performance objectives, and baselines and models for expected process performance exist.

2. A defined process is used for the activities performed to achieve these goals.

These items are exactly what would need to be established for maturity level 4, based on the CMMI staged representation. Consequently, to be rated at maturity level 4, some subprocesses in some process areas must be statistically managed, but it is not possible to specify in advance which process areas are targeted. In a real-life capability

Figure 5-5: *Target profile 4*

profile for an organization at maturity level 4, the capability level of at least one process area would be at level 4.

The equivalent staging for maturity level 5 is handled in a similar way (Figure 5-6). In this manner, the user of the continuous representation

Table 5-4: *Maturity Level 4 Process Areas and Goals*

Process Area	Specific Goals
Quantitative Project Management (QPM)	SG 1: The project is quantitatively managed using quality and process performance objectives. SG 2: The performance of selected sub-processes within the project's defined process is statistically managed.
Organizational Process Performance (OPP)	SG 1: Baselines and models that characterize the expected process performance of the organization's set of standard processes are established and maintained.

Figure 5-6: *Target profile 5*

could establish a maturity level rating, if desired, for any maturity level (1 through 5).

For CMMI, if an organization wanted to have a single-number rating of a maturity level, it could choose a CMMI staged representation. Of course, because of this equivalent staging comprising a set of four target profiles, the organization could also choose a CMMI continuous representation.

Chapter 6

CMMI Dimensions for Measuring Improvement

Catch, then, oh catch the transient hour;
Improve each moment as it flies!
Samuel Johnson, *Winter. An Ode* **(1709–1784)**

Anyone who isn't confused really doesn't understand the situation.
Edward R. Murrow (1908–1965)

Chapter 5 presented some basic information about the two representations (continuous and staged) that are provided for every Capability Maturity Model Integration (CMMI) model. This chapter continues to explore the relationships between the two representations by taking a more detailed look at how the capability and maturity dimensions are implemented in CMMI.[1] Essentially, the differences in the two

---

1. At some point in our description of the two CMMI architectural representations, you may ask, "Which representation should I use?" When that point comes, you may wish to turn to Chapter 9 on picking a representation. In Chapter 6, we focus on building a good understanding of these structures and their implementation in CMMI.

representations reflect the methods used to describe the process dimension for each capability or maturity level. Rest assured that while the mechanics of the descriptions may differ, both representations achieve the same improvement purposes through the use of generic goals and practices as required and expected model elements.

Continuous models describe improvement through the capability of process areas, singly or collectively. A capability level includes a generic goal and its associated generic practices that are added to the specific goals and practices within the process area. When the organization meets the process area specific goals and generic goals, it achieves the capability level for that process area.[2]

Staged models describe the maturity of organizations through successful implementation of ordered groups of process areas. These groups, or stages, improve processes together, based on achievements in the previous stage. Each process area in the staged model includes the appropriate generic goals and practices for its stage.

The remainder of this chapter discusses in detail the characteristics and mechanisms used by CMMI in defining the capability dimension, the maturity dimension, generic practices, and staging. Chapter 7 addresses the process dimensions for both representations.

6.1 Capability Dimension

The capability dimension is used in the continuous representation of CMMI, just as it was in CMMI's predecessor source model, EIA/IS 731 (see Section 3.3.2). In this section we describe the levels and summarize the mechanism of capability improvement. Section 6.3 offers a more detailed discussion of the individual generic practices.

CMMI includes six levels of process area capability, imaginatively called *capability levels (CLs)*, and numbered 0 through 5. These CLs indicate how well the organization performs in an individual process area. As shown in Figure 6-1, capability level zero (CL 0) indicates that the processes are *Not Performed*, which means that one or more of the specific goals of the process area are not satisfied. The capability levels

---

2. If a continuous model contains advanced practices, then for a capability level to be achieved, all advanced practices specified at or below that level must also be met.

Figure 6-1: *Capability dimension*

increase up to capability level five (CL 5), where the process is per-formed well and is being continuously improved.

Table 6-1 shows the generic goal statements for each capability level. As the table shows, no generic goal exists for CL 0 (*Not Performed*). A process area is at CL 0 when it fails to reach CL 1. The reason for not having a goal is that this level simply signifies "not yet CL 1."[3]

Capability level 1 is called *Performed,* and the generic goal for this level focuses on the achievement of the specific goals of the process area. Two generic practices are mapped to the CL 1 generic goal. One speci-fies that the base practices of the process area are performed at this level of capability. The other specifies that a process area at CL 1 identi-fies and communicates the scope of the work to be performed. Even though 1 is a lowly number, reaching CL 1 represents a significant achievement for an organization; if a process area is at CL 1, then the specific goals of the process area are satisfied. The added capabilities

---

3. It is highly recommended that when describing an organization's capability as zero that the words "not yet level 1" be substituted—no one wants to be considered as being at level 0.

Table 6-1: *Generic Goals*

Capability Level	Generic Goal
CL 0	No goal.
CL 1	GG 1: The process supports and enables achievement of the specific goals of the process area by transforming identifiable input work products to produce identifiable output work products.
CL 2	GG 2: The process is institutionalized as a managed process.
CL 3	GG 3: The process is institutionalized as a defined process.
CL 4	GG 4: The process is institutionalized as a quantitatively managed process.
CL 5	GG 5: The process is institutionalized as an optimizing process.

for CL 2 through CL 5 depend on the specific practices within a process area being performed at their capability level; only when they are performed can they be improved by satisfying higher-level generic goals. Figure 6-2 illustrates how a process increases in capability.

Capability level 2 is called *Managed,* and its generic goal focuses on institutionalization as a managed process. Ten generic practices are mapped to the CL 2 generic goal. A managed process has increased capability over a performed process; the 10 generic practices provide a definition for that increased capability. In general, a process operating at CL 2 has an organizational policy stating which processes will be used. The projects follow a documented plan and process description. They apply adequate and appropriate resources (including funding, people, and tools) and maintain appropriate assignment of responsibility and authority. In addition, the projects allow for training of the people performing and supporting the process. Work products are placed under appropriate levels of configuration management. All relevant stakeholders are identified and involved as appropriate. Personnel monitor and control the performance of the process and take corrective action

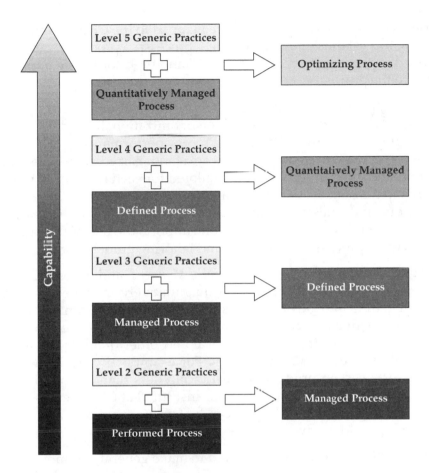

Figure 6-2: *Building capability*

when needed. They objectively evaluate the process, its work products, and its services, addressing any noncompliance with corrective actions. The activities, status, and results of the process activities are reviewed with appropriate levels of management, and corrective action is taken if necessary. Thanks to this robust set of generic practices at CL 2, mostly targeted at individual projects, a *managed* process represents a significant advance relative to a *performed* process.

Capability level 3 is called *Defined*, and the generic goal for this level focuses on institutionalization as a defined process. In layman's terms, for each process area considered, each project in an organization will have a managed process (like that created under CL 2) that is tailored from an organization's standard processes using standard tailoring guidelines.[4] Two generic practices are mapped to the CL 3 generic goal. Besides the establishment of defined processes, process assets and process measurements must be collected and used for future improvements to the process.

Whereas capability level 2 targets the capability of individual process instances,[5] capability level 3 focuses on organizational standardization and deployment of the processes. Process performance is stabilized across the projects because processes are standardized across the organization; the standard processes are tailored for each instance in which that process is needed. Personnel can readily apply their process-based knowledge and skills across multiple instances of the process without expensive retraining. The organization supports the use of the process by providing process asset libraries and tailoring guidelines.

Capability level 4 is called *Quantitatively Managed,* and its generic goal focuses on institutionalization as a quantitatively managed process. Without getting into the finer points of statistical process control, a CL 4 process is a defined process (like that created under CL 3—see how this inheritance works?) that uses statistical and other quantitative methods to control selected subprocesses. For example, if you know that defects for a certain product are historically less than 5% of the total volume and your process measures (as instituted at CL 3) deviate from that percentage significantly, you can be fairly certain that a problem exists and should be investigated.

Because of the overhead involved and to make general common sense, the process measures selected for CL 4 relate to individual subprocesses—not necessarily all processes or even entire processes. Obviously, the organization should quantitatively manage only those subprocesses that are important to its business needs and objectives.

Capability level 5 is called *Optimizing,* and the generic goal for this level focuses on institutionalization as an optimizing process. CL 5 is a bit tricky, because it essentially requires the organization to constantly adapt the quantitatively managed subprocesses established at CL 4 based on their measures and established objectives for quality and process performance. This requirement doesn't just mean fixing problems (such as the quality anomaly cited earlier), but entails analyzing

---

4. This example assumes the process area considered is a project-related process area—that is, from the Project Management process area category.

5. Usually, each instance of the process is associated with a project.

trends, surveying technical practice, addressing common causes of process variation, and then determining how best to adapt the process to changing business needs. This procedure could result in either evolutionary or revolutionary action.

6.2 Maturity Dimension

The maturity dimension of a CMMI model is described in the staged representation. Five levels of maturity exist, each of which indicates the process maturity of the organization. Figure 6-3 shows the *maturity levels (MLs)* and their characteristics.

Note the overlap in the names for maturity levels 2 through 5 and the names for capability levels 2 through 5. Although these capability levels and maturity levels have the same names, a fundamental difference separates them. Capability levels are independently applied to any individual process area, whereas a maturity level specifies a set of process areas whose combined set of goals must be achieved. Furthermore, generic goals and practices follow different inclusion rules in the staged representation than they do in the continuous representation. They are included in the process areas according to the level where the process area is staged. Process areas staged at maturity level 2 use the CL 2 generic goal and its associated generic practices. Process areas

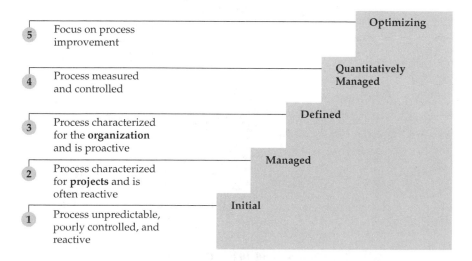

Figure 6-3: *Staged maturity levels*

staged at maturity levels 3 through 5 include the CL 3 generic goal, plus the generic practices from both capability levels 2 and 3. CL 1, 4, and 5 generic goals and practices are not used in the maturity level definitions—no process areas are staged at level 1, and the generic goals for levels 4 and 5 are addressed by the specific goals and practices of the four process areas staged at those levels.

Note that maturity level 1 has a different name (*Initial*) from that assigned to capability level 1 (*Performed*). In the staged representation, ML 1 is similar to CL 0 in its negative connotation; that is, an organization at ML 1 is one that has not reached ML 2. No goals need to be met to qualify for ML 1. Unlike CL 1, ML 1 does not connote any significant achievement for an organization.

Figure 6-4 shows the structure of a maturity level. In the staged representation, each process area exists at a maturity level. The process areas

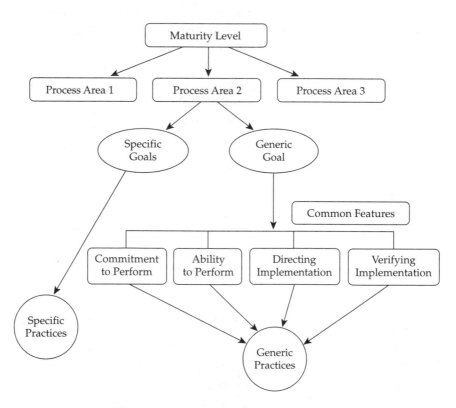

Figure 6-4: *Maturity level structure*

required for each staged level were shown in Chapter 5. In Chapter 7, we will describe each of the process areas.

6.3 Generic Practices in the Capability Dimension

In the previous two sections, we saw how generic goals and practices are used to define both capability levels and maturity levels. The continuous representation includes 18 generic practices grouped by capability levels 1 through 5. As stated earlier, only the capability level 2 and 3 generic practices are included in the staged representation. These 12 generic practices are grouped by their *Common Feature* category, using a terminology that was carried over from the SW-CMM. This section takes a more detailed look at the full set of generic practices used in the continuous representation. Section 6.4 scrutinizes the partial set of generic practices used in the staged representation.

6.3.1 Capability Level 0 Generic Practices

Capability level 0 does not have any generic practices. It is the *Not Performed* level, which means that the specific goals for a process area are not satisfied.

6.3.2 Capability Level 1 Generic Practices

Table 6-2 shows the capability level 1 generic practices. When GP 1.1 is applied to a process area, the people performing the work understand

Table 6-2: *Generic Practices from Capability Level 1*

Name	Generic Practice
GP 1.1 Identify Work Scope	Identify the scope of the work to be performed and work products or services to be produced, and communicate this information to those performing the work.
GP 1.2 Perform Base Practices	Perform the base practices of the process to develop work products and provide services to achieve the specific goals of the process area.

the processes associated with the process area and the work products to be produced. This idea is the basic premise of any work. When GP 1.2 is applied to a process area, the base specific practices of the process area are performed.[6] Most of the specific practices in the CMMI models are base practices, with the only exceptions involving some advanced practices in the Engineering process areas.

6.3.3 Capability Level 2 Generic Practices

Table 6-3 shows the capability level 2 generic practices.

When GP 2.1 is applied to a process area, it establishes an organizational policy that requires planning and execution of the process area. Organizational policies need not be labeled with the term "policy," but senior management sponsorship must be documented in a manner that requires planning and the use of the processes associated with the process area.

Implementing GP 2.2 establishes the requirements and objectives for the processes associated with the process area, and it forms the basis for process planning. This GP has five subpractices that provide information on how this feat could be accomplished, dealing with management sponsorship, documenting the process, planning for performing the process, reviewing the process with relevant stakeholders, and revising it as necessary.

This "Plan the Process" generic practice can create confusion when it is applied to the Project Planning process area, as it seems to entail a need to "plan the plan." This result is desired; the planning of the activities for the Project Planning process area is a logical and necessary set of tasks in any project. The process for planning a project is one that, like any other process, should be planned.[7]

Another potential source of confusion is the fact that some process areas include a goal or specific practices to establish a strategy or a specific plan. This concept differs from the generic practice, because a specific practice for planning addresses detailed product or product component strategies and plans—not planning across the full scope of

---

6. In the CMMI continuous representation, a *base practice* is a specific practice that resides at CL 1; it is distinguished from an advanced practice that resides at CL 2 or higher. Section 7.3 provides further discussion of base and advanced practices.

7. Only one level of "recursion" exists. Nothing in the model requires one to "plan to plan the plan."

Table 6-3: *Generic Practices from Capability Level 2*

Name	Generic Practice
GP 2.1 Establish an Organizational Policy	Establish and maintain an organizational policy for planning and performing the process.
GP 2.2 Plan the Process	Establish and maintain the requirements and objectives, and plan for performing the process.
GP 2.3 Provide Resources	Provide adequate resources for performing the process, developing the work products, and providing the services of the process.
GP 2.4 Assign Responsibility	Assign responsibility and authority for performing the process, developing the work products, and providing the services of the process.
GP 2.5 Train People	Train the people performing or supporting the process as needed.
GP 2.6 Manage Configurations	Place designated work products of the process under appropriate levels of configuration management.
GP 2.7 Identify and Involve Relevant Stakeholders	Identify and involve the relevant stakeholders as planned.
GP 2.8 Monitor and Control the Process	Monitor and control the process against the plan and take appropriate corrective action.
GP 2.9 Objectively Evaluate Adherence	Objectively evaluate adherence of the process and the work products and services of the process to the applicable requirements, objectives, and standards, and address noncompliance.
GP 2.10 Review Status with Higher-Level Management	Review the activities, status, and results of the process with higher-level management and resolve issues.

process area activities. For example, in the Verification process area, the first specific practice establishes and maintains a verification strategy for selected work products, and the third specific practice establishes and maintains detailed verification plans for the selected work products. In contrast, the generic practice expects that all of these activities will be planned, along with the other verification practices.

GP 2.3 is a favorite of all project and program managers. When applied to a process area, it ensures that adequate resources are allocated for carrying out the processes associated with the process area. This practice includes developing the work products of the process area and providing the services associated with the process, as well as the need for funding, facilities, people, and tools.

When a project applies GP 2.4 to a process area, responsibility and authority are assigned to perform the processes associated with that area. The three subpractices cover assigning responsibility for personnel who are in charge of the process as well as workers who perform the tasks of the process, and confirming that those individuals understand their responsibilities.

Ensuring that process participants are trained correctly is the focus of GP 2.5. It includes training of the people performing and supporting the process so that both groups understand the process sufficiently to perform or support it. The Organizational Training process area provides guidance on how to develop an organizational training program that supports this generic practice. The generic practice and the process area differ, however, in that the process area provides training practices at the organizational level whereas the generic practice addresses training for each process. Of course, a project may choose to rely on organizational training assets to the extent that they are available.

When a project applies GP 2.6 to a process area, it ensures that the appropriate level of configuration management is maintained for the process work products. Formal configuration management may or may not be expected, and a work product may be subject to different levels of configuration management at different points in time. The Configuration Management process area provides the specific practices needed to manage the selected work products for each project-related process area.

GP 2.7 requires involving all of the affected entities. The relevant stakeholders are specifically identified and drawn into the process associated with the process area.[8] The three subpractices identify stakeholders, let project planners know who these stakeholders are, and get the stakeholders involved. Although much of the CMMI material relevant to Integrated Product and Process Development is staged at maturity level 3, this CL 2 practice is important in both an integrated and a nonintegrated environment.

GP 2.8 monitors the plan for executing the process (which was defined in GP 2.2) and ensures that corrective actions are implemented when necessary. It has seven subpractices that provide more detailed information on how to monitor and control processes. The Project Monitoring and Control process area supports this generic practice by providing specific goals and practices for monitoring and taking corrective actions.

Objective evaluation of process and work product performance is provided to a process area through GP 2.9. While a quality assurance group or department may be used to perform the evaluations, the CMMI does not assume any particular organizational structure. Note, however, that people not directly responsible for managing or performing the process should perform the evaluation. The Process and Product Quality Assurance process area supports this generic practice by providing guidance on how to accomplish independent evaluations.

When a project applies GP 2.10 to a process area, its higher-level management reviews the activities, status, and process results and resolves any outstanding issues with the process performance. Each level of management may have its own needs for information about the process performance. The reviews should be both periodic and event-driven.

6.3.4 Capability Level 3 Generic Practices

Table 6-4 shows the capability level 3 generic practices.

GP 3.1 supports institutionalization of processes by requiring that projects establish and maintain a defined process tailored from the organization's standard processes. Defined processes may be established for a project or an organizational group; although various parts of the organization may have different defined processes, all will be based on the

---

8. A relevant stakeholder is a person or role that is affected by or accountable for a process outcome, and whose involvement in a particular activity is planned.

Table 6-4: *Generic Practices from Capability Level 3*

Name	Generic Practice
GP 3.1 Establish a Defined Process	Establish and maintain the description of a defined process.
GP 3.2 Collect Improvement Information	Collect work products, measures, measurement results, and improvement information derived from planning and performing the process to support the future use and improvement of the organization's processes and process assets.

standard processes. This tailoring provides flexibility to companies that have similar units that are organized differently, while ensuring that the standard processes remain truly standard across the enterprise.

GP 3.1 has five subpractices that support the establishment of the defined process that is associated with the process area. The Organizational Process Definition process area supports GP 3.1 by providing specific goals and practices related to the establishment of standard processes. The Integrated Project Management process area is also closely related to this generic practice. The notes in the model on individual specific practices offer more information on the use of these processes in an organization.

GP 3.2 represents a key to further process improvement, because it requires the organization to collect example work products, measures, and other data about the process for future use. Without such historical data, the process may become difficult to plan and impossible to manage quantitatively—the focus of CL 4. Three of the subpractices provide information on the contents of the process library. The fourth subpractice captures proposed improvements to the process assets. The Organizational Process Focus process area supports this generic practice by addressing process asset deployment and incorporating process-related experiences into the organizational process assets.

6.3.5 Capability Level 4 Generic Practices

Table 6-5 shows the capability level 4 generic practices.

Table 6-5: *Generic Practices from Capability Level 4*

Name	Generic Practice
GP 4.1 Establish Quality Objectives	Establish and maintain quantitative objectives for the process about quality and process performance based on customer needs and business objectives.
GP 4.2 Stabilize Subprocess Performance	Stabilize the performance of one or more subprocesses of the process to determine its ability to achieve the established quantitative quality and process performance objectives

GP 4.1 expects an organization to use its business objectives to define process performance and quality objectives. All relevant stakeholders should be included in this activity, which entails making use of the CL 2 generic practice. Once established, quantitative objectives are allocated to the processes. The processes may be related to process areas or a set of process areas. The Quantitative Project Management process area encompasses quantitatively managing processes, so the information in that area is extremely useful in implementing this generic practice, especially in project-related process areas.

In implementing GP 4.2, the organization uses the quality and process performance objectives to statistically manage selected subprocesses. A strong rationale for choosing the particular subprocesses should exist, and the organization needs to demonstrate how those subprocesses are managed to meet the intent of the generic practice. The Quantitative Project Management process area also supports this generic practice.

6.3.6 Capability Level 5 Generic Practices

Table 6-6 shows the capability level 5 generic practices.

Implementing GP 5.1 drives the organization to select and deploy process and technology improvements that contribute to its ability to meet quality and performance objectives for the process. The Organizational Innovation and Deployment process area provides more information in terms of goals and practices on ways to implement this generic practice.

Table 6-6: *Generic Practices from Capability Level 5*

Name	Generic Practice
GP 5.1 Ensure Continuous Process Improvement	Ensure continuous improvement of the process in fulfilling the relevant business goals of the organization.
GP 5.2 Correct Common Cause of Problems	Identify and correct the root causes of defects and other problems in the process.

The root causes of defects in the process are identified and corrected through GP 5.2.[9] Without this practice, organizations would find it difficult to gain the agility needed to rapidly solve problems and to effectively evolve their processes. Goals and practices that can be applied in implementing GP 5.2 appear in the Causal Analysis and Resolution process area.

6.4 Generic Practices in the Maturity Dimension

The maturity dimension is used in the staged representation for the model. As discussed in Section 6.2, only the generic practices from capability levels 2 and 3 are used in establishing the maturity dimension.

Although they are grouped as common features rather than as capability levels, the generic practices have the same meaning here that they have in the capability dimension. While this grouping mixes the generic practices of different capability levels, no special meaning is implied—it is simply a different way of grouping the practices. The nomenclature in Table 6-7[10] appears in the staged representation and provides a means to relate the generic practices of both representations.

---

9. The concept of a *root cause* is frequently misunderstood. Clearly, it is not a cause for which no preceding cause exists; only a god or the "big bang" would be a candidate to meet that definition. Rather, a root cause is an antecedent cause of a problem or defect such that, if it were removed, the problem or defect would be lessened or eliminated.

10. For brevity, Table 6-7 shows the generic practices for maturity levels 3 through 5. The generic practices are the same for ML 2, except that GP 3.1 and GP 3.2 are not found in the ML 2 process areas. In this case, AB 1 in Table 6-7 is GP 2.2, and there are four GPs in the Ability to Perform common feature.

Table 6-7: *Common Features and Generic Practices*

Commitment to Perform	
GP 2.1 (CO 1)	Establish and maintain an organizational policy for planning and performing the process.
Ability to Perform	
GP 3.1 (AB 1)	Establish and maintain the description of a defined process.
GP 2.2 (AB 2)	Establish and maintain the requirements and objectives, and plan for performing the process.
GP 2.3 (AB 3)	Provide adequate resources for performing the process, developing the work products, and providing the services of the process.
GP 2.4 (AB 4)	Assign responsibility and authority for performing the process, developing the work products, and providing the services of the process.
GP 2.5 (AB 5)	Train the people performing or supporting the process as needed.
Directing Implementation	
GP 2.6 (DI 1)	Place designated work products of the process under appropriate levels of configuration management.
GP 2.7 (DI 2)	Identify and involve the relevant stakeholders as planned.
GP 2.8 (DI 3)	Monitor and control the process against the plan and take appropriate corrective action.
GP 3.2 (DI 4)	Collect work products, measures, measurement results, and improvement information derived from planning and performing the process to support the future use and improvement of the organization's processes and process assets.

(continued)

Table 6-7: *Common Features and Generic Practices (cont.)*

Verifying Implementation	
GP 2.9 (VI 1)	Objectively evaluate adherence of the process and the work products and services of the process to the applicable requirements, objectives, and standards, and address non-compliance.
GP 2.10 (VI 2)	Review the activities, status, and results of the process with higher-level management and resolve issues.

6.5 Organizational Capability Evolution

Users of staged models (especially the CMM for Software) often have difficulty in understanding how a continuous model measures organizational progress. When one is accustomed to a model in which process areas build on one another, it is not obvious how possibly unrelated process areas might be improved without some kind of staging. It may also be unclear when work should be carried out in a particular process area. Although the Software CMM does not explicitly prohibit addressing higher-level key process areas (KPA) before lower-level KPAs, it implies that this sequence should not be the normal way of proceeding. In EIA/IS 731 (a continuous model), this implication would be meaningless; the focus areas in the Systems Engineering Capability Model (SECM) were not staged. The following example may help explain how an ML 4 process area fits into the capability level used in the CMMI model.

Quantitative Project Management (QPM) is an ML 4 process area. Obviously, it doesn't make sense for an organization to start its process improvement journey with this particular process area. In fact, cautionary statements in the Introductory Notes section of the process area warn against this approach. The continuous representation, however, does not dictate the time or state that must be reached before delving into this process area. When an organization initially establishes a QPM process, it may be rated at CL 1. By adding generic goals and practices, it may improve its capability to CL 5 if deemed appropriate by the organization. In contrast, strict adherence to the staging in the staged representation would not look at QPM until ML 4.[11] The bottom line is that the two means of achieving the advanced capability are striving for the same objective: quantitatively managed processes.

---

11. In EIA/IS 731, the practices in QPM are addressed as advanced practices in other focus areas.

Chapter 7

CMMI Process Areas

*Never tell people how to do things. Tell them what to do
and they will surprise you with their ingenuity.*
General George S. Patton (1885–1945)

*In theory, there is no difference between theory
and practice. In practice there is.*
Yogi Berra (1925–   )

The CMMI-SE/SW/IPPD model includes 24 process areas that define
the process dimension of the model. These process areas are the same
in both Capability Maturity Model Integration (CMMI) architectural
representations. This chapter provides a brief description of each process
area, focusing on its purpose, goals, and specific practices. It also points
out some of the inherent relationships between the process areas, which
are important in planning process improvement activities.

In the continuous representation, the process areas are grouped by category: Process Management, Project Management, Engineering, and
Support. The process areas in three of the four categories (Support is
the exception) are related to one another. The Support process areas
are independent of each other as well as all other process areas. In the
staged representation, the process areas are grouped into maturity levels 2 through 5. Table 7-1 shows the process areas grouped by category
and labeled with their maturity level (ML).

Table 7-1: *Process Areas by Category with Maturity Level*

Category	Process Area	Maturity Level
Process Management	Organizational Process Definition	3
	Organizational Process Focus	3
	Organizational Training	3
	Organizational Process Performance	4
	Organizational Innovation and Deployment	5
Project Management	Project Planning	2
	Project Monitoring and Control	2
	Supplier Agreement Management	2
	Integrated Project Management	3
	Risk Management	3
	Integrated Teaming	3
	Quantitative Project Management	4
Engineering	Requirements Management	2
	Requirements Development	3
	Technical Solution	3
	Product Integration	3
	Verification	3
	Validation	3

Category	Process Area	Maturity Level
Support	Configuration Management	2
	Process and Product Quality Management	2
	Measurement and Analysis	2
	Decision Analysis and Resolution	3
	Organizational Environment for Integration	3
	Causal Analysis and Resolution	5

In our review of each process area, we will follow the groupings provided by the four categories of the continuous representation. This strategy should clarify the process area relationships that emerge when planning a successful process improvement strategy.

7.1 Process Management Process Areas

The five process areas that make up the Process Management category contain the cross-project practices related to defining, planning, resourcing, deploying, implementing, monitoring, controlling, verifying, measuring, and improving processes. They are

- Organizational Process Definition (OPD)
- Organizational Process Focus (OPF)
- Organizational Process Performance (OPP)
- Organizational Innovation and Deployment (OID)
- Organizational Training (OT)

As shown in Figure 7-1, a close relationship exists between four of these process areas. OPP builds on the capabilities in OPF and OPD. OID builds on the capabilities of the other process areas. This relationship is defined in the staged representation with OPF and OPD at ML 3, OPP at ML 4, and OID at ML 5. In EIA/IS 731, this ordering was accomplished by designating specific practices at higher capability levels within a

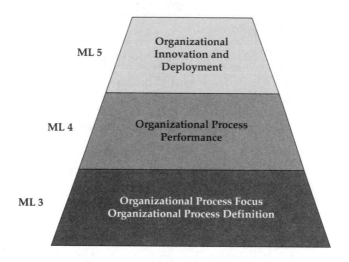

Figure 7-1: *Process Management process area relationships*

focus area. In CMMI, however, all of the specific practices for these four process areas are at capability level 1 (CL 1). When using the CMMI continuous representation for process improvement, you should understand these relationships and plan your improvement projects accordingly. For example, you should not seek a capability level in OPP that is greater than what you have achieved in both OPF and OPD.

7.1.1 Organizational Process Definition

The purpose of Organizational Process Definition is to establish and maintain a usable set of organizational process assets. OPD (see Figure 7-2)[1] has two specific goals: to create organizational process assets and to make supporting assets available. OPD and OPF work together in that the former provides guidance for an organization on creating processes and their supporting assets, while the latter provides guidance on identifying and planning process improvements.

The first OPD goal—creating organizational process assets—is accomplished with three specific practices. The first establishes descriptions of life-cycle models that may be used by each project. These models are also used as the basis for establishing the organization's standard

---

1. We will begin our description of each process area with a context diagram and the purpose statement from the model. The context diagrams are drawn from Introduction to CMMI-SE/ SW-Continuous V1.0 Module.

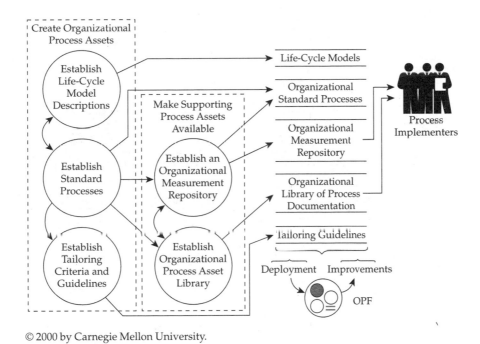

Figure 7-2: *Organizational Process Definition context diagram*

processes in the second practice. The third practice provides tailoring guidelines and criteria for the standard processes, which are in turn used by the projects during the planning phases of the project life cycle.

The second OPD goal—making assets available—includes a specific practice for establishing a repository for organizational process measurements and a specific practice for establishing process assets that are used by the projects. An organizational measurement repository supports process performance and quantitative process management as the organization's capability and maturity improve. The repository also supports the use of historical data in establishing estimates. The process asset library supports projects in planning their project-unique processes through tailoring and implementing the standard processes, with resultant cost savings. This library may contain document templates, example plans, work products, policies, and other process enablers.

7.1.2 Organizational Process Focus

The purpose of Organizational Process Focus is to establish and maintain an understanding of the organization's processes and process assets, and to identify,

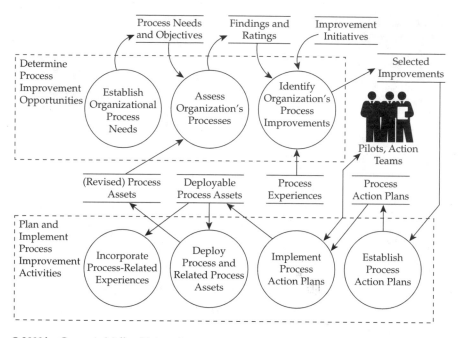

© 2000 by Carnegie Mellon University.

Figure 7-3: *Organizational Process Focus context diagram*

plan, and implement the organization's process improvement activities. OPF (see Figure 7-3) uses two specific goals to achieve this purpose: one for determining improvement opportunities and another for planning and implementing selected improvements. The specific practices mapped to each of these goals are shown in the context diagram.

For the first goal, determining process improvement opportunities, the organization establishes and maintains its process needs and objectives. These pieces of information are used when assessing the processes, with the assessment generating findings and ratings that are used along with improvement initiatives to identify the organization's needed process improvements. The organization can then select which improvements to make.

The second goal—planning and implementing those process improvement activities—is carried out with four specific practices. The organization uses selected improvements to establish process action plans. Next, the plans are implemented, resulting in process assets that are subsequently deployed and incorporated into the process assets library.

Note that the context diagram in Figure 7-3 (and others in this chapter) shows how typical work products of the practices may be used. In this book we will not attempt to discuss every specific practice or every arrow to or from a typical work product in the context diagram. For further information, refer to the model itself or take a formal CMMI training course. Our objective here is simply to introduce some of the details within each process area.

7.1.3 Organizational Process Performance

The purpose of Organizational Process Performance is to establish and maintain a quantitative understanding of the performance of the organization's set of standard processes, and to provide the process performance data, baselines, and models to quantitatively manage the organization's projects. OPP (see Figure 7-4) has one specific goal to establish these performance baselines and models. This "advanced" process area builds on both OPD and OPF by establishing expectations and objectives for the quantitative management of process performance. Selected processes or subprocesses are analyzed, perhaps by examining both performance

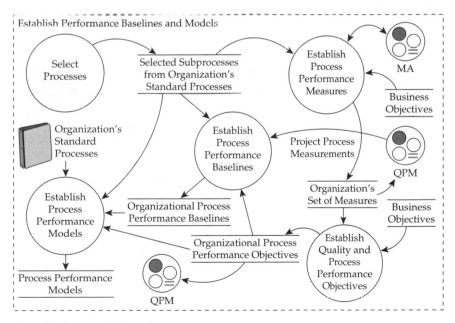

© 2000 by Carnegie Mellon University.

Figure 7-4: *Organizational Process Performance context diagram*

measures and product measures (for example, quality). Process performance baselines and models are then established. The baselines measure the performance of the organization's standard processes at various levels of detail. Tailoring and other factors (such as product line, complexity, application domain, or team size and experience) can significantly affect the baselines. As a result, the organization may need several performance baselines.

7.1.4 Organizational Innovation and Deployment

The purpose of Organizational Innovation and Deployment is to select and deploy incremental and innovative improvements that measurably improve the organization's processes and technologies. The improvements support the organization's quality and process performance objectives, as established in OPP and derived from the organization's business objectives. OID (see Figure 7-5) adds further capability to OPD, OPF, and OPP with its two goals: systematically selecting improvements and systematically deploying them.

The CMMI models include technology in the OID process area. Technology is also addressed, at least at the subprocess level and dealing

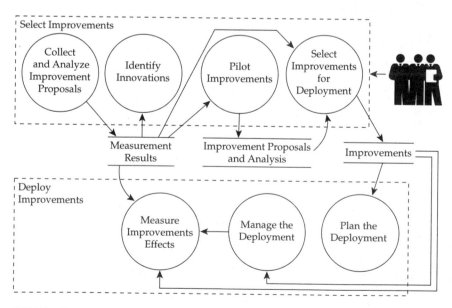

© 2000 by Carnegie Mellon University.

Figure 7-5: *Organizational Innovation and Deployment context diagram*

with product technology, in the Technical Solution (TS) process area. In EIA/IS 731, the Manage Technology focus area deals with product technology. In OID, however, both product- and process-related technology are deployed to improve the total organization.

The first OID goal—selecting improvements—involves collecting and analyzing process and technology improvement proposals. Innovations are identified and analyzed, evaluated through pilot projects, and then selected for deployment. The improvements may be incremental or innovative. The second goal—deploying improvements—includes planning the deployment and then measuring the effectiveness of the new process or technology as well as its effects on other management objectives.

7.1.5 Organizational Training

The purpose of Organizational Training is to develop the skills and knowledge of people so they can perform their roles effectively and efficiently. OT (see Figure 7-6) has two specific goals: one for identifying training needs

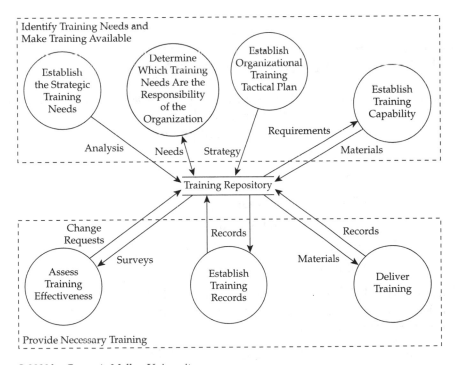

Figure 7-6: *Organizational Training context diagram*

and making training available, and another for providing necessary training. This process area does not build on the capability level of any other Process Management process area. Rather, OT focuses on the organization's strategic and cross-project training needs.

The first goal—identifying training needs and making training available—includes four specific practices. First, strategic training needs are established to guide the overall organizational training. Second, responsibility for each need is assigned, to either the organization or the project. Third, a tactical plan is established to ensure that training needs are met. This plan should explain how each of the organization's training needs will be addressed. The fourth practice addresses the actual establishment of the organization's training capability, such as developing or obtaining training materials.

Under the second goal, providing necessary training, the specific practices focus on delivery of training to the target audiences, measurement of the training's effectiveness, and creation of training records for the employees.

7.2 Project Management Process Areas

The Project Management process areas cover the activities related to planning, monitoring, and controlling the project. The CMMI-SE/SW model includes six project management process areas:

- Project Planning (PP)
- Project Monitoring and Control (PMC)
- Integrated Project Management (IPM)
- Quantitative Project Management (QPM)
- Supplier Agreement Management (SAM)
- Risk Management (RSKM)

The SE/SW/IPPD model includes one additional process area under Project Management and an expanded version of the Integrated Project Management process area:

- Integrated Project Management (IPM [IPPD])
- Integrated Teaming (IT)

This section describes the Project Management process areas in the CMMI-SE/SW model. Section 7.5 covers the process areas in the IPPD model extension.

As shown in Figure 7-7, a close relationship exists between four of these process areas. IPM and QPM build on the capabilities of PP and PMC. This relationship is defined in the staged representation with PP and PMC at ML 2, IPM at ML 3, and QPM at ML 4. When using the continuous representation for process improvement, you should understand this relationship and plan your improvement projects accordingly.

7.2.1 Project Planning

The purpose of Project Planning is to establish and maintain plans that define project activities. PP (see Figure 7-8) has three specific goals: to establish estimates, to develop a project plan, and to obtain commitments. PP and PMC work together, in that the former involves the creation of the project plan, and the latter involves tracking progress against the plans, thereby ensuring that any corrective actions are managed to closure.

In the first goal, establishing estimates for the project, the scope of the project is estimated based on a work breakdown structure, and project attributes for work products and tasks are estimated. To set the scope of the planning effort, a project life cycle is defined. Estimates of effort and

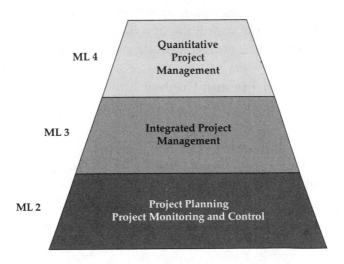

Figure 7-7: *Project Management process area relationships*

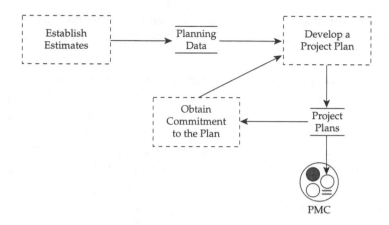

Figure 7-8: *Project Planning context diagram*

cost can then be developed. These estimates are used as the basis for developing the project plans in the second goal: budgets and schedules are established, risks are identified, and plans are created for data management, resources, knowledge and skills needed, and stakeholder involvement.

For the third goal, the project obtains commitment to the project plans by reviewing the subordinate plans to understand project commitments, reconciling the project plan to reflect available and projected resources, and obtaining commitments from relevant stakeholders responsible for performing and supporting plan execution.

7.2.2 Project Monitoring and Control

The purpose of Project Monitoring and Control is to provide understanding into the project's progress so that appropriate corrective actions can be taken when the project's performance deviates significantly from the plan. PMC (see Figure 7-9) has two specific goals: one on monitoring actual performance, and another on managing corrective actions.

The first goal (monitor the project against the plan) has five practices that identify what should be monitored and two practices that deal with reviews. The monitoring focuses on the following:

- Project planning parameters
- Commitments

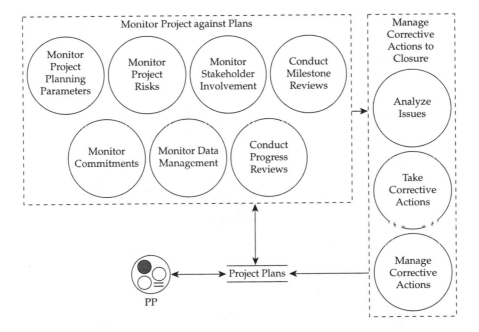

Figure 7-9: *Project Monitoring and Control context diagram*

- Project risks
- Data management
- Stakeholder involvement

These monitoring efforts are reviewed at both progress reviews and milestone reviews. Whenever these practices identify needed corrective actions, the second goal provides specific practices to analyze the issues, take the necessary action, and manage the the corrective action to closure. Note that other CMMI process areas (such as Verification, Supplier Agreement Management, and Configuration Management) refer to this PMC goal and its practices to obtain information about managing corrective actions.

7.2.3 Integrated Project Management

The purpose of Integrated Project Management is to establish and manage the project and the involvement of the relevant stakeholders according to an integrated and defined process that is tailored from the organization's set of standard processes. IPM (see Figure 7-10) has two specific goals in the

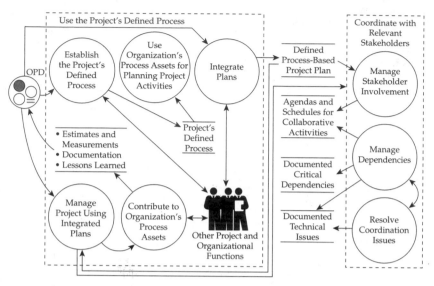

Figure 7-10: *Integrated Project Management (without IPPD)*
context diagram

CMMI-SE/SW model. Adding IPPD provides two more specific goals. The two basic specific goals relate to using a defined process for the project and coordinating activities with relevant stakeholders. These goals build on the planning covered in PP, by making sure that the appropriate organizations and people are involved in managing the project. The organization's standard processes, which were developed in the Organizational Process Definition process area, are the basis for the project's defined process.

The first IPM goal has five practices that address how the project follows a defined process. Establishing the project's defined process is the first step, with the organization's standard processes serving as a starting point. Next, the organizational process assets from the organizational process asset library are used for planning project activities, integrating all plans to describe the defined process, and managing using the integrated plans. Finally, the project contributes its work products to the organization's process assets for use by future projects and process improvement activities.

The second basic goal—coordination and collaboration with relevant stakeholders—has three practices, which focus on managing the involvement of stakeholders to satisfy commitments and resolve misunderstandings, tracking critical project dependencies, and resolving outstanding issues.

The addition of IPPD brings two more specific goals: using the project's shared vision and organizing integrated teams. The first goal (Figure 7-11), which is dubbed SG 3 in the IPPD version, defines a shared vision context that is used to establish a shared vision for the project and evaluates the use and effectiveness of that vision. The second goal, called SG 4 in the IPPD version, organizes integrated teams by determining team structure for a project, developing a plan for distributing requirements to the team, and establishing the teams.

7.2.4 Quantitative Project Management

The purpose of the Quantitative Project Management process area is to quantitatively manage the project's defined process to achieve the project's established quality and process performance objectives. QPM (see Figure 7-12) has two specific goals that build on the goals of PP, PMC, and IPM: using performance objectives to quantitatively manage the project and statistically managing selected subprocesses. The first goal is achieved by specific practices that establish performance objectives, analyze and select candidate subprocesses, and monitor the project's performance objectives

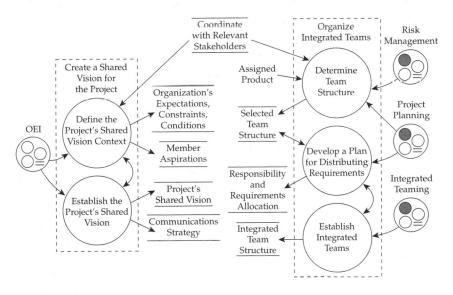

© 2000 by Carnegie Mellon University.

Figure 7-11: *Integrated Project Management (IPPD) context diagram*

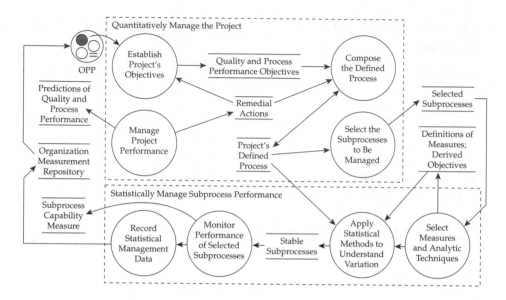

© 2000 by Carnegie Mellon University.

Figure 7-12: *Quantitative Project Management context diagram*

to determine whether they have been satisfied. The second goal is achieved by specific practices that select measures and analytical techniques, understand variation, monitor the selected subprocesses, and record the resulting data in a measurement repository for the organization. In this way, QPM builds on PMC by ensuring that the organizations uses statistical management practices as well as historical data to determine objectives and select the subprocesses that will be quantitatively managed.

7.2.5 Supplier Agreement Management

The purpose of Supplier Agreement Management is to manage the acquisition of products and services from suppliers external to the project for which there exists a formal agreement. SAM (see Figure 7-13) has two specific goals: one for establishing supplier agreements and another for satisfying them. This process area works in cooperation with the Technical Solution process area, in which the organization decides whether to make or buy. Once a decision to buy is made, SAM creates the agreement and then manages it from the purchaser's viewpoint. Product component requirements are developed in the Requirements Development process area.

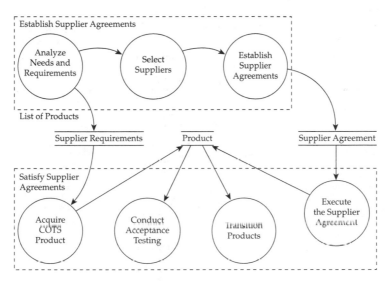

© 2000 by Carnegie Mellon University.

Figure 7-13: *Supplier Agreement Management context diagram*

To establish supplier agreements, the project analyzes the acquisition options to see how well they meet the needs and requirements. Suppliers are then identified and selected, and an agreement is established. To satisfy those supplier agreements, the project acquires commercial off-the-shelf (COTS) products, performs the activities mandated in the supplier agreements, conducts acceptance tests for the acquired products, and transitions the acquired products into the project integration effort.

7.2.6 Risk Management

The purpose of Risk Management is to identify potential problems before they occur, so that risk-handling activities may be planned and invoked as needed across the life cycle to mitigate adverse impacts on achieving objectives. RSKM (see Figure 7-14) actually builds on part of the PP process area, as a specific practice in PP identifies and analyzes project risks, and the project plan should document those risks. However, PP is less systematic and less proactive than the requirements noted in RSKM. Furthermore, RSKM could be applied outside of the project context to manage organizational risks (if desired). Several other process areas reference RSKM.

RSKM has three specific goals that involve preparation for risk management, identification and analysis of the risks, and handling and mitigation of risks as appropriate. The preparation steps include determining

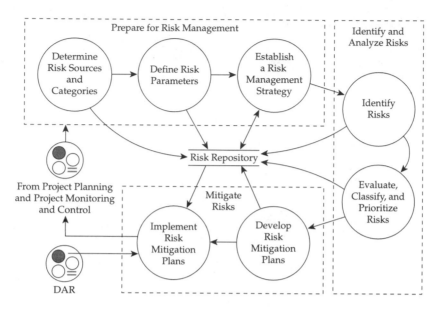

© 2000 by Carnegie Mellon University.

Figure 7-14: *Risk Management context diagram*

risk sources and the categories used for organizing risks by "bins," establishing the parameters used to analyze and classify risks, and developing a risk strategy. The identification and analysis steps focus on determining the relative priority of the risks based on the analysis parameters. The handling and mitigation of the risks encompass developing and implementing risk mitigation plans.

7.3 Engineering Process Areas

In both the Process Management and Project Management categories, (some of) the process areas build upon and presuppose others. In contrast, the Engineering category lacks one-directional, "build upon" relationships between process areas. Instead, it is assumed that all of the process areas are used together in an integrated manner. In CMMI, the Engineering process areas integrate software and systems engineering processes into a "product-oriented" set of process areas. Improving product development processes means targeting essential business objectives, rather than the more narrow objectives of specific disciplines. That is, the Engineering process areas are constructed to discourage the tendency toward a "stovepiped" set of processes. After trying to include both software and systems engineering process areas, the CMMI Product Development Team discovered that the practices overlapped almost completely. The first attempt to integrate the SW-CMM Software Product Engineering key process area and the EIA/IS 731 Technical focus areas resulted in version 0.2 of the CMMI. It included more goals and practices than are currently found in CMMI version 1.0.

The Engineering process areas apply to the development of any product or service in the engineering development domain (for example, software products, hardware products, services, or processes). They address all development using the term "product" rather than "system." This choice was made to avoid problems with that terminology. The process areas apply recursively at all levels of product development. The term "product component" designates the building blocks of the "product."

These process areas are constructed to apply to many different types of organizations, not just those responsible for the initial systems engineering and software development work. For example, a software maintenance organization that provides software updates to a system may not have been part of the initial development effort. Such a group may review the CMMI Engineering process areas and decide that Requirements Development doesn't apply to it; someone else handled those activities. In reality, any engineering change request is based on some need. That need should be elicited, new requirements should be determined based on it, and alternative solutions should be considered before the selected solution is designed, implemented, verified, and validated. In this way, the technical control based on these principles ensures that all maintenance actions are necessary and meet the user's needs.

The requirement for the model to support both continuous and staged representations, however, caused some problems. One architectural feature of CMMI is that only the Engineering process areas are allowed to contain advanced practices—that is, specific practices assigned to a capability level greater than CL 1.[2] In the CMMI models that have been

---

2. The discussions on the CMMI Product Development Team regarding advanced practices were highly contentious. Some team members wanted no advanced practices; others wanted them throughout the model. The decision to put them in only the Engineering process areas represented a "middle-ground" decision based on the fact that many of the advanced practices in EIA/IS 731 resided in these process areas. It also reflected the hope that practical application of CMMI models would enable the community to determine how useful advanced practices are for process improvement, thereby deciding the fate of this model construct.

released to date, the advanced practices in the Engineering process areas are all at CL 2 or CL 3. In EIA/IS 731, the specific practices spanned all capability levels. In contrast, in the SW-CMM, advanced practices are not used and all practices are base practices (at CL 1). Because the CMMI lacks advanced practices in process areas other than Engineering, the definition of the capability levels is complicated, especially in the Process Management and Project Management categories, where some of the process areas build on each other.[3]

Six Engineering process areas exist:

- Requirements Management (REQM)
- Requirements Development (RD)
- Technical Solution (TS)
- Product Integration (PI)
- Verification (VER)
- Validation (VAL)

In this section, descriptions of the specific practices will identify advanced practices with the capability level in parentheses, such as (CL 2).

7.3.1 Requirements Management

The purpose of Requirements Management is to manage the requirements of the project's products and product components and to identify inconsistencies between those requirements and the project's plans and work products. REQM (see Figure 7-15) has one specific goal: to manage requirements and identify inconsistencies with plans and work products. It is the only Engineering process area that is staged at ML 2; all other process areas are staged at ML 3. The SW-CMM had a Requirements Management process area at ML 2 that led to the inclusion of this process area at ML 2 in CMMI.

REQM has five specific practices, including two advanced practices at CL 2. Neither of these advanced practices builds on a lower-level

---

3. The argument in favor of advanced practices states that they help define the capability levels within a process area and identify a clear path of process improvement. Specific goals become complicated, however, because they are defined as covering all specific practices at all capability levels. Thus a specific goal takes on an expanded meaning as one moves from one capability level to the next. Some find this flexibility problematic; others do not.

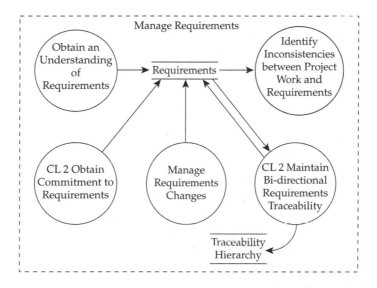

© 2000 by Carnegie Mellon University.

Figure 7-15: *Requirements Management context diagram*

practice.[4] To achieve CL 1 in REQM with the CMMI continuous representation, the single specific goal of managing requirements can be met with just the three expected specific practices at CL 1 (that is, ignoring the other two specific practices). To achieve CL 2 in REQM, the goal must be met with all five expected specific practices. At either CL 1 or CL 2, if alternative practices were used to satisfy the goal, an expanded set of alternative practices would be needed for CL 2 compared with CL 1, so as to match the expanded expectation.[5]

Here and in other Engineering process areas we will present all specific practices as a group. We take the viewpoint of the higher capability levels and explicitly note all advanced practices.

To manage requirements, the person or team that receives them needs to develop an understanding of what they mean before doing anything

---

4. Some Engineering process areas include a base practice that says to do something, plus an advanced practice that says to do the same thing better. In this way, an advanced practice "builds on" a lower-level practice. Not all advanced practices follow this pattern, as the examples here from REQM show.

5. When advanced practices are mapped to a goal, the satisfaction of the goal is not a binary affair. A basic way of satisfying the goal exists, as does a more advanced way of satisfying the same goal. Some critics have labeled this phenomenon "chameleonic goals."

with the requirements. It should obtain a commitment from the people who implement the requirements (CL 2). Once the requirements are received and understood, and a commitment is obtained, all changes to the requirements should be managed, including recording change histories and evaluating change impacts. The project should provide for bidirectional traceability of the requirement and the associated plans and work products (CL 2). Tracing the requirements provides a better basis for determining the ramifications of changes, and it ensures that all requirements have a parent and that the product design covers all high-level requirements. Finally, the project should identify inconsistencies between the requirements and the project plans and work products. Any corrective action required to fix inconsistencies is accomplished in the requirements development process, the project planning process, or possibly other processes.

7.3.2 Requirements Development

The purpose of Requirements Development is to produce and analyze customer, product, and product component requirements. RD (see Figure 7-16) has three specific goals: developing customer requirements, developing product requirements, and analyzing and validating requirements to produce a definition of the required functionality. This process area contains all of the practices related to generating product and product component requirements. It is recursive with TS, with alternative solutions being developed to help determine lower-level product requirements.

© 2000 by Carnegie Mellon University.

Figure 7-16: *Requirements Development context diagram*

Figure 7-16 shows a simplified context diagram for RD, because this process area contains too many specific practices to include clearly. Furthermore, Figure 7-16 does not really illustrate how the requirements are developed. The analysis tasks are performed concurrently with the development tasks. Processes developed from RD practices should be designed to meet the needs of the organization. They can represent several different product life-cycle models, such as waterfall, iterative, incremental, and multilevel models.

The development process needs a starting point, and RD's first goal provides it by developing customer requirements. The first two specific practices call for the collection (CL 1) and elicitation (CL 2) of stakeholder needs, expectations, constraints, and interfaces. Providing information on needs allows the customer (and other stakeholders) to describe the product's desired function, performance, appearance, and other characteristics. In the third specific practice, the stakeholders' needs, expectations, constraints, and interfaces are translated into customer requirements.

In the staged representation, only the second (elicit needs) and third (transform into customer requirements) specific practices are expected; the first specific practice (collect needs) is listed as informative only. Why does this difference arise if both representations are really two views of the same model? How can a specific practice be an expected item in one representation but not in the other? Actually, this discrepancy is not difficult to understand. When (as here) an advanced practice builds on a lower-level practice, which makes sense for distinguishing two capability levels in a continuous representation, only the advanced practice appears in the staged representation. In a process area that exists at just one maturity level, it would be awkward to have two specific practices where one subsumes the other: (1) do x and (2) do x better. Because you cannot successfully perform the advanced practice and yet fail to meet the base practice, the latter is not needed in the staged world.

RD's second goal addresses the use of customer requirements to develop the product-level and product-component-level requirements. In some cases, these requirements may consist of a system and its subsystems, boxes, boards, software configuration items, software components, and modules. In other cases, they may include processes, subprocesses, or service-related products. The three specific practices focus on translating the customer requirements into the more technical form of product requirements, allocating the requirements to each component of the product, and identifying interface requirements. One way of handling interfaces is to treat them as if they were the same as the other requirements. Note, however, that a lack of attention to the interfaces often results in defects, which can lead to rework, cost overruns, and schedule slips.

In RD's third goal, the requirements are analyzed and validated as they are developed; this step is critical for the success of a product. The six specific practices that map to this goal involve preparation, analysis, and validation. To get started, a good way to undertake the analysis is to develop operational concepts and scenarios that detail the way the product will be used, stored, transported, and so forth. The operational concepts help define the requirements from a broad, in-use point of view, and they help establish a definition of the required functionality. Analysis of allocated requirements ensures that they are necessary and sufficient to meet the objectives of the higher-level requirements. In addition, requirements are analyzed to reduce the life-cycle cost, schedule, and risk of product development (CL 3). Two specific practices address validating requirements—one at CL 1 and one at CL 2. The first base practice ensures that the resulting product will perform appropriately in its intended use environment. The second builds on the first, adding the use of multiple techniques to further reduce the risks of proceeding. Only the advanced practice is expected in the staged representation.

7.3.3 Technical Solution

The purpose of Technical Solution is to develop, design, and implement solutions to requirements. Solutions, designs and implementations encompass products, product components, and product related processes either singly or in combinations as appropriate. TS (see Figure 7-17) has three specific goals that address selecting product component solutions, developing the design, and implementing the design. The context diagram in Figure 7-16 is high-level, showing only the goals. In the first goal, alternative solutions are developed and analyzed, and the one that best satisfies the criteria is selected. The selected alternative may be used to develop more detailed requirements in the RD process area or designed in the second goal of TS. After the product components are designed, they are implemented together with support documentation in the third goal of TS.

The first TS goal includes four specific practices, the second of which (at CL 2) builds on the first: develop alternative solutions and develop detailed alternative solutions. In the CMMI glossary, a "detailed

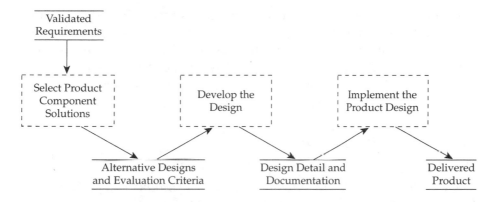

Figure 7-17: *Technical Solution context diagram*

alternative solution" is defined as having a list of specific things to be included. This choice reduced the number of specific practices in the model; an alternative would have been to add several specific practices to address the listed items. The specific practice to evolve the operational concepts and scenarios based on the alternative solutions (CL 2) helps determine which alternative to select, along with the other criteria that have been established. For the fourth specific practice, the engineer or team selects the solution that best satisfies the established criteria.

For the second goal of developing the product or product component designs, six specific practices exist. Because the model can be used for many different products, a specific practice calls for establishing and using effective design methods. Indeed, design methods may vary greatly even when developing the same type of product. The third specific practice (at CL 3) builds on the second (at CL 1): develop a technical data package and establish a complete technical data package. The CMMI glossary defines the content of a "complete technical data package" as the minimum expected for the CL 3 practice. Because specific practices are expected (not required) and alternative practices are possible, the user could apply this concept to the defined complete technical data package. The fifth specific practice (at CL 3) builds on the fourth (at CL 1): establish product component interface solutions, and do so in terms of established criteria. In the final specific practice (at CL 3), the project evaluates whether the product components should be developed, purchased, or reused. If it decides to purchase a component, the SAM process area establishes the agreement and manages it.

The third goal—implementing the product components and generating associated support documentation—has two specific practices. For the first, the project implements the designs for all types of product components—software, hardware, and so on. For the second, it establishes and maintains the end-use support documentation that describes how to install, operate, and maintain the product.

7.3.4 Product Integration

The purpose of Product Integration is to assemble the product from the product components, ensure that the product, as integrated, functions properly, and deliver the product. PI (see Figure 7-18) has three specific goals that address establishing an integration strategy, ensuring interface compatibility, and assembling the product components for delivery.

The first goal—establishing and maintaining a strategy for integration—includes three specific practices. First, the project develops the strategy for integration early in the life cycle, which assists in the overall planning effort. Second, it establishes the environment for integration (CL 2). Finally, it defines the detailed procedures and criteria for integration (CL 3).

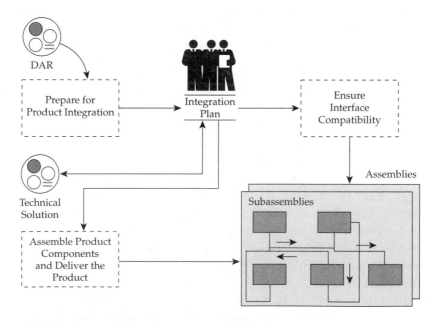

© 2000 by Carnegie Mellon University.

Figure 7-18: *Product Integration context diagram*

The second goal—ensuring that the interfaces (both internal and external) are compatible—has two specific practices. First, the project reviews the interface descriptions for coverage and completeness. Note that interfaces to the environment are included in this practice. Then, it manages the interface definitions, designs, and changes for the product and product components to maintain consistency and resolve issues.

Four specific practices exist for the third goal, verifying that product components are assembled and that the integrated, verified, and validated product is delivered. After the product components are implemented and unit testing is complete, the integration process begins. The lowest levels of the product are usually integrated first, with the product being assembled in successive stages. In the CMMI, the delivery of the product occurs in the PI process area. First, the project confirms that each component has been properly identified and functions according to its description and that the interfaces comply with their descriptions. This step helps avoid problems during assembly of the product components, which occurs in the next specific practice. Personnel then check out the assembly according to the strategy and procedures. Finally, they package the product and deliver it to the appropriate customer.

7.3.5 Verification

The purpose of Verification is to assure that selected work products meet their specified requirements. VER (see Figure 7-19) has three specific goals that

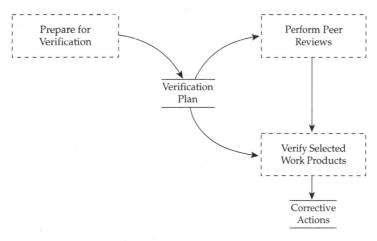

© 2000 by Carnegie Mellon University.

Figure 7-19: *Verification context diagram*

address preparing for verification, performing peer reviews on selected work products, and verifying selected work products. The three specific practices for the first goal regarding preparation resemble the PI specific practices: develop the strategy for verification early in the project, establish the environment for verification (CL 2), and define the detailed procedures and criteria for verification (CL 3). The verification strategy is established early in the project, because many of the activities associated with requirements development and design (such as analyses, reviews, and demonstrations) involve ensuring that the requirements are, in fact, verifiable.

Three practices are included to meet the peer review goal. Peer reviews comprise a specialized verification activity intended to reduce defects in selected product components. Among software developers, they are perceived to be a highly valued technique. In fact, the SW-CMM devoted an entire key process area to peer reviews. Although EIA/IS 731 did not explicitly include peer reviews, there is value in including them in the verification strategy for other development disciplines. For the specific practices, the project first prepares for the peer reviews, then conducts them, and finally (at CL 2) analyzes the results. Selection is a critical step in the preparation stage; the cost of conducting the reviews means that they should remain limited to key work products.

For the third goal, executing the verification strategy, three specific practices exist. First, personnel perform verification according to the verification strategy, capturing results and associated action items. Then (at CL 2) they analyze the results and further identify needed corrective actions based on established verification criteria. Finally, they reverify corrected work products, ensuring that they have not been negatively affected. This verification may involve regression tests.

7.3.6 Validation

The purpose of Validation is to demonstrate that a product or product component fulfills its intended use when placed in its intended environment. VAL (see Figure 7-20) has two specific goals that address preparing for validation and validating the product or product components. The validation practices are similar to those used in verification, but the two process areas focus on different topics. Validation addresses those activities needed to show that a product fulfills its intended use when it

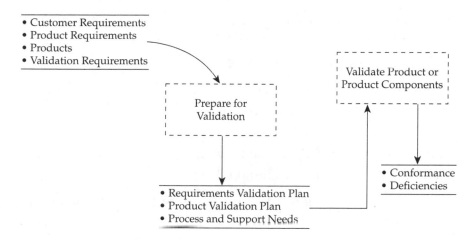

Figure 7-20: *Validation context diagram*

is placed in its intended environment, whereas verification shows that the work products meet their specified requirements.

The goal of preparing for validation has three specific practices, which mirror those in PI and VER. First, the project develops its strategy for validation early in the life cycle. Next, it establishes the environment for validation (CL 2). Finally, personnel define the detailed procedures and criteria for validation (CL 3).

The goal of actually performing the validation has two specific practices. First, workers perform the validation according to the strategy to show that the product or product component performs as intended. Then, they capture and analyze the validation results, identifying any problems or unresolved issues.

7.4 Support Process Areas

The Support process areas provide essential processes that are used by other CMMI process areas; in addition they are used by the CMMI generic practices. In general, these process areas are targeted toward the project (except for Process and Product Quality Assurance). When necessary, however, they can be applied more generally to the organization. For example, Process and Product Quality Assurance can be used with all other process areas to provide an objective review of the processes and work products described in them.

The SE/SW model includes five Support process areas:

- Configuration Management (CM)
- Process and Product Quality Assurance (PPQA)
- Measurement and Analysis (MA)
- Causal Analysis and Resolution (CAR)
- Decision Analysis and Resolution (DAR)

The SE/SW/IPPD model includes one additional process area for the Support category:

- Organizational Environment for Integration (OEI)

This section describes the Support process areas in the SE/SW model. Section 7.5 provides a description of the process areas in the IPPD model extension.

7.4.1 Configuration Management

The purpose of Configuration Management is to establish and maintain the integrity of work products using configuration identification, configuration control, configuration status accounting, and configuration audits. CM (see Figure 7-21) has three specific goals that address establishing baselines, tracking and controlling changes, and establishing the integrity of baselines. It is assumed that configuration management can occur at multiple levels of granularity and formality. This process area is closely connected with the generic practice at CL 2 to manage configurations; it provides the process to be used when applying that generic practice.

The first goal—establishing baselines for work products—has three specific practices: identifying the items to be placed under configuration management, establishing a configuration management and change management system, and creating and releasing the baselines. Once baselines are established using a configuration management system, all changes are tracked and controlled in the second goal with two specific practices. The first tracks the requests for changes, and the second tracks content changes to the configuration items. The third goal—establishing the integrity of the baselines—has two specific practices: one for keeping records on the configuration items, and another for performing configuration audits to ensure that the baselines are correct.

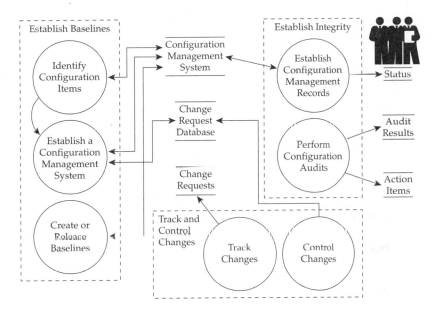

Figure 7-21: *Configuration Management context diagram*

7.4.2 Process and Product Quality Assurance

The purpose of Process and Product Quality Assurance is to provide staff and management with objective insight into the processes and associated work products. PPQA (see Figure 7-22) has two specific goals: objectively evaluating adherence to process descriptions, standards, and procedures; and resolving noncompliance issues. To achieve objective evaluation, some organizations may strive for independent oversight of the processes and work products, perhaps via a Quality Assurance department. Other organizations may embed the quality assurance function within the process, placing greater emphasis on evaluation by peers. CMMI supports both options. This process area is closely connected with the generic practice at CL 2 to objectively evaluate adherence; it provides the process to be used when applying that generic practice.

The first goal—objectively evaluating adherence of the performed process and associated work products and services to applicable process descriptions, standards, and procedures—is addressed with two specific practices. One conducts an objective evaluation of the performed process, and the other performs an objective evaluation of designated work products. The second goal—resolving noncompliance

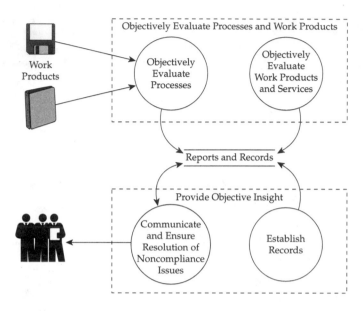

© 2000 by Carnegie Mellon University.

Figure 7-22: *Process and Product Quality Assurance context diagram*

issues—is also addressed by two specific practices. The first communicates noncompliance issues with relevant stakeholders and ensures their resolution by progressive escalation, and the second establishes and maintains records of quality assurance activities.

7.4.3 Measurement and Analysis

The purpose of Measurement and Analysis is to develop and sustain a measurement capability that is used to support management information needs. MA (see Figure 7-23) has two specific goals: one for aligning measurement activities with information needs, and one for providing measurement results that satisfy those needs. This process area is loosely connected with two generic practices at CL 2. That is, planning the process includes defining measurement objectives, and monitoring and controlling the process encompasses measuring performance against the plan.

The practices of the two MA goals provide an eight-step measurement process with four specific practices mapped to each of the two goals. For the first goal, personnel define the objectives to meet the information

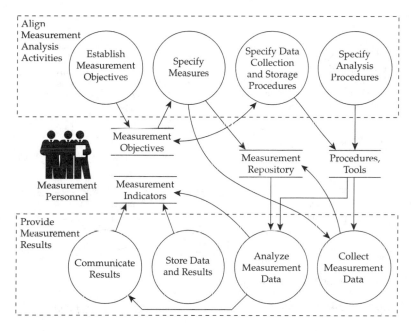

© 2000 by Carnegie Mellon University.

Figure 7-23: *Measurement and Analysis context diagram*

needs, specify the measures that will be needed to meet the objectives, indicate how the data will be obtained and stored, and determine how the data will be analyzed and reported. For the second goal, they collect the data, analyze and interpret the information gathered, manage and store both the data and the analysis results, and communicate the results to the stakeholders.

7.4.4 Decision Analysis and Resolution

The purpose of Decision Analysis and Resolution is to make decisions using a structured approach that evaluates identified alternatives against established criteria. DAR (see Figure 7-24) has one specific goal, related to evaluating alternatives using established criteria. Only the key issues for a project would warrant the structured decision-making process of DAR. Possible examples might include architectural or design alternatives, make–buy decisions, and tool selection.

The practices of this process area identify a six-step process for making decisions in a structured manner:

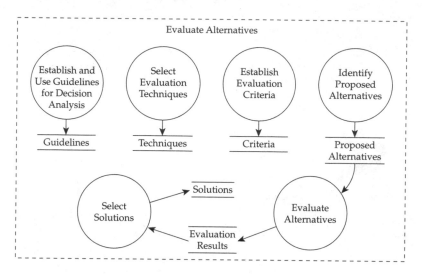

© 2000 by Carnegie Mellon University.

Figure 7-24: *Decision Analysis and Resolution context diagram*

1. Establish and use guidelines to determine which issues are subject to DAR.

2. For a given issue, select an appropriate decision-making technique.

3. Establish the criteria on which the decision will be based and their relative ranking.

4. Identify proposed alternatives.

5. Evaluate the alternatives based on the criteria.

6. Select a solution, documenting its results and rationale.

An organization can use DAR for any significant decision that needs to be made. Typically, it would be employed for making technical decisions, such as those related to trade studies. DAR should *not* be used for making insignificant decisions, such as buying pencils or paper. In reality, some process is used even in low-level decisions; it just isn't required or expected by the CMMI models.

7.4.5 Causal Analysis and Resolution

The purpose of Causal Analysis and Resolution is to identify causes of defects and other problems and take action to prevent them from occurring in the future. CAR (see Figure 7-25) has two specific goals: one for determining the

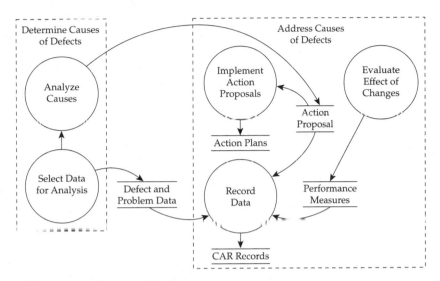

Figure 7-25: *Causal Analysis and Resolution context diagram*

root causes of defects, and another for addressing these causes to prevent the future occurrence of those defects. This process area is closely related to the generic practice at capability level 5 that seeks to identify and correct the root causes of defects and other process-related problems; the processes of CAR should be used when applying that generic practice.

For the first goal of determining root causes, two specific practices exist: select the defects for analysis, and perform causal analysis and propose actions to address these problems. For the second goal of addressing the root causes of defects and other problems, three specific practices are provided: implement the action proposals, evaluate the effects of the changes on process performance, and record the data from the CAR activities for subsequent use by other projects in the organization.

7.5 Integrated Product and Process Development Process Areas

Integrated Product and Process Development (IPPD) represents a systematic approach to product development that achieves a timely collaboration of relevant stakeholders throughout the product life cycle so as to better satisfy customer needs. When an organization chooses to use

IPPD in the CMMI model, two new process areas and two new specific goals in the Integrated Project Management (IPM) process area are added to the model. Several new amplifications of other model elements and an additional front matter section are added as well. This section describes IPPD process areas.

7.5.1 Integrated Teaming

The purpose of Integrated Teaming is to form and sustain an integrated team for the development of work products. Integrated Teaming[6] (IT), as shown in Figure 7-26, has two specific goals related to establishing team composition so as to provide needed knowledge and skills and governing the operation of the team.

The first goal—establishing team composition—has three specific practices. First, personnel identify and define the specific internal tasks needed to generate the team's expected output. Second, they identify the knowledge, skills, and functional expertise needed to perform those tasks. Third, the organization assigns the appropriate personnel

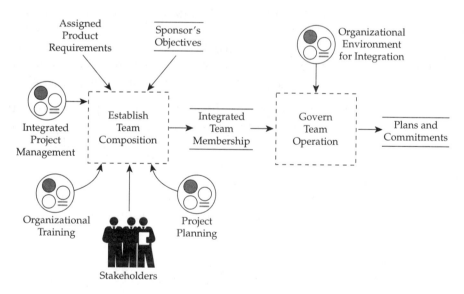

© 2000 by Carnegie Mellon University.

Figure 7-26: *Integrated Teaming context diagram*

---

6. Although Integrated Teaming is categorized as a Project Management process area in the continuous representation, the authors decided to discuss it in a separate IPPD section.

to be team members, based on those employees having the required knowledge and skills.

The second goal—operating the integrated team according to established principles—has five specific practices. First, the integrated team establishes and maintains a shared vision that is aligned with its overarching or higher-level vision; a team with a shared vision is more likely to function with unity of purpose. Next, it establishes and maintains a team charter—a "contract" related to the expected work and the level of performance—based on the integrated team's shared vision and overall objectives. Then, it clearly defines each team member's roles and responsibilities based on the charter. The team then establishes operating procedures, and finally collaborates with other teams as necessary.

7.5.2 Organizational Environment for Integration

The purpose of Organizational Environment for Integration is to establish an organizational infrastructure and organizational process assets that are unique to IPPD. Organizational Environment for Integration[7] (OEI), as shown in Figure 7-27, has two specific goals: providing an IPPD infrastructure and managing people so as to nurture successful IPPD behavior.

For the first goal, providing an infrastructure that maximizes the productivity of people and effects the collaboration necessary for integration, three specific practices exist. First, the organization establishes a shared vision, including a mission, objectives, expected behavior, and values. Next, it creates an integrated work environment that supports IPPD by enabling collaboration and concurrent development. Finally, it identifies the unique skills needed to support the IPPD environment.

For the second goal, managing people so as to nurture the integrative and collaborative behaviors of an IPPD environment, three specific practices apply. First, the organization establishes leadership mechanisms to enable timely collaboration. Next, it specifies incentives for adopting and demonstrating integrative and collaborative behaviors at all levels of the organization. Finally, organizational guidelines are developed that seek to balance team and home organization responsibilities. The *home organization* includes the part of the organization to which personnel are assigned when they are members of an integrated team. It may also be called the "functional organization," "home base,"

---

7. Organizational Environment for Integration is considered as a Support process area in the continuous representation.

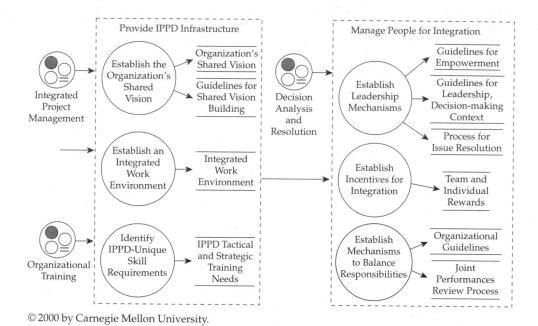

© 2000 by Carnegie Mellon University.

Figure 7-27: *Organizational Environment for Integration context diagram*

"home office," "homeroom," or "direct organization." Whatever its title, the home organization is often responsible for the career growth of the personnel assigned to it; for example, it may provide performance appraisals and training to maintain functional and discipline expertise.

7.6 Acquisition Process Areas

Acquisition is considered as a discipline in CMMI. This process area focuses on managing the acquisition of products and services, rather than developing them. Several "acquisition amplifications" in other process areas describe how those practices should be interpreted when using them for acquisition projects or portions of a project that purchase (rather than make) product components. The user should constantly keep one question in mind: "How do I interpret these words in the context of acquisition?"

CMMI version 1.02d included three new process areas for acquisition. This pilotable release provided the CMMI Product Team with the ability to test the proposed content. The first full release of the Acquisition process area is planned for version 1.1.

Three acquisition-unique process areas exist:

- Supplier Selection and Monitoring (SSM)
- Integrated Supplier Management (ISM)
- Quantitative Supplier Management (QSM)

A clear relationship exists among these process areas, as indicated by their staged levels: SSM is level 2, ISM is level 3, and QSM is level 4. This approach to structuring a discipline differs significantly from the tack taken in SE/SW/IPPD. The process area capabilities are built on top of lower levels by adding a higher-level process area. The Engineering process areas handled this situation by providing advanced practices. In contrast, the Acquisition process areas follow a much more obvious course than that employed in the Process Management and Project Management categories. A close relationship also exists between ISM and IPM, with both addressing integrated management. QSM and QPM are related in a similar fashion.

This version of the model omits Supplier Agreement Management, replacing it with Supplier Selection and Monitoring. This substitution creates some conflict in terms of how the model is used. If you start process improvement without acquisition, then you will use SAM for managing your supplier agreements. If you later decide to include acquisition, SAM disappears and is replaced by three new process areas at three levels. The final resolution of this issue may be determined through the pilot program before the release of CMMI version 1.1. Also, note that these process areas do not provide the same level of informative material as the other process areas, which may leave some questions unanswered. The work performed between the writing of this book and the release of a model with acquisition may change the following sections significantly.

7.6.1 Supplier Selection and Monitoring Process Area

The purpose of Supplier Selection and Monitoring is to manage the acquisition of products and services from sources external to the project. SSM includes three specific goals that address establishing agreement requirements, selecting suppliers, and establishing and satisfying agreements.

The first goal entails determining outsourcing options for the product and establishing the agreement requirements for this outsourcing. Notice the strong overlap between this goal and the Requirements Development goals; it may not survive the piloting evaluations being conducted prior to the release of version 1.1. From the acquisition development team's point of view, adding amplifications to RD and other process areas may not prove strong enough. That is, amplifications are informative, but acquisition may necessitate required and expected components. The CMMI-SE/SW/IPPD eliminated almost all overlaps in the model. Currently, the acquisition process areas add many overlapping practices.

The second goal selects the suppliers to satisfy the agreement requirements by preparing solicitations and selecting suppliers based on an evaluation of the supplier's ability to meet the requirements.

The third goal establishes agreements with the selected suppliers and ensures that those agreements are satisfied. It is accomplished by first creating an agreement that communicates the requirements, expectations, and verification methods and then monitoring and evaluating the supplier's performance relative to the agreement. Another practice expects informal and formal reviews to be conducted according to the agreement. In CMMI, this practice would normally be covered by the generic practice on monitoring and controlling the process. Few specific practices expect the project to carry out reviews. This theme continues, however, in additional specific practices that expect verification to be performed on the product. Two more specific practices expect the organization to carry out acceptance verifications and validations and to manage the transition of the product from the supplier.

7.6.2 Integrated Supplier Management

The purpose of Integrated Supplier Management is to proactively identify potential sources and manage suppliers while maintaining a cooperative relationship. ISM has three goals that address analyzing sources of products, monitoring and analyzing suppliers of custom-made products, and establishing a cooperative relationship with suppliers.

The first goal analyzes the sourcing options that best fit the needs of the acquisition. The project analyzes and selects off-the-shelf products that may satisfy the requirements, analyzes and identifies sources of custom-made products, and performs trade-off studies to determine the sources of products to be acquired.

The second goal monitors the quality of the supplier's process and custom-made products throughout the agreement's period of performance. It is accomplished by monitoring and analyzing the supplier's engineering process and its results, and by tailoring the acquisition process to accommodate the supplier-related risk.

The third goal encourages a cooperative and productive relationship between the customer, supplier, and project. The customer and end user became involved in monitoring the evolving products and performing activities that foster a cooperative and productive relationship between project personnel and the supplier.

7.6.3 Quantitative Supplier Management

The purpose of Quantitative Supplier Management is to manage the acquisition effort through the application of quantitative methods. QSM has two goals: defining quantitative objectives for the acquisition and quantitatively managing the acquisition effort. The first goal initially determines and defines the quantitative objectives for the acquisition effort and then incorporates them into the solicitation package. The second goal uses quantitative methods and techniques by measuring, analyzing, and comparing the evolving product using the quantitative objectives; applying those measures in the review and oversight of the supplier; identifying and analyzing special causes of variances from the quantitative objectives; and implementing changes to eliminate those sources of variance.

7.7 Relationships within CMMI Components

While the internal references in the CMMI models did not undergo the rigorous peer reviews to which the required and expected components were subjected, they nevertheless represent valuable information about how the processes work together to achieve improvement. Two major sources of relationships are found in the models: those between process areas and those between process areas and generic practices.

7.7.1 Relationships among Process Areas

Table 7-2 describes the key relationships among process areas by summarizing the references from the "Related Process Areas" section of each process area. The models discuss key relationships between process areas in the categories but don't provide such a summary. Specific information about relationships between lower-level components,

Table 7-2: *CMMI Related Process Areas*

Process Area	Related Process Areas
Organizational Process Focus	OPD
Organizational Process Definition	OPF
Organizational Training	OPD, PP, DAR
Organizational Process Performance	QPM, MA
Organizational Innovation and Deployment	OPF, OPD, OPP, OT, MA, IPM (IPPD)
Project Planning	RD, REQM, RSKM, TS, MA, SAM
Project Monitoring and Control	PP, MA
Supplier Agreement Management	PMC, RD, REQM, TS
Integrated Project Management (IPPD)	PP, PMC, VER, OPD, MA, IT, OEI
Risk Management	PP, PMC, DAR
Integrated Teaming	PP, OEI, IPM (IPPD)
Quantitative Project Management	PMC, MA, OPP, OPD, IPM (IPPD), CAR, OID
Requirements Management	RD, TS, PP, CM, PMC
Requirements Development	REQM, TS, PI, VER, VAL, RSKM, CM
Technical Solution	RD, VER, DAR, REQM, OID
Product Integration	RD, TS, VER, VAL, RSKM, DAR, CM, SAM
Verification	IPM (IPPD), RD, VAL, REQM
Validation	RD, TS, VER, DAR
Configuration Management	PP, CAR, PMC

Process Area	Related Process Areas
Process and Product Quality Assurance	PP, VER
Measurement and Analysis	PP, PMC, CM, RD, REQM, OPD, QPM
Decision Analysis and Resolution	PP, IPM (IPPD), RSKM
Organizational Environment for Integration	IPM (IPPD), OPD, OT
Causal Analysis and Resolution	QPM, OID, MA

such as specific practices and subpractices, is also included in the models, but a summary at that level is beyond the scope of this book.

We can make several observations after looking at Table 7.2. First, note the strong interrelationship within the Engineering process areas. Not surprisingly, Project Planning and Measurement and Analysis are key to successful implementation of a variety of process areas.

The references reveal the fundamental interrelationships within the management processes through the number and type of cross references within the Process Management category. Notice that the higher-capability-level process areas reference the lower-level process areas. Thus the higher-level process areas depend heavily on the lower-level process areas for implementation. The same type of relationship links Quantitative Project Management to the other Project Management process areas.

Probably the most telling observation is the lack of stand-alone process areas. This view of the model clearly indicates that an organization should pay close attention to its business objectives and ensure that its tailored model considers all aspects of the model at the appropriate time.

7.7.2 Relationships between Generic Practices and Process Areas

The references between the generic practices and process areas identify close relationships between those model components, as shown in Table 7-3. A close look at the generic practices reveals practices that are

Table 7-3: *Generic Practice References*

Generic Practice	Process Area
GP 2.6 Manage Configurations	CM
GP 2.7 Identify and Involve Relevant Stakeholders	PP
GP 2.8 Monitor and Control the Process	MA
GP 2.9 Objectively Evaluate Adherence	PPQA
GP 3.1 Establish a Defined Process	OPD
GP 3.2 Collect Improvement Information	OPD
GP 4.1 Establish Quality Objectives	QPM
GP 5.2 Correct Common Cause of Problems	CAR

almost identical to those specified in the process areas. Because the process areas provide the "detailed what to do" for implementing the generic practices, they may be thought of as "enabling" process areas. Notice, also, that each generic practice resides at the same capability level as the process area that enables it. This correspondence is not a random artifact, but was crafted in such a manner to provide the mechanism for staging.

The process area provides detailed guidance on how to implement the generic practice, which raises some interesting questions about capability and maturity levels. For example, can you be at CL 3 in Configuration Management if GP 2.6 is not met in other process areas? The answer is yes. The generic practices indicate a level of institutionalization separate from the capability level of the process areas. Another interesting question is, Can you tailor an enabling process area? Possibly, but it would argue against the underlying theory of the models. Also, it would certainly make it more difficult to improve other processes by using the generic practices.

7.7.3 Relationships, Complexity, and Common Sense

Clearly, complex relationships exist among the elements of the CMMI models. Many of these stem from the theoretical bases of model-based process improvement, especially those that deal with organizational maturity. Others, like the relationships between the Engineering process areas and the relationships between the generic practice and enabling process areas, have roots in the source models and the work conducted in integrating the various representations.

Remember, however, that the models are merely guides and are intended to help—not mystify. When you encounter a seeming conundrum, you can either consult the process improvement experts or simply make a reasonable decision that solves your immediate problem. Although some occasions will call for special expertise, usually a commonsense, "Gordian knot" approach will provide an answer that meets your needs.

Lewis and Clark Party at Three Forks
Detail from painting by E. S. Paxson,
Missoula County Courthouse, Missoula, Montana
© 2000–2001 *www.arttoday.com*

Part III

Using CMMI

On their historic journey of exploration, Meriwether Lewis and William Clark learned from the Nez Perce tribe and from Sacagawea that success in unknown territory often depends on having a knowledgeable guide. The CMMI, while not actually an untamed wilderness, does present a landscape where pitfalls and risks can confront the unwary user. Part III attempts to provide help in selecting the best routes based on your organization's particular process improvement needs.

Part III Contents

161

Chapter 10. Assessments with CMMI

In which the authors present the CMMI assessment methods. A discussion of their use is provided as well as some advice on tailoring the models.

Chapter 8

Selecting the
Appropriate
Disciplines

Inclination snatches arguments to make indulgence seem judicious choice.
George Eliot, *Spanish Gypsy* (1868)

A little too late is much too late.
German proverb

The Capability Maturity Model Integration (CMMI) Product Suite offers a growing number of multi- and single-discipline models, all developed with integrated process improvement in mind. The best combination of disciplines for your organization will depend on its business, organization, environment, and process improvement objectives. This chapter discusses ways to select the disciplines best suited to your situation. It focuses on the use of model extensions for Integrated Product and Process Development (IPPD) and for acquisition.

8.1 The Discipline Dilemma

Because of the close integration of software and systems engineering in the CMMI models by the Product Development Team, the initial versions offer somewhat limited discipline choices. Software-only or systems-engineering-only models are available by just ignoring in the CMMI-SE/SW model the discipline amplifications that do not apply. An Integrated Product and Process Development (IPPD) extension to the basic CMMI-SE/SW model is available in version 1.0. A "pilotable" version of a CMMI model that includes Acquisition as a discipline is also available, with a formal release of version 1.1 planned for 2002.[1] As the CMMI Product Suite matures, other disciplines will be added to the official set or become available through other sources, such as after-market model developers or professional societies. When this proliferation occurs, the choice may become more complex.

For each CMMI discipline that you add, your organization must meet and assess more process requirements. The CMM for Software described slightly more than 300 practices or activities. The CMMI-SE/SW version 1.0 model describes 431 practices in the staged representation.[2] Consider the difference between assessing 300 and 431 practices, and you can easily see why the selection of disciplines is so important.

8.2 Your Situation

You do not need a book written by "outsiders" to tell you about the situation that you confront in your own organization. We provide this section just as a reminder of some factors that are relevant to your selection of CMMI disciplines.

8.2.1 Your Core Business

Your organization's fundamental activities, business objectives, and organizational culture all influence the choice of the appropriate CMMI model. First, you should consider the disciplines used in producing the products or services that are central to your organization:

---

1. For the current status of the CMMI discipline options, consult the Software Engineering Institute's (SEI's) Web site or solicit information directly from the SEI.

2. 12 generic practices × 22 process areas + 167 specific practices.

- Do you develop software?
- Do you establish requirements?
- Do you acquire or subcontract for key components?
- Do you integrate commercial materials or products created by others?
- Do you provide a service?
- Is some engineering specialty fundamental to your success?
- Are you constrained by security requirements?

All of these issues may have a bearing on which disciplines you choose. Ideally, you should choose the disciplines that are most critical to your business success. Of course, those may be difficult to define in a fast-changing business environment.

8.2.2 Your Organization

It is also crucial to understand how your organization affects the selection of disciplines. This consideration is especially important with the IPPD extensions, as they are based on the premise that you want to move toward an integrated or concurrent operation. You may want to consider the following questions:

- Do some groups want to independently improve and measure their process improvement?
- Does your organization support independent cost centers that may compete with each other?
- Are you moving toward an integrated way of doing business, perhaps by using enterprise tools?

You may find it helpful to align your process improvement plans with any organizational changes that are concurrently under way. The IPPD extensions are particularly useful in change management.

8.2.3 Your Business Environment

The disciplines you choose should, of course, support your business environment. For example, if long-term projects and a stable workforce characterize your environment, your organization can generally support the efforts needed for multidiscipline process improvement over the spectrum of its business activities. On the other hand, if the organization faces a rapid development environment where projects are short, intense, and schedule-driven, it may need to focus on one specific discipline (or even just a few process areas) to realize a quick return on process improvement investment.

Your customer base may also influence the choice of disciplines. Customers who have critical requirements for complex systems may force you to adopt certain disciplines to match their processes. This possibility is particularly likely in large U.S. Department of Defense contracts, where current government policy demands SW-CMM maturity level 3 or equivalent for the software discipline.

8.2.4 Your Process Improvement Scope and Objectives

Disciplines provide the special subject matter for your process improvement. Consequently, you should understand the kind of processes you want to improve and the objectives for your process improvement before selecting a model. For example, the software and systems engineering disciplines describe the requirements for standard technical processes, so they can be used in a variety of engineering environments. On the other hand, the core CMMI Process Management and Project Management process areas and the corresponding generic practices provide a rich language and a consistent model to improve any process, regardless of its technical content.[3]

If your organization's objectives are entirely related to internal process improvement, you have considerable leeway in selecting which disciplines to address. If the objective is to demonstrate to others the maturity of your organization's processes for specific disciplines (for example, by adding a level indication in your marketing material or bidding on U.S. Department of Defense contracts), however, you must approach discipline selection in a stricter, more dogmatic manner.

8.3 The IPPD Extension

Selecting the IPPD extension with the CMMI-SE/SW model provides two additional process areas (Integrated Teaming and Organizational Environment for Integration), plus one expanded process area (Integrated Project Management). The content of this material was described

---

3. Many debates occurred regarding the application of CMMI outside the engineering world. It will be interesting to discover the extent to which interest in CMMI arises in nonengineering areas, such as manufacturing and services like medicine and law.

in Section 7.5. Note that all of these materials are staged at maturity level 3.

The following questions address some of the issues associated with IPPD:

- Do you use teams for any aspect of your projects?
- Does your organization need to know how to use teams effectively?
- Does your organization have difficulty in organizing and planning projects around teams?
- Does your organization have problems in communicating between disciplines or groups?
- Does your organization need to know how to promote integration by providing an environment that supports it?
- Do you want people to work together to get the maximum benefit of collaboration, even at a cost of some efficiency or schedule?
- Does your organization need to know how to nurture the integrative and collaborative behaviors of an IPPD environment?

Answering yes to these questions indicates that your organization could benefit from using the IPPD extension of the CMMI.

8.4 The Acquisition Extension

Although no formal release of a CMMI model has specifically targeted acquisition organizations, a version of CMMI-SE/SW/IPPD/A (where the "/A" indicates "acquisition") is available for piloting purposes. The plan (as of this book's publication) was to gain some experience with a proposed CMMI acquisition extension that was advanced enough to be "pilotable," prior to its formal release with version 1.1. Here we present a brief description of the version that will be available for piloting and some of the reasons for choosing to use it.[4]

---

4. This section was correct as of January 2001. In the past, however, versions of CMMI models for piloting purposes have changed to reflect the experiences in the early pilot projects, or to test alternative approaches. Readers who need more up-to-date information should contact the CMMI Steward at the SEI.

Three process areas have been proposed for the acquisition extension:

- Supplier Selection and Monitoring (SSM)
- Integrated Supplier Management (ISM)
- Quantitative Supplier Management (QSM)

In SSM, which is staged at maturity level 2, three goals focus on managing the acquisition of products and services from an external source.[5] They include establishing requirements for supplied products, selecting suppliers, creating supplier agreements, and performing needed tasks to bring the agreements to a successful conclusion.

ISM, which is staged at maturity level 3, includes three goals that build on SSM and focus on a more "proactive" acquisition. They include performing detailed analyses of sourcing options, careful monitoring of both the supplier's process and the resulting products, and working to create cooperative and productive relationships among all relevant stakeholders.

In QSM, which is staged at maturity level 4, two goals guide the application of quantitative methods to the acquisition of products and services. They include first defining quantitative objectives for the acquisition, and then using quantitative methods to manage the acquisition.

Obviously, you will have a keen interest in this model extension if you are a part of an acquisition-oriented organization or participate in a project where the acquisition of products and services from an external source is a central issue of concern.

Uncertainty has arisen regarding whether the addition of the SSM, ISM, and QSM process areas to the CMMI model to cover the topic of acquisition will persist in future model revisions. Some have argued that the more "proactive" acquisition activities are better handled (architecturally) with some combination of discipline amplifications to process areas from the CMMI-SE/SW/IPPD model and advanced practices. In addition, having two nearly identical (though slightly different) process areas staged at maturity level 2 (SAM and SSM) creates unnecessary confusion and potential configuration management problems. The authors would suggest that CMMI should include just one

---

5. SSM is an offshoot of, and an attempt to improve upon, Supplier Agreement Management (SAM); SAM is, in turn, a part of the basic CMMI-SE/SW model. Indeed, in the CMMI-SE/SW/IPPD/A model, SAM has been replaced by SSM.

acquisition-related process area at maturity level 2. Making a commitment to an integrated model means trying to avoid the creation of process area variants for changing selections of disciplines. Just as CMMI has one process area for managing requirements, so should there be one process area for managing suppliers.

In the end, the architectural approach to include acquisition topics within the CMMI framework more adequately is of less importance than the fact that a tool is available now for organizations that provide acquisition functions, so that they begin on a process improvement path. The material in the three additional process areas provides excellent guidance in this realm.

8.5 Selecting the Appropriate Model

In deciding whether to use the IPPD extension or the Acquisition extension, you will need to understand your organization's core business and to focus your process improvement efforts where they will most dramatically affect your key operating parameters. Consider your business environment, and don't overtax personnel by attempting to improve too many areas at the same time. Make sure your efforts remain in synch with your customers' activities and requirements. Decide on your objectives, and then align the disciplines selected with your organization's business strategy.

Selecting the disciplines is an integral step in ensuring the success of your process improvement initiatives. Another critical step is the selection of the type of model representation employed. Chapter 9 examines this decision in detail.

Chapter 9

Picking a Representation

You must choose . . . but choose wisely.
The Grail Knight, *Indiana Jones and the Last Crusade* (1989)

We choose our joys and sorrows long before we experience them.
Kahlil Gibran, *Sand and Foam* (1926)

So far, you have selected (based on guidance from Chapter 8) a set of disciplines from the options provided in the Capability Maturity Model Integration (CMMI) product suite, a set that is appropriate for the scope of your planned process improvement efforts. Your next important decision is to pick an architectural representation: continuous or staged. In Chapter 5, we described the distinguishing features of staged and continuous models, including some basic information about how CMMI provides these two alternative representations in its integrated suite of model products.

Each of the two architectural representations can provide a solid foundation for process improvement. For some people, however, the preference for one representation is deeply rooted and emotionally charged; they may simply mistrust the other representation. For other people, the preference is based on habit and grounded in the source model to which they are accustomed. For most users, this preference will ideally be developed through a comprehensive understanding of the benefits (in their organization's specific environment) provided by each representation. Perhaps this choice merits the use of a structured decision-making process and the application of the CMMI process area for Decision Analysis and Resolution. While each organization must explore this issue for itself, this chapter highlights some important issues and considerations in making that decision.

This chapter is arranged so as to start you on the path to making the best decision for your organization. The first two sections address the representations individually and present (for undecided voters or independents) the salient arguments offered by the proponents of each representation. The third section brings these general considerations into the CMMI context.

9.1 Reasons for Liking Staged Models

The Software CMM is a staged model that has been used successfully and with proven results for many years. This fact heads the list of reasons for using staged models; it is a powerful argument. Like Washington, D.C., insiders, staged model users can claim "Real Experience, Real Results." The path from an immature organization to a mature one has been demonstrated repeatedly with the Software CMM, and it is marked by the following benefits:

- An ability to manage processes across the organization
- Good communication about process among employees
- Improved accuracy of project estimates
- Improved cost and quality control
- The use of measurable data to guide problem analysis and improvement efforts

These results are made possible and supported by a process infrastructure that provides discipline and motivation for both project and organizational process improvement.

For an organization that is just beginning its journey to greater process maturity, a staged model provides a well-defined and proven path.

First, the organization's personnel work at process areas that facilitate improved project management (maturity level 2), then they provide organization-wide process definition (ML 3), and finally they use the standardized process definitions to support quantitative analysis for improving (ML 4) and optimizing (ML 5) process behavior. By building the staging of the process areas into its architecture, the model offers a clear path for improvement that can be followed without a lot of discussion and debate.

Consider the analogy of a child who is told to clean his room. There are toys everywhere with nary any floor to be seen. The child just looks at the problem. It seems so overwhelming that he doesn't know where to start. If he is told to pick up the blocks, however, he can sort through the mess and put all of the blocks away. Next, he can be told to pick up the balls, and so on, until the room is tidy. The approach taken by the staged model is similar, in that the model architects (rather than the model users) decide on the best order for process improvement.

Having a single system for defining process maturity facilitates making comparisons across organizations. The maturity level numbers are broadly understood, so that (proponents would argue) there is a single meaning (more or less) regarding what it means to be a maturity level 2 organization, for example.[1]

For all of these reasons (and others), the Software CMM—the premier staged model—has been used by organizations to achieve notable success in support of their efforts related to process improvement. An excellent source of information and data on the use of this model is the Software Engineering Information Repository (SEIR), which is housed at the Software Engineering Institute (SEI) of Carnegie Mellon University.[2]

---

1. By having each process area reside at a specified maturity level and hence at a well-understood position in the path to organizational maturity, the model authors can create more uniform process areas. For example, in a staged model, a process area that is written for maturity level 2 would differ from a similar process area that is written for maturity level 3. When assessments are conducted, the intended scope and application for the process area become very clear, as they are based on the staged level.

2. The Web address for the Software Engineering Information Repository is http://seir.sei.cmu.edu/

Proven Path, Truth, and Untruth

To speak of a single path to process improvement with a staged model involves both truth and untruth.

The truth is that the maturity levels define plateau stages for process improvement, providing a common general structure for all model users and a predefined ordering of the process areas within a small, finite number of maturity levels. The single path is defined by first requiring the satisfaction of all goals at maturity level 2, and continuing stepwise (as appropriate) to the satisfaction of goals that reside at higher maturity levels.

The untruth is any suggestion that within this general structure, all organizations will do things in the same way. For example, the requirement to perform peer reviews on selected work products must be a part of achieving maturity level 3. The exact time when this issue is addressed prior to achieving ML 3 and the selection of products for peer review are both items that can vary greatly among organizations. Thus, when we speak of a single path to improvement with a staged model, understand that we intend to speak the truth, not the untruth.

9.2 Reasons for Liking Continuous Models

The concept of a continuous model for process improvement precedes the development of staged models. The writings of Phillip Crosby, for example, define levels for improvement within individual areas.[3] In spite of this heritage, continuous process improvement models have been used less often than staged models, and there has been no systematic data collection on the results of continuous model usage. Nonetheless, there is no shortage of proponents for the continuous approach, especially among systems engineers.

---

3. The five levels of Crosby's Quality Management Maturity Grid are: Stage I—Uncertainty; Stage II—Awakening; Stage III—Enlightenment; Stage IV—Wisdom; and Stage V—Certainty. See Crosby, Philip B. *Quality Is Free: The Art of Making Quality Certain*. New York: McGraw-Hill, 1979.

Proponents cite two fundamental reasons for using a continuous (as opposed to a staged) model: freedom and visibility. Unlike a staged model, which provides a single improvement path for all model users, a continuous model offers additional freedom for users, who can select the order for process improvement activities based on organizational business objectives.[4] With a continuous model, individual organizations or organizational groups have the option of defining organizational maturity and an ordering for the process areas which (they may believe) are a better fit for their unique business environment. They may wish to achieve given capability levels for the process areas in an alternative order, rather than accepting the constraints of the "one size fits all" philosophy of the staged models.

As multiple capability levels are defined for each process area, an assessment based on a continuous model may provide increased visibility into process improvement strengths and weaknesses. The greater transparency comes from the way in which the results are reported, rather than the model content. Despite the unflattering portrayal of managers in the cartoon world of "Dilbert," those with more detailed process data can make more informed decisions. For instance, a capability level profile with a separate rating number for each individual process area could provide greater insight than a single maturity level number.[5] Even a manager who initially may prefer the simplicity of a single number could, in time, develop greater appreciation for the capability profile that only a continuous representation provides. In the end, managers may want both.

By providing more detailed insight that is tailored to the individual business environment, an organization can benefit from

- The complete application of all generic practices in each process area
- A clearer focus on risks that are specific to individual process areas

---

4. Just as a staged model allows for many choices and options, the wise use of a continuous model requires an understanding of the many inherent ordering relationships between various model elements. As with any freedom, the situation for the user of a continuous model is not "anything goes." In the CMMI continuous representation, for example, the organization needs to reach CL 1 in the Configuration Management process area before it applies the generic practice on configuration management, which resides at CL 2, to any process area. Even without a staging of process areas, CMMI continuous representations have many such ordering constraints. Chapter 7 highlighted some of these constraints.

5. While a staged model assessment doesn't normally report a profile, it does provide organizational strengths and weaknesses on a process-area-by-process-area basis.

- A structure that is more immediately compatible with ISO/IEC 15504
- A structure that more easily facilitates the addition of new process areas with minimal effects on the existing model structure

For managers who have used and found benefit in a single maturity level number, a continuous model can provide the same information. With any continuous model, a "staging" is possible. Fundamentally and simply, a staging comprises a set of rules of the following form: For an organization to be at maturity level x, it must achieve capability level y in process areas PA_1, PA_2, . . . , PA_n.[6] To produce a single maturity level number, the model need not have a staged architecture; it requires only an algorithm to produce the maturity rating based on a set of staging rules that define the maturity levels in terms of capability levels. As described in Section 5.3.3, CMMI includes an equivalent staging for users of the continuous representation.

As long as two organizations follow the same staging rules, their maturity level ratings may be compared, just as is possible with a staged model. For organizations that want or need a predefined path for process improvement, a staging on a continuous model provides the same guidance as a staged model. If some groups support different staging schemes, however, then model users must choose *a* path for process improvement; they will not be given *the* path.

9.3 Reasons for Choosing a CMMI Representation

Based on the considerations cited in the preceding sections for liking either a staged or continuous architectural representation, a decision to favor one or the other would seem to involve almost philosophical musings. On the one hand, all other things being equal, having a single number rating score and a single standard path for process improvement would seem to have many potential benefits. Many organizations would prefer to avoid the "anything goes" approach to process improvement that the continuous representation may seem (incorrectly) to engender. On the other hand, a rating profile may ultimately prove more useful than a single number. Furthermore, recognizing the realities of different

---

6. A more complex rule is possible. For example, to be at maturity level x, you must reach capability level y in one set of process areas and capability level z in another set of process areas.

business environments may lead to multiple approaches to process improvement, all of which are equally valid.[7] Most of us would likely prefer to receive the benefits available on both sides. That is, it would be nice to have a relatively small number of choices in process improvement paths (one of which is the most common in any given business environment). Likewise, it would be nice to have clear recognition that one predefined path may not be appropriate for the entire world and all business environments. Finally, it would be nice to have a single number rating for some contexts and a rating profile for other contexts.

CMMI holds out the promise of the benefits from both sides. A close examination reveals that the differences between the staged representation and the continuous representation are less pronounced in CMMI and the choice of representation is less polarized than is the case with the legacy models that are either staged or continuous, but not both.[8] In an effort to ensure that each representation would be just an alternative view of the same base model, the CMMI Product Development Team duplicated the required and expected material in both representations. Thus the process areas in both are the same. The goals (the required items) are the same, except for the fact that the generic goals residing at capability levels 1, 4, and 5 are not needed in the staged representation. The specific practices (the expected items from individual process areas) are the same, except for cases where an advanced practice supercedes a lower-level specific practice. The generic practices are the same for maturity level 2 and 3 generic goals. In the staged representation, process areas staged at maturity level 2 use the level 2 generic practices only, whereas all process areas staged at maturity level 3 or higher use the level 2 and 3 generic practices.

Because the two representations are so closely aligned, and because both contain most of the good material from all of the source models,

---

7. Within the Department of Defense environment, for example, personnel are not far removed from the debates that raged about the programming language Ada. While many claimed that having a single programming language within the Department offered strong potential benefits, others demurred, citing a need to recognize alternative valid approaches in different kinds of systems. For example, the software in a management information system and that in a real-time weapon system may be very different. Trade studies of widely varying system types relating to the best choice for a programming language would not rate any one language as always preferable. Sometimes the best place in standardization efforts is a middle ground, somewhere between one (at one extreme) and hundreds (at the other extreme); perhaps three, or seven, would keep everyone happy.

8. The IPD CMM (the Integrated Product Development model, which served as the third source model for the initial CMMI work) was a hybrid model, as is the FAA-iCMM (the Federal Aviation Administration's model).

the reasons for preferring one over the other become more practical and less philosophical. Will your organization need less of a training effort with one representation than with the other due to legacy issues? Is the staging that is integral to the staged architecture and provided in the equivalent staging for the continuous architecture the better one for your business environment? Does management need the detail provided by a capability profile? Questions such as these may not have easy answers, but they can be investigated across all organizational components that seek to develop an integrated process improvement strategy.

Because the two architectural representations in CMMI are not dramatically different, in some ways you cannot make a bad choice; the fundamentals are the same. Perhaps, in time, the use of CMMI will show that two distinct representations are not necessary at all.

Chapter 10

Assessments with CMMI

*Not everything that can be counted counts, and
not everything that counts can be counted.*
Albert Einstein (1879–1955)

Good, Fast, Cheap; Pick any two.
Sign in Print Shop

*If you don't like something, change it. If you can't change it,
change your attitude. Don't complain.*
Maya Angelou (1928–   )

Just as the three source models provided the basis for the integrated
Capability Maturity Model Integration (CMMI) models, two assess-
ment methods provided the basis for the initial CMMI assessment
method. The method used with the Systems Engineering Capability
Model (SECM) of EIA/IS 731-1 was the SECM Appraisal Method, or
EIS/IS 731-2.[1] The method used with the Software CMM was the

---

1. *EIA Interim Standard, Systems Engineering Capability.* EIA/IS 731, Part 2: Appraisal Method,
EIA/IS 731-2, version 1.0, 1999.

CMM-Based Appraisal for Internal Process Improvement (CBA IPI).[2] The initial CMMI assessment method (SCAMPI) traces the majority of its features to the CBA IPI.[3]

A complete discussion of process assessment, its history, its role in the source models, and the many details about how it is addressed in CMMI would warrant another book. The goal of this chapter is more modest: to briefly introduce the initial assessment products in the CMMI product suite, as well as some of the primary concepts and issues regarding their use, to help orient the reader for further explorations in this area. Preparing for an assessment includes tailoring the model, so we include a brief discussion of tailoring at the end of this chapter.

10.1 Assessment Requirements for CMMI

One part of the CMMI product suite that deals with assessment is the *Assessment Requirements for CMMI, version 1.0* (ARC, V1.0). This document comprises 40 "requirements" that provide a mixed set of requirements and design constraints on an assessment method.[4] As such, it is perhaps of more interest to the designers of an assessment method than to organizations seeking an assessment to evaluate their capabilities. We discuss it here briefly to provide insight into the approach to assessment taken to date by the CMMI project and to suggest promising future directions.

The ARC includes seven categories of requirements:

1. *Responsibilities.* Lists responsibilities of the assessment sponsor and the leader of the assessment team.

2. *Assessment Method Documentation.* Provides items of guidance that should be included in the documentation of a method. As examples,

---

2. *CMM-Based Appraisal for Internal Process Improvement (CBA IPI): Method Description*, CMU/SEI-1996-TR-007. There is also a guide for lead assessors on using the CBA IPI method.

3. *SCAMPI, V1.0, Standard CMMI Assessment Method for Process Improvement: Method Description, version 1.0*, CMU/SEI-2000-TR-009. See SCAMPI Appendix B, p. 47, for a comparison of the source appraisal methods.

4. A method that satisfies all 40 requirements is considered to be a Class A method as defined in the ARC. Two other class types, B and C, are defined with lesser sets of requirements. The discussion here focuses on a "full" Class A method—the only type that offers the option of capability level (CL) or maturity level (ML) ratings.

guidance should be provided for identifying the assessment's purpose, model scope, organizational scope, team qualifications, team size, team member roles, resource estimation, logistics, data collection, findings, data protection, nonattribution, and assessment records.

3. *Planning and Preparing for the Assessment.* Identifies a minimum set of assessment preparation activities and the items needed in an assessment plan.

4. *Assessment Data Collection.* Requires the use of three methods for the collection of data: administering instruments (for example, questionnaires, surveys), conducting interviews, and reviewing documentation.

5. *Data Consolidation and Validation.* Specifies constraints on the way in which an assessment method provides for the consolidation and validation of the data collected. The topics required include team consensus leading to findings and ratings, validated observations from at least two different sources on each specific and generic practice, sufficiency of coverage for each practice, a mechanism to determine strengths and weaknesses relative to the CMMI model being used, and feedback of assessment findings to the assessment participants.

6. *Rating.* Provides more specific constraints on what is needed for a capability level or maturity level rating. The topics required include the prerequisite of valid observations for each practice prior to the rating of goals, a judgment that goals are "satisfied" only when "no significant weaknesses" have been uncovered, and the satisfaction of all relevant goals as the basis for a capability level or maturity level rating.

7. *Reporting Results.* Requires documentation of the findings for the assessment sponsor and a report made to the CMMI Steward (the Software Engineering Institute).

In three of these seven areas (data collection, data consolidation and validation, and rating), some of the ARC "requirements" seem to be method design constraints rather than true performance requirements. The performance requirements in this area would focus on issues such as accuracy, repeatability, stability, usefulness, and efficiency. The ARC authors placed design constraints in these areas for two reasons: to aid in meeting the challenge of specifying real performance requirements, and to assure the accuracy and repeatability of the assessment results

The Authors' Perspective

The three authors of this book believe that user requirements for assessment performance should be specified to address adequate reliability of results and cost control, in addition to the usefulness of assessment results for process improvement. Then there would exist a basis to verify the extent to which a specific design for an assessment method met those requirements. Currently, no ARC requirements address cost efficiency. While ratings to benchmark a process are emphasized, there is insufficient weight placed on the development of findings useful for process improvement.

Two distinct, but not unrelated, reasons for conducting an assessment exist. One is to accurately diagnose internal process problems and areas for process improvement; the other is to provide a benchmark for process capability or process maturity relative to a larger community. These two purposes can pull in opposite directions. The identification of process improvement opportunities requires exposing process weaknesses, whereas the effort made to achieve a benchmark score may encourage the hiding of process weaknesses and the "gaming" of numbers.

In the trade-offs between reliability, accuracy, repeatability, cost, and other factors, we believe, ARC V1.0 places too much emphasis on reliability and too little emphasis on cost. This choice is not unrelated to the issue on process improvement versus benchmark. For a benchmark, reliability is a central concern; for process improvement, a somewhat lesser level of reliability may be acceptable if cost is significantly less. The ARC requirements should not be written so that trying to focus on process improvement and reduction of cost means using a "less than full" (that is, less "good") method. In the months and years ahead, the CMMI user community needs to collect data on various assessment methods that make the cost and reliability trade-off in different ways. Eventually, we will have an empirical basis for knowing how much accuracy, reliability, and usefulness of findings is produced at what cost for a proposed assessment method.

and ratings. If we could deepen our understanding of what the performance requirements really should be and how to best measure results against those requirements, then perhaps the ARC might be recast to allow for more flexibility in developing methods that trade off differently between the various quality factors and efficiency.

10.2 Standard CMMI Assessment Method for Process Improvement

Another part of the CMMI product suite that deals with assessment is the Standard CMMI Assessment Method for Process Improvement (SCAMPI). This assessment method was developed by the CMMI Product Development Team to meet the full set of ARC requirements. As published, the SCAMPI document provides a "high-level overview" of SCAMPI; a more complete process description has not yet been produced.

Because CMMI models are integrated across disciplines, SCAMPI provides options for assessments against multiple disciplines with either separate or combined results. Some of the key principles of SCAMPI follow:

- Senior management sponsorship
- Focus on the organization's business goals
- Use of a documented assessment method
- Use of a process reference model (for example, a CMMI model)
- Confidentiality for interviewees
- Collaborative team approach
- Focus on follow-up actions for process improvement

A SCAMPI assessment is divided into three phases: (1) initial planning and preparation, (2) on-site assessment, and (3) reporting of results. Each phase includes multiple steps. The first phase involves identifying the assessment scope, developing a plan, preparing the team, briefing the participants, administering an appraisal questionnaire and examining the responses, and conducting an initial document review. The second phase focuses on holding an opening meeting for the on-site visit, conducting interviews, consolidating information, preparing and

Table 10-1: *Effort Estimates for SCAMPI*

Person	Effort Required
Assessment team leader	30 days
Sponsor	8 days
Organizational unit coordinator	25 days
Assessment team member	16 days each
Assessment participant (interviewed by assessment team)	0.17 day each

presenting draft findings, consolidating the findings and (optionally) determining ratings and preparing for the presentation of the final findings. The third phase involves the presentation of the final findings to the sponsor and (optionally) to the senior site manager as well as the collection of all information needed by the CMMI Steward (the SEI).

Only a SCAMPI lead assessor, who has been trained and authorized by the CMMI Steward, may lead a SCAMPI assessment. To be a lead assessor, an individual must have relevant discipline experience, knowledge of CMMI models, and training in assessment techniques. Assessment team members are also selected based on their knowledge, experience, and skills. There must be at least four members of a SCAMPI assessment team, and a maximum of 10 is recommended.

Table 10-1 shows the initial estimates from the CMMI team regarding the effort required for conducting a SCAMPI assessment, assuming two disciplines and using the full model scope.[5] It should not be too long before we have some real data against which to judge the accuracy of these estimates.

For organizations that seek to conform to ISO/IEC TR 15504, the emerging international standard on process assessment, SCAMPI is designed for conformance.

---

5. See *SCAMPI V1.0*, p. 32, Table 3.

10.3 Using Assessments in Process Improvement

The ARC allows three classes of assessments, as shown in Figure 10-1. The level of effort for each class varies based on the scope of the assessment. In general, however, a Class C assessment takes much less time than a Class B or A assessment. The "quick look" approach is designed to provide guidance on process improvements that would not require a full assessment. Such assessments can be performed on small parts of an organization several times so as to prepare for a Class B assessment.

The Class B assessment provides a more in-depth look at the organization. In most cases, it does not go into as much depth or detail as a Class A assessment. As a result, it can generally be completed within a week. A Class B assessment may be performed on limited parts of an organization in preparation for a Class A assessment.

Figure 10-2 depicts an example timeline for an organization. To start an improvement program that leads to a full SCAMPI assessment, an organization could use several Class C assessments leading up to a Class B assessment. Process improvements are made based on the findings of the quick looks at parts of the organization. The lessons learned in this way can be used to provide broader organizational improvements. As improvements indicate that the part of the organization is

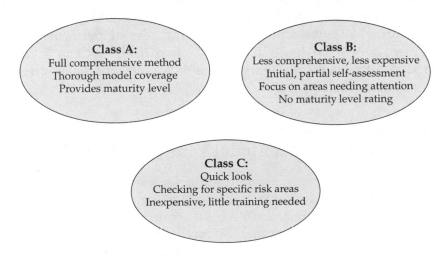

Figure 10-1: *ARC assessment classes*

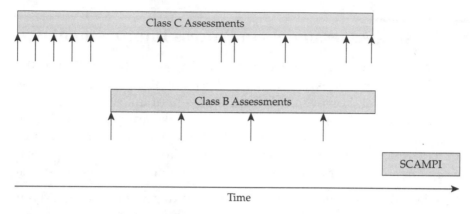

Figure 10-2: *Sample assessment timeline*

ready for the next step, a Class B assessment can be performed, and its findings subsequently used to prepare for the full SCAMPI assessment. To spot-check improvements, the organization may perform additional Class C assessments. Other parts of the organization can use the same process and assessment tools to prepare for the SCAMPI benchmark assessment. The actual time needed to prepare for a SCAMPI assessment will, of course, depend on several factors such as resources, budgets for process improvement, size of the organization, previous process improvement results, and management commitment.

Depending on the purpose of your assessment, you will select a method from the appropriate method class. If you could use a Class C method to achieve your purpose, then the cost of performing the assessment would be lower than that when using a Class B or A method. A different purpose might require the selection of an alternative assessment method.

10.4 Making a CMMI Model Your Own (Tailoring)

The model also represents a significant factor in the assessments. The more of the model that you use, the greater the effort needed for an assessment. Whether you have selected a continuous representation or a staged representation, you may perceive a benefit from "tailoring" some pieces of the model. For example, you may feel that the Supplier Agreement Management process area, which is staged at ML 2, does not apply to your project because you have no supplier agreements. In this case, you will identify the entire process area as "not applicable." In other cases you may identify a part of a process area, such as a specific goal and its associated specific practices, as "not applicable."

An example of a goal that is not applicable might be the first goal of the Requirements Development process area, which addresses the transformation of stakeholder needs into customer requirements. Perhaps in your business the customer requirements are just provided to you, and in your judgment they represent your starting point. Remember, however, that requirements can come from internal customers as well as external customers, so the transformation of internal customer needs into requirements may be critical to your business. For this reason, you should not rush to judgment when you suspect a goal is not applicable.

In another case, you might be inclined to declare one or more specific practices as "not applicable," even though the goal remains. As noted earlier, with any CMMI model a practice is an "expected" model element. Thus you may prefer to replace one or more practices with "alternative practices" that may represent a better path to achieving the goal for your organization.

Whenever you decide to customize or replace a model element that is required or expected (that is, a goal or a practice), a set of risks must be considered. First, from the perspective of process improvement, have you tailored an item that is really essential to developing an effective strategy for process improvement? Second, from the perspective of rating, have you modified an item that may undercut the accuracy, objectivity, or comparability of a rating number (either a capability level rating or a maturity level rating)? While the first of these risks is no doubt the most important in terms of the long-term success of your process improvement program, the second area—especially maturity level ratings—tends to generate the most emotion. Indeed, a given assessment method (for example, SCAMPI) will have rules for producing ratings that address what kind of tailoring of a CMMI model is or is not allowed.

A clear understanding of business objectives or goals is critical to developing effective processes. Similarly, an organization's business objectives should be considered when tailoring a CMMI model for internal use. The tailored model can then be used to guide process improvement activities. An advantage to this approach is that the model should remain stable for several years while the processes undergo continuous improvement. The model also provides a good measure of process capability that is based on the organization's business objectives and goals.

Business models can also serve as a basis for tailoring the CMMI product suite. For example, they may help an organization determine the order in which process areas should be implemented. Such business models may help determine requirements for processes or the tailoring of the CMMI as well.

Resources for process improvement can guide an organization during tailoring. They may be limited, which would indicate a need to customize the model in a series of smaller stages. Tailoring can aid in making the process improvement activities match the resources that are available. Limited tailoring may be possible when adequate resources are available to support the broader process improvement activities dictated by the CMMI model.

Tailoring of the model and of the assessment method is discussed in the model itself in the "Understanding the Model" section of Version 1.0. This section describes ways to customize model components for both process improvement and benchmarking purposes. Tailoring allows you to select the process areas that align most closely with your business objectives, business model, and resources. Version 1 of SCAMPI does not allow the tailoring of goals for an assessment. If it meets your purpose, however, tailoring at this level can reduce the cost of interim assessments—that is, those leading up to a full SCAMPI assessment.

Luckily, the assessment tools can be tailored to meet almost any need that you might envision. For example, if your organization is not responsible for any of the standard process management processes, you might decide to ignore all practices in the Process Management category except those that deal with saving process-related assets in a library. If your organization is primarily responsible for project management, then you might concentrate your assessment on the appropriate Project Management category process areas. The engineering department of your organization might select the planning and monitoring process areas along with the Engineering category process areas.

Finally, note that some organizations establish a standard process with traceability to models, such as CMMI, as well as other sources of process requirements (for example, standards, customers). This correspondence identifies where model components and process requirements are represented in the standard process. Should parts of the model be deemed not applicable to the organization, they may be eliminated from the process definition. Thus organizations assessing conformance to the standard process indirectly assess their work against the model and other requirement sources. Of course, tailored material may jeopardize the comparability of the assessment results.

The Delphic Sybil
Michaelangelo Buonarotti
Cappella Sistina, II Vaticano
Scala/Art Resource, NY

Part IV

The Future of CMMI

The historian Herodotus gave an account of King Croesus of Lydia (circa 546 BCE), who asked the Oracle at Delphi to consult the gods, look into the future, and determine whether he should invade Persian territory. The Oracle answered that, if he crossed a river, "Croesus will destroy a great empire." Croesus, thinking he would be victorious, invaded Persia. Unfortunately, it was his own empire that fell and was subsequently destroyed.

Prediction has always been risky. The evolution of process improvement to date has certainly been rapid and contentious. In Part IV, the authors don their mystical robes and stare deeply into their scrying crystals in an attempt to predict how CMMI may change in the future.

Part IV Contents

191

Chapter 11

Evolving CMMI

The rung of a ladder was never meant to rest upon, but only to hold a man's foot long enough to enable him to put the other somewhat higher.
Thomas Henry Huxley, *Life and Letters of Thomas Huxley (1825–1895)*

Beware becoming change-averse change agents!
Barry Boehm, SEI Symposium 2000 Keynote Address

When we blindly adopt a religion, a political system, a literary dogma, we become automatons. We cease to grow.
Anaïs Nin, *The Diaries of Anaïs Nin (1903–1977)*

What lies ahead for the architecture of Capability Maturity Model Integration (CMMI) and how might it evolve? How might having only one architectural representation for the CMMI model affect process improvement and assessments? What are some of the other issues for CMMI that were not addressed in version 1.0? Our discussion of (and musings on) these questions in this final chapter may be of greatest interest to those readers who are, in their heart of hearts, architects or system designers. Perhaps as you reflected on our description of the CMMI product suite in earlier chapters, you found yourself thinking: "Why did they do it that way?", or "I would have done it differently." "What *were* they thinking?" If this description fits you, read on. In contrast, if your interest is focused (quite legitimately) on learning about and using the current CMMI products, then you may prefer to make

193

this chapter a "quick read" on your way to the Afterword, which contains our concluding remarks.

11.1 Single versus Dual Representations

Many people, in discussing CMMI and its two architectural representations (continuous and staged), have expressed the viewpoint that in the future the CMMI models should move toward a single representation. After all, a close study of the two representations shows that while they have differences, they are much more alike than different. With two representations, an organization must endure confusion and (perhaps) wasted effort before deciding which one to use. Having two representations also affects the choice of assessment method. The generic practices are handled differently depending on whether you are doing a staged or continuous assessment.[1] Why not consolidate the two representations?

In response to such concerns, we present three ideas regarding how this merger might be achieved. While the authors agree that movement in this direction should be explored, we do not intend to propose any specific, defined timetable for when this investigation would or should occur. Nor do we want to endorse strongly any one option over the others. Clearly, a larger community of users would need to gain experience with the current dual-representation model and to provide feedback to the CMMI sponsors and Steward (the Software Engineering Institute) before any decisions could be made. Options in this area other than the ones detailed in this chapter exist, as do multiple variations of the options presented here. The goal here is to stimulate thought and lay a foundation for some of these deliberations as well as to encourage continued movement in this direction.

11.1.1 A Partially Staged CMMI Model

The phrase "partially staged" refers to a model in which a subset of CMMI process areas (derived from the full set) is used to define a common understanding for stages and maturity levels (MLs). Currently, in the CMMI staged representations (and in the equivalent staging for the

---

1. The Standard CMMI Assessment Method for Process Integration (SCAMPI) differs only in the final steps: determining the ratings for the maturity level or the capability profile.

continuous representations), all process areas are staged at one of the maturity levels. In a partially staged model, some—but not all—of the process areas would be staged at a maturity level. Process areas that were not staged at a maturity level or used in their definition for a maturity-level rating would be available (either individually or collectively) for other types of rating, such as capability levels (CLs).

The path to creating a partially staged CMMI model would be strewn with many options and decisions, and here we speculate regarding only a small number of those possibilities. Our goal is not to provide a complete vision regarding what partial staging would mean to CMMI, but to stimulate exploration, discussion, and debate in this area.

The following principle would be important to observe in creating a partially staged model: If a process area could be tailored out in some organizations, then it would not be a part of the subset that defines the model staging. For example, the Supplier Agreement Management (SAM) process area often may be identified in a process assessment as "not applicable." Some organizations or projects lack important supplier relationships that must be managed and hence have no supplier agreements to establish, maintain, or satisfy. When SAM is applicable, it can be a significant process area that should not be ignored; managing suppliers can prove central to the success of a project, especially if the suppliers provide critical system components. As SAM does not have universal applicability, however, it should not be included in the partial staging. In general, process areas related to acquisition and the relationship between acquirers and suppliers would not be staged. They would not apply in every situation and would, therefore, be subject to "tailoring out."

Reporting the rating results from an assessment with a partially staged model is not as simple as reporting with a fully staged model and its single-digit maturity level; likewise, it is not as complex as reporting with a continuous model and its capability profile, in which each process area is rated individually. To continue with the prior example, consider a CMMI staged representation for which all process areas are staged as dictated in version 1.0, with the exception of SAM. In such a case, an organization could be rated at ML 3 based on everything but SAM, and its process for supplier management would be rated at a capability level, (for example, CL 3). Then regardless of whether the organization had suppliers, you could have a comparable maturity level rating across a larger set of organizations. Furthermore, you would have a vehicle for reporting an additional capability in the area of managing suppliers.[2]

In a partially staged CMMI model, what could be done with the process areas in the Engineering category? If you think of the CMMI model primarily as geared toward supporting process improvement for engineering development and maintenance, then the process areas (at least most of them) could be included in the partial staging. The Engineering process areas, however, comprise an interrelated group that could perhaps benefit from a rating other than a general process maturity rating. Furthermore, if you think of CMMI models as having potential application in domains outside of engineering (for example, manufacturing), then engineering development should not be an essential part of the maturity level definitions. To accomplish this transformation, you could think about a collective engineering capability rating outside of the basic maturity staging. While the maturity staging would remain focused on process management (in the context of projects, and making use of support processes), a collective "engineering capability rating" could be defined to include most of the material in the Engineering process areas.[3]

If the process areas in the Engineering category were not staged, how would the organization report the results of an assessment? As an example, an organization might have achieved ML 2 in basic process management (with project management and support), an engineering CL 3, a Validation CL 3, and a supplier management CL 2. This result becomes even more complicated than a single maturity-level number, but perhaps would not be all that bad, really. Such an understandable (and small) collection of ratings paints a picture of overall capability and maturity in an organization—one that is much easier to comprehend than a 22- or 24-number capability profile—and simultaneously reveals more than the single maturity-level number.

---

2. The CMMI Product Development Team had no shortage of discussion and debate regarding the key process area from the Software CMM version 2(c) related to product lines. Some team members who strongly opposed its inclusion as a process area in CMMI were nevertheless among the strongest advocates of product-line development. They simply did not believe that a product-line approach had sufficiently universal application to warrant inclusion in a fully staged model. If partial staging had been an option, the contents of this process area would likely have appeared in CMMI, but not as a part of the maturity staging.

3. If some items had less than universal applicability (for example, Validation or the goal in Requirements Development on transforming stakeholder needs into customer requirements), then they could be omitted from the engineering capability rating. In this way, the rating would have more general applicability across a wider range of organizations.

Sample Requirements for CMMI Partial Staging

Following is a candidate list of requirements or principles that might be followed on the path to creating a single, partially staged CMMI representation:

1. There is just one integrated CMMI model.

2. There is just one architectural representation of this model.

3. The CMMI model includes all process areas that are available in all possible discipline combinations.

4. A discipline combination (for example, CMMI-SE/SW, CMMI-SE/SW/IPPD, or CMMI-SE/SW/IPPD/A) provides a view of the single integrated model.

5. A discipline view may encompass a set of process areas that is a subset of all the process areas in the base CMMI model.

6. CMMI process areas are constructed to avoid duplication of the required or expected material in two or more process areas.

7. Only one version of any CMMI process area exists at any given time.

8. Every process area in the CMMI model has capability levels that define an improvement path within that individual area. The process areas that are included in a discipline view are available for rating, either individually or collectively, with capability levels.

9. One partial staging for the one integrated CMMI model exists, and it defines organizational maturity levels.

10. The set of process areas that define the organizational maturity levels constitutes "the core CMMI process areas."

11. Those who do not wish to adopt the single definition of CMMI organizational maturity levels, for whatever reason, may rely on capability level ratings (singly or in groups) that are available in each CMMI process area. They may not redefine the meaning of the maturity level ratings based on an alternative partial staging.

(continued)

Sample Requirements for CMMI Partial Staging (*cont.*)

12. Generally speaking, the scope of the core CMMI process areas includes the categories of process management processes, project management process, and support processes.

13. Generally speaking, the scope of the core CMMI process areas does not include the categories of engineering processes or acquisition processes.

14. Generally speaking, the scope of the core CMMI process areas includes only those process areas (within the categories of process management processes, project management processes, and support processes) that have universal applicability. That is, a wide spectrum of organizations should not have good grounds for wanting to eliminate any process area or goal from the core CMMI process areas as not applicable to them.

15. Every discipline view encompasses the core CMMI process areas, and a label such as "a CMMI maturity level 2 organization" has only one meaning.

16. A discipline view may identify some of the noncore process areas as "essential" for that view and other noncore process areas as "optional."

17. A discipline view may identify collections of noncore process areas that are subject to a collective capability level rating (for example, engineering capability, Integrated Product and Process Development [IPPD] capability, or acquisition capability). That is, an organization may be at maturity level i, with an engineering capability of j or an acquisition capability of k.

18. References between process areas do not change with discipline views. An amplification-like entry after a reference may indicate that the CMMI process area cited is not included in the particular discipline view.

11.1.2 A Unified CMMI Model

While the "partially staged" model represents a step in the downsizing of the CMMI core components, other ideas have been raised that move farther along that continuum. Several members of the CMMI Product Development Team have long advocated a simpler, more streamlined approach to CMMI. Dubbed the "Unified CMMI" (U-CMMI), the idea is to produce a model consisting of only generic practices and the process areas that "enable" or support them.[4] Written in a conceptual, extensible manner, those components, accompanied by a template for defining organization-specific target processes, would define a model that could apply to any process—engineering or otherwise. Capability levels would be process capability levels and would be measured by the implementation of generic practices. Maturity levels would be based on the staging of the enabling process areas in the same way as the equivalent staging described earlier. Figure 11-1 shows a possible unified configuration.

As an example, suppose that a printing company wanted to apply the U-CMMI to its processes. It would first need to establish its "core discipline" processes—perhaps layout, printing, finishing, and delivery—according to the template provided with the U-CMMI. Once these processes were defined, the company could begin improvement with the level 2 generic practices and their enabling process areas.

Although the unified model would be similar to the existing CMMI models, its lack of an engineering orientation would provide two broad benefits. First, it could act as a process improvement model for a much wider range of enterprises, such as banking, consulting services, light industry, government, and retail. Second, it could provide a layman's view of process improvement that could be taught in undergraduate management and business curricula. Additionally, because of its lean structure, U-CMMI would not require the complex support infrastructure needed by existing models or the large development teams to apply to additional disciplines.

This approach may have some drawbacks, however. It is not clear that the language in the model could be suitably simplified so as to apply universally. Some question might arise as to the comparability of level ratings, given the variation in the organization-specific processes. Of

---

4. For example, a process area for configuration management that supports the Configuration Management generic practice at CL 2.

Figure 11-1: *A unified CMMI*

course, training and assessment materials would be needed that were as simple and clear as the model language, plus trainers and assessors available to support its use.

The automated framework of CMMI could support the production of such a model, but it is still too early to predict whether the will to simplify could ever extend this far.

11.1.3 More CMMI Model Options

As the CMMI model evolved from the first integration efforts to version 1.0, the two representations began to look increasingly similar. Having a single representation of the model, with guidelines on its use in both continuous and staged manners, may be one objective for the evolving CMMI.

The key architectural differences that prevent us from having a single representation are the use of goals, specific practices, and generic practices (all of the required and expected elements). Specific goals are an issue because in the continuous representation, they must encompass additional specific practices as the capability level increases. Note that EIA/IS 731 did not have goals; assessments based on this systems engineering model used the specific practices as the rated elements, and each specific practice was defined at a specified capability level. In CMMI, practices are merely expected; goals are the required element and serve as the basis for ratings. In the CMMI continuous representations, this approach causes the scope of the specific practices mapped to a goal to increase as the capability level increases.[5]

To maintain an unchanging mapping of the set of specific practices to specific goals, one might designate every specific practice at a capability level. The entire model architecture would then look like the current Engineering process areas, including both base and advanced specific practices. The specific goals would be used only at the capability level that was equal to the staged maturity level of the process area. In a continuous assessment, the specific practices (not the goals) would define the process dimension at the lower capability levels. This option represents a step toward a single representation, and it allows the staged users to work with the process areas in exactly the way they do now. It also defines the capability levels in a clear manner and satisfies the intention of a continuous process improvement scenario.

Removing goals entirely from the model would represent a major change. Nevertheless, it might be an attractive option for a single representation model. It would reduce the three levels of model elements to two levels. Specific practices would continue as part of the model, but the "required" and "expected" terms used to describe the current goals and specific practices, respectively, would be replaced with one new term, such as "normative." The "normative" specific practices would permit the use of alternative practices, reduce the number of steps in the assessment method, and make the appraisal questionnaire easier to complete. The definition of capability levels might resemble that employed in the EIA/IS 731 model. Maturity levels would be defined not as a set of process areas, but rather as a set of specific practices at specific capability levels. This option diminishes the importance of

---

5. One option to resolve this issue would be to add specific goals at each capability level. This option is not very attractive because the size and complexity of the model is increased significantly.

process areas in the model. Process areas could be combined in certain categories to reduce the complexity of assessment of generic practices, and it would be a straightforward task to relate maturity levels to capability levels.

11.2 Collection of Issues for Version 1.1 and Beyond

The public review period for CMMI version 0.2 in 1999 resulted in about 2500 change requests to the model and the "books" that represent the model. Of these requests, approximately 400 were classified as "minor" and 500 were considered "global" (affecting several process areas or other elements). The remaining change requests were classified as being "local" to the individual model elements. For several of the change requests in the global and local categories, the Product Development Team lacked sufficient time to deal with them properly. Instead, they were placed on a list of potentially good ideas warranting more exploration. One such request called for a single architectural representation for the model, as discussed in Section 11.1. In this section, we discuss a few of the other major open issues—that is, issues deferred for consideration to version 1.1 or later.

11.2.1 Advanced Practices

As mentioned in Section 11.1, moving to a single representation would perhaps entail some change in the way advanced practices are treated in the model. Even if the dual-representation concept were maintained, however, some change in the area of advanced practices may be needed. It may seem somewhat odd that version 1.0 allowed advanced practices in the Engineering category but not in the other process area categories.

For the future, we would expect that as the model is used one of two things would occur. First, process improvement in the Engineering process areas might be aided by the presence of advanced practices, prompting users of this model to seek the expansion of this concept across the entire model. Alternatively, the value that advanced practices may have for process improvement might be viewed as insufficient to justify the architectural complexity they introduce, prompting model users to ask for their elimination across the entire model. The decision within the Product Development Team to put them into the initial model releases in a limited way was intended to lay the foundation for feedback either in favor of or opposed to advanced practices, as the team could not reach a consensus view. This disagreement was a part of the debate between proponents of staged versus continuous architectures.

11.2.2 Enterprise Viewpoints

As disciplines are added to CMMI and the potential scope of an integrated model increases, the initial vision of CMMI as providing an integrated engineering development model may face challenges. Its applicability may come to be viewed from a broader viewpoint than just engineering development—for example, acquisition is not engineering development. The more expansion that occurs, the more inevitable that questions will arise regarding CMMI's role in other process-related initiatives and activities within an enterprise, of which engineering development is just one part. In the manufacturing world, much attention has focused on "lean" initiatives as a way to improve processes by eliminating waste. Enterprise modeling is used to understand the implications of change and improve an enterprise's response to change. The interface of CMMI to such initiatives needs clarification and development—and potentially integration.

11.2.3 Generic Attributes

EIA/IS 731 contains generic attributes, an aspect of process improvement that is not included in any other source model. Generic attributes address the effectiveness of the process and the value of the work products produced by it. Proponents of generic attributes on the CMMI Product Development Team generated a proposal for CMMI generic attributes by improving the objectivity of the generic attributes in EIA/IS 731. In the end, however, that proposal was not adopted.

The generic attributes add a significant aspect to process improvement that is not addressed by the capability dimension or the process dimension: How effective are the processes in your environment, and do they produce work products that the stakeholders find valuable? Some organizations have developed the ability to evaluate this process improvement dimension by adopting the "lean" initiative. For CMMI, the question remains: Would the inclusion of generic attributes in a CMMI assessment be of sufficient value, given the issue of their objectivity?

11.2.4 Relationship to Other Process Areas

CMMI version 1.0 includes a section in each process area titled "Related Process Areas," which contains (not surprisingly) references to other process areas. At the current time, these references are not used consistently across all process areas. A recommendation was made and accepted by the Product Development Team (but not implemented in version 1.0) to change the title of this section to "Relationships with Other Process Areas," and to make its content more consistent across the model.[6]

The needs related to this issue are as follows:

- Model users need to understand the high-level (key) relationships between process areas.
- Those who develop CMMI training materials need a mechanism to generate a high-level diagram to show relationships between process areas.
- Model users need to understand the difference between references at different levels (components) of the model.

The following guidelines were defined to restrict the use of the initial reference section in each process area to "key" process area interfaces:

- Change the title of "Related Process Areas" to "Relationships with Other Process Areas."
- Use the "Reference" architectural component but change the structure of the reference, in this section only, to an active statement of the relationship with other process areas.
- Allow one to three sentences for each relationship description.
- Include only key relationships (that is, what the user needs to see at a high level).
- Retain the normal references in the model from other components.
- Generate a view in the Product Suite Repository that shows these relationships.

---

6. An earlier version of CMMI (predating version 1.0) used two levels of reference: the currently used "informative" reference and a stronger reference. The stronger reference invoked another process area, stating "Use the X process areas to achieve y." The application of the "Use" reference was not consistent across the model, confused model users, and raised issues in the area of assessment. It was not clear exactly what was implied by the stronger relationship between process areas. Given the many calls to reduce the model's complexity and of the time to adequately study the issue, the stronger reference was eliminated in version 1.0. Whether anyone will make the case to revive multiple forms of reference in CMMI remains to be seen.

The CMMI Product Team has recommended such a change for each process area as a part of the next release of CMMI.

Example Update to Relationships Section

The following example is a proposed update to the Technical Solution process area:

Relationship with Other Process Areas

The Requirements Development process area provides product component requirements to this process area so that alternative solutions can be developed.

The Requirements Development process area receives technical solutions, selected from the alternatives, to refine the product component requirements.

The Work Product Verification process area verifies that the product components meet their requirements. As verification issues are identified, the design may need to change. This is an iterative process and occurs throughout the development of the product.

The Decision Analysis and Resolution process area provides structured decision-making practices that are used in selecting a technical solution from the alternative solutions.

The Product Integration process area receives the product components following their implementation.

The Product Integration process area provides integration test deficiencies to this process area for corrective action.

The Validation process area provides validation deficiencies to this process area for corrective action.

The Product Integration process area provides integration test deficiencies to this process area for corrective action.

The Supplier Agreement Management process area handles the acquisition of all product components once the purchase decision is made in this process area.

Afterword

There is, and always will be, tension between the desire to improve, change, and grow, and the desire for stability and an avoidance of moving targets. This choice should not apply to Capability Maturity Model Integration (CMMI), however; both change and stability are fundamental to process improvement. The CMMI models must have sufficient stability so that an investment in process improvement is not undercut by radical and pervasive changes to the models. At the same time, the CMMI models must change to incorporate new knowledge, proven experience, and the continuous creativity of those who practice and preach process improvement.

As we said at the beginning of this book, the task of producing integrated models was a largely unprecedented task. The likelihood that the Product Development Team got everything "right," even after more than two years of diligent work, is not high. Furthermore, as every proponent of process improvement knows, change focused on making improvements never ends. Surely this axiom applies to process improvement models just as much as it does to engineering development processes.

Of course, the determination of whether a given change proposed is too radical or pervasive lies somewhat in the eye of the beholder. For some, moving to a single representation would be a significant change with significant impact. For others, who are perhaps struck by the degree of commonality between the existing two CMMI representational architectures, it seems a logical step that would not undermine process improvement for anyone. By discussing such possible evolutionary paths for CMMI, we do not intend to diminish the stability or the acceptance of the model. It is our view that making a good thing better would only improve its acceptance in the community.

Throughout this book, we have tried to distill our experiences in responding to the need for integrated process improvement and participating in a major initiative aimed at developing innovative products. Some readers may have an opportunity to enjoy a similar opportunity, and we wish you well. For the rest of you, we hope that you can understand the hard work, difficult decisions, intellectual fireworks, and friendships that are an integral part of any such endeavor. We also hope that we have provided an accessible view into the results of the CMMI project so that you can make more informed decisions about applying this model in your organization. As CMMI evolves, whether along the paths that we have suggested or some other course, we will continue to update this information through the Addison-Wesley Web site.

Chapter 1 began with a quote from W. Edwards Deming, which proves as useful at this juncture as it did for our opening act: "It is not necessary to change. Survival is not mandatory." As you have survived your reading of this book, please let us know whether it has helped you on your path to integrated process improvement. Like engineering development processes and process improvement models, books about these topics can be improved. We look forward to hearing and using your suggestions in future editions.

The Charge of the CMMI Product Team

Richard Turner (with apologies to Alfred, Lord Tennyson)

The following poem is dedicated to the men and women of the CMMI Product Development Team. These brave souls spent far more hours on airplanes and in hotel rooms than they bargained for at the outset. They also endured interminable meetings, sometimes covering arcane concepts and important but obscure minutiae, all in an effort to create an architecture and bind together the various CMMI source models. In particular, the project managers, Dr. Jack Ferguson and Dr. Mike Phillips, and the chief architect, Dr. Roger Bate, are to be cheered for leading the charge and keeping the troops together.

Omnia vincit labor

Half a line, half a line,
Half a line onward,
All in the valley of words
Wrote the sage hundred.
"Forward, the Product Team!
Merge them to one!" the theme.
Into the valley of words
Wrote the sage hundred.

"Forward the Product team!"
Was there a one did scream?
Not tho' the authors knew
Someone would blunder.
Theirs to make each reply,
Theirs doomed to reason why,
Theirs but to write and sigh.
Into the valley of words
Wrote the sage hundred.

Models to right of them,
Models to left of them,
Models in front of them,
Merged and sundered.
Consider, let reason tell,

Boldly they wrote, and well
Into the laws of words,
Into the model Hell
Wrote the sage hundred.

Flashed all their laptops bare,
Flashed as they worked in air,
Making way, here and there,
Charging the hours, while
Companies wondered.
Writing through battery smoke,
Cheering when genius stroke,
Fully debated,
Blossomed, and answers woke
Almost as fated.
Then they pushed on, but not,
Not the same hundred.

Models to right of them,
Models to left of them,
Models behind them,
Practices thunder'd.
Stormed at with verb and goal,
Road warriors feeling old,
They that had writ so bold
Came through the laws of words,
Back from the model Hell,
Bloodied, not bowed they came,
Came the sage hundred.

When can their glory fade?
Oh, the grand work they made!
The process world wonder'd.
Honor CMMI!
Honor that team so wise,
Noble sage hundred.

Appendix A

Summary of CMMI-SE/SW/IPPD Models

Summary of Continuous Representation

Process Management

ORGANIZATIONAL PROCESS FOCUS

Establish and maintain an understanding of the organization's processes and process assets, and to identify, plan, and implement the organization's process improvement activities.

Strengths, weaknesses, and improvement opportunities for the organization's processes are identified periodically and as needed. SG 1

Establish and maintain the description of the process needs and objectives for the organization. SP 1.1-1

Assess the processes of the organization periodically and as needed to maintain an understanding of their strengths and weaknesses. SP 1.2-1

Identify improvements to the organization's processes and related process assets. SP 1.3-1

Improvements are planned and implemented, process assets are deployed, and process-related experiences are incorporated into the organization's process assets. SG 2

Establish and maintain process action plans to address improvements to the organization's processes and related process assets. SP 2.1-1

Implement process action plans across the organization. SP 2.2-1

Deploy the process and related process assets across the organization. SP 2.3-1

Incorporate process-related work products, measures, and improvement information derived from planning and performing the process into the organization's process assets. SP 2.4-1

Organizational Process Definition

Establish and maintain a usable set of organizational process assets.

A set of organizational process assets is available. SG 1

Establish and maintain the organization's set of standard processes. SP 1.1-1

Establish and maintain descriptions of the life-cycle process models approved for use in the organization. SP 1.2-1

Establish and maintain the tailoring criteria and guidelines for the organization's set of standard processes. SP 1.3-1

Process assets that support the use of the organization's set of standard processes are available. SG 2

Establish and maintain an organizational measurement repository. SP 2.1-1

Establish and maintain the organization's library of process-related assets. SP 2.2-1

ORGANIZATIONAL TRAINING

Develop the skills and knowledge of people so they can perform their roles effectively and efficiently.

Training to support the organization's management and technical roles is identified and made available. SG 1

Establish and maintain the strategic training needs of the organization. SP 1.1-1

Determine which training needs are the responsibility of the organization and which will be left to the individual project or support group. SP 1.2-1

Establish and maintain an organizational training tactical plan. SP 1.3-1

Establish and maintain training capability to address organizational training needs. SP 1.4-1

Training necessary for individuals to perform their roles effectively is provided. SG 2

Deliver the training following an organizational training plan. SP 2.1-1

Establish and maintain records of the organizational training. SP 2.2 1

Assess the effectiveness of the organization's training program. SP 2.3-1

ORGANIZATIONAL PROCESS PERFORMANCE

Establish and maintain a quantitative understanding of the performance of the organization's set of standard processes, and to provide the process performance data, baselines, and models to quantitatively manage the organization's projects.

Baselines and models that characterize the expected process performance of the organization's set of standard processes are established and maintained. SG 1

Select the processes or process elements in the organization's set of standard processes that are to be included in the organization's process performance analyses. SP 1.1-1

Establish and maintain definitions of the measures that are to be included in the organization's process performance analyses. SP 1.2-1

Establish and maintain quantitative objectives for quality and process performance for the organization. SP 1.3-1

Establish and maintain the organization's process performance baselines. SP 1.4-1

Establish and maintain the process performance models for the organization's set of standard processes. SP 1.5-1

ORGANIZATIONAL INNOVATION AND DEPLOYMENT

Select and deploy incremental and innovative improvements that measurably improve the organization's processes and technologies. The improvements support the organization's quality and process performance objectives as derived from the organization's business objectives.

Process and technology improvements that contribute to meeting quality and process performance objectives are selected. SG 1

Collect and analyze process and technology improvement proposals. SP 1.1-1

Identify innovative improvements that would increase the organization's quality and process performance. SP 1.2-1

Pilot process and technology improvements to select which ones to implement. SP 1.3-1

Select process and technology improvement proposals for deployment across the organization. SP 1.4-1

Measurable improvements to the organization's processes and technologies are continually and systematically deployed. SG 2

Establish and maintain the plans for deploying the selected process and technology improvements. SP 2.1-1

Manage the deployment of the selected process and technology improvements. SP 2.2-1

Measure the effects of the deployed process and technology improvements. SP 2.3-1

Project Management

PROJECT PLANNING
Establish and maintain plans that define project activities.

Estimates of project planning parameters are established and maintained. SG 1

> Establish and maintain a top-level work breakdown structure (WBS) to estimate of the scope of the project. SP 1.1-1
>
> Establish and document estimates of the attributes of the work products and tasks. SP 1.2-1
>
> Define the project life-cycle phases upon which to scope the planning effort. SP 1.3-1
>
> Estimate the project effort and cost for the attributes of the work products and tasks based on estimation rationale. SP 1.4-1

A project plan is established and maintained as the basis for managing the project. SG 2

> Establish and maintain the project's budget and schedule. SP 2.1-1
>
> Identify and analyze project risks. SP 2.2-1
>
> Plan for the management of project data. SP 2.3-1
>
> Plan for necessary resources to perform the project. SP 2.4-1
>
> Plan for knowledge and skills needed to perform the project. SP 2.5-1
>
> Plan the involvement with identified stakeholders. SP 2.6-1
>
> Establish and maintain the overall project plan content. SP 2.7-1

Commitments to the project plan are established and maintained. SG 3

> Review subordinate plans to understand project commitments. SP 3.1-1
>
> Reconcile the project plan to reflect available and projected resources. SP 3.2-1
>
> Obtain commitment from relevant stakeholders responsible for performing and supporting plan execution. SP 3.3-1

PROJECT MONITORING AND CONTROL

Provide understanding into the project's progress so that appropriate corrective actions can be taken when the project's performance deviates significantly from the plan.

Actual performance and progress of the project is monitored against the project plan.

Monitor the actual values of the project planning parameters against the project plan. SP 1.1-1

Monitor commitments against those identified in the project plan. SP 1.2-1

Monitor risks against those identified in the project plan. SP 1.3-1

Monitor the management of project data. SP 1.4-1

Monitor stakeholder involvement against the project plan. SP 1.5-1

Periodically review the project's progress, performance, and issues. SP 1.6-1

Review the accomplishments and results of the project at selected project milestones. SP 1.7-1

Corrective actions are managed to closure when the project's performance or results deviate significantly from the plan. SG 2

Collect and analyze the issues and determine the corrective actions necessary to address the issues. SP 2.1-1

Take corrective action on identified issues. SP 2.2-1

Manage corrective actions to closure. SP 2.3-1

SUPPLIER AGREEMENT MANAGEMENT

Manage the acquisition of products and services from suppliers external to the project for which there exists a formal agreement.

Agreements with the suppliers are established and maintained. SG 1

Analyze the project's needs and requirements that will be fulfilled by sources outside the project to determine how the needs and requirements will be satisfied. SP 1.1-1

Select suppliers based on an evaluation of their ability to meet the specified requirements and established criteria. SP 1.2-1

Establish and maintain formal agreements with the supplier. SP 1.3-1

Agreements with the suppliers are satisfied by both the project and the supplier. SG 2

Acquire COTS products to satisfy the specified requirements that are covered under a supplier agreement. SP 2.1-1

Perform activities with the supplier as specified in the supplier agreement. SP 2.2-1

Ensure that the supplier agreement is satisfied before accepting the acquired product. SP 2.3-1

Transition the acquired products from the supplier to the project. SP 2.4-1

Integrated Project Management (IPPD)

Establish and manage the project and the involvement of the relevant stakeholders according to an integrated and defined process that is tailored from the organization's set of standard processes. It also covers the establishment of a shared vision for the project and a team structure for integrated teams that will carry out the objectives of the project.

The project is conducted using a defined process that is tailored from the organization's set of standard processes. SG 1

Establish and maintain the project's defined process. SP 1.1-1

Use the organization's process assets and measurement repository for estimating and planning the project's activities. SP 1.2-1

Integrate the project plan and the subordinate plans to describe the project's defined process. SP 1.3-1

Manage the project using the project plan, the subordinate plans, and the project's defined process. SP 1.4-1

Contribute work products, measures, and documented experiences to the organization's process assets. SP 1.5-1

Coordination and collaboration of the project with relevant stakeholders is conducted. SG 2

Manage the involvement of the relevant stakeholders in the project. SP 2.1-1

Participate with relevant stakeholders to identify, negotiate, and track critical dependencies. SP 2.2-1

Resolve issues with relevant stakeholders. SP 2.3-1

The project is conducted using the project's shared vision. SG 3

Identify expectations, constraints, interfaces, and operational conditions applicable to the project's shared vision. SP 3.1-1

Establish and maintain a shared vision for the project. SP 3.2-1

The integrated teams needed to execute the project are identified, defined, structured, and tasked. SG 4

Determine the integrated team structure that will best meet the project objectives and constraints. SP 4.1-1

Develop a preliminary distribution of requirements, responsibilities, authorities, tasks, and interfaces to teams in the selected integrated team structure. SP 4.2-1

Establish and maintain teams in the integrated team structure. SP 4.3-1

RISK MANAGEMENT

Identify potential problems before they occur, so that risk-handling activities may be planned and invoked as needed across the life cycle to mitigate adverse impacts on achieving objectives.

Preparation for risk management is conducted. SG 1

Determine risk sources and categories. SP 1.1-1

Define the parameters used to analyze and classify risks, and the parameters used to control the risk management effort. SP 1.2-1

Establish and maintain the strategy and methods to be used for risk management. SP 1.3-1

Risks are identified and analyzed to determine their relative importance. SG 2

Identify and document the risks. SP 2.1-1

Evaluate and classify each identified risk using the defined risk categories and parameters, and determine its relative priority. SP 2.2-1

Risks are handled and mitigated, where appropriate, to reduce adverse impacts on achieving objectives. SG 3

Develop a risk mitigation plan for the most important risks to the project, as defined by the risk management strategy. SP 3.1-1

Monitor the status of each risk periodically and implement the risk mitigation plan as appropriate. SP 3.2-1

INTEGRATED TEAMING

Form and sustain an integrated team for the development of work products.

Team composition that provides the knowledge and skills required to deliver the team's product is established and maintained. SG 1

Identify and define the team's specific internal tasks to generate the team's expected output. SP 1.1-1

Identify the knowledge, skills, and functional expertise needed to perform team tasks. SP 1.2-1

Assign the appropriate personnel to be team members based on required knowledge and skills. SP 1.3-1

Operation of the integrated team is governed according to established principles. SG 2

Establish and maintain a shared vision for the integrated team that is aligned with any overarching or higher-level vision. SP 2.1-1

Establish and maintain a team charter based on the integrated team's shared vision and overall team objectives. SP 2.2-1

Clearly define and maintain each team member's roles and responsibilities. SP 2.3-1

Establish and maintain integrated team operating procedures. SP 2.4-1

Establish and maintain collaboration among interfacing teams. SP 2.5-1

QUANTITATIVE PROJECT MANAGEMENT

Quantitatively manage the project's defined process to achieve the project's established quality and process performance objectives.

The project is quantitatively managed using quality and process performance objectives. SG 1

Establish and maintain the project's quality and process performance objectives. SP 1.1-1

Select the processes and process elements that comprise the project's defined process based on historical stability and capability data. SP 1.2-1

Select the subprocesses of the project's defined process that will be statistically managed. SP 1.3-1

Monitor the project to determine whether the project's objectives for quality and process performance will be satisfied, and take corrective action as appropriate. SP 1.4-1

The performance of selected subprocesses within the project's defined process is statistically managed. SG 2

Select the measures and analytic techniques to be used in statistically managing the selected subprocesses. SP 2.1-1

Establish and maintain an understanding of the variance of the selected subprocesses using the selected measures and analytic techniques. SP 2.2-1

Monitor the performance of the selected subprocesses to determine their capability to satisfy their quality and process performance objectives, and take corrective action as necessary. SP 2.3-1

Record statistical and quality management data in the organization's measurement repository. SP 2.4-1

Engineering

REQUIREMENTS MANAGEMENT

Manage the requirements of the project's products and product components and to identify inconsistencies between those requirements and the project's plans and work products.

Requirements are managed and inconsistencies with project plans and work products are identified. SG 1

Develop an understanding with the requirements providers on the meaning of the requirements. SP 1.1-1

Obtain commitment to the requirements from the project participants. SP 1.2-2

Manage changes to the requirements as they evolve during the project. SP 1.3-1

Maintain bi-directional traceability among the requirements and the project plans and work products. SP 1.4-2

Identify inconsistencies between the project plans and work products and the requirements. SP 1.5-1

REQUIREMENTS DEVELOPMENT

Produce and analyze customer, product, and product component requirements.

Stakeholder needs, expectations, constraints, and interfaces are collected and translated into customer requirements. SG 1

Identify and collect stakeholder needs, expectations, constraints, and interfaces for all phases of the product's life cycle. SP 1.1-1

Elicit stakeholder needs, expectations, constraints, and interfaces for all phases of the product's life cycle. SP 1.1-2

Transform stakeholder needs, expectations, constraints, and interfaces into customer requirements. SP 1.2-1

Customer requirements are refined and elaborated to develop product and product component requirements for the product life cycle. SG 2

Establish and maintain, from the customer requirements, product and product component requirements essential to product and product component effectiveness and affordability. SP 2.1-1

Allocate the requirements for each product component. SP 2.2-1

Identify interface requirements. SP 2.3-1

The requirements are analyzed and validated, and a definition of required functionality is developed. SG 3

Establish and maintain operational concepts and scenarios. SP 3.1-1

Establish and maintain a definition of required functionality. SP 3.2-1

Analyze derived requirements to ensure that they are necessary and sufficient. SP 3.3-1

Analyze requirements with the purpose of reducing the life-cycle cost, schedule and risk of product development. SP 3.4-3

Validate requirements to ensure the resulting product will perform appropriately in its intended use environment. SP 3.5-1

Validate requirements to ensure the resulting product will perform as intended in the user's environment using multiple techniques as appropriate. SP 3.5-2

TECHNICAL SOLUTION

Develop, design, and implement solutions to requirements. Solutions, designs and implementations encompass products, product components, and product related processes either singly or in combinations as appropriate.

Product or product component solutions, including applicable product related processes, are selected from alternative solutions. SG 1

Develop alternative solutions and establish selection criteria. SP 1.1-1

Develop detailed alternative solutions and selection criteria. SP 1.1-2

Evolve the operational concept, scenarios, and environments to describe the conditions, operating modes, and operating states specific to each product component. SP 1.2-2

Select the product component solutions that best satisfy the criteria established. SP 1.3-1

Product or product component designs are developed. SG 2

Establish and use effective design methods. SP 2.1-1

Develop a product or product component technical data package. SP 2.2-1

Establish and maintain a complete technical data package. SP 2.2-3

Establish and maintain the solution for product component interfaces. SP 2.3-1

Design product component interfaces in terms of established and maintained criteria. SP 2.3-3

Evaluate whether the product components should be developed, purchased, or reused based on established criteria. SP 2.4-3

Product components, and associated support documentation, are implemented from their designs. SG 3

Implement the designs of the product components. SP 3.1-1

Establish and maintain the end-use documentation. SP 3.2-1

PRODUCT INTEGRATION

Assemble the product from the product components, ensure that the product, as integrated, functions properly, and deliver the product.

The strategy for conducting product integration is established and maintained. SG 1

Establish and maintain a strategy for integration of the product components. SP 1.1-1

Establish and maintain the environment needed to support the integration of the product components. SP 1.2-2

Define detailed procedures and criteria for integration of the product components. SP 1.3-3

The product component interfaces, both internal and external, are compatible. SG 2

Review interface descriptions for coverage and completeness. SP 2.1-1

Manage internal and external interface definitions, designs, and changes for products and product components. SP 2.2-1

Verified product components are assembled and the integrated, verified, and validated product is delivered. SG 3

Confirm, prior to assembly, that each product component required to assemble the product has been properly identifed, functions according to its description, and that the product component interfaces comply with the interface descriptions. SP 3.1-1

Assemble product components according to the product integration strategy. SP 3.2-1

Checkout an assembly of product components. SP 3.3-1

Package the assembled product or product component and deliver it to the appropriate customer. SP 3.4-1

Verification

Assure that selected work products meet their specified requirements.

Preparation for verification is conducted. SG 1

Establish and maintain a verification strategy for selected work products. SP 1.1-1

Establish and maintain the environment needed to support verification. SP 1.2-2

Establish and maintain detailed verification plans for selected work products. SP 1.3-3

Peer reviews are performed on selected work products. SG 2

Prepare for peer reviews of selected work products. SP 2.1-1

Conduct peer reviews on selected work products and identify issues resulting from the peer review. SP 2.2-1

Analyze data about preparation, conduct, and results of the peer reviews. SP 2.3-2

Selected work products are verified against their specified requirements. SG 3

Perform verification according to the verification strategy. SP 3.1-1

Analyze the results of all verification activities and identify corrective action. SP 3.2-2

Perform re-verification of corrected work products and ensure that work products have not been negatively impacted. SP 3.3-1

VALIDATION

Demonstrate that a product or product component fulfills its intended use when placed in its intended environment.

Preparation for validation is conducted. SG 1

Establish and maintain a validation strategy. SP 1.1-1

Establish and maintain the environment needed to support validation. SP 1.2-2

Define detailed procedures and criteria for validation. SP 1.3-3

The product or product components are validated to ensure that they are suitable for use in their intended operating environment. SG 2

Perform validation according to the validation strategy. SP 2.1-1

Capture and analyze the results of the validation activities and identify issues. SP 2.2-1

Support

CONFIGURATION MANAGEMENT

Establish and maintain the integrity of work products using configuration identification, configuration control, configuration status accounting, and configuration audits.

Baselines of identified work products are established and maintained. SG 1

Identify the configuration items, components, and related work products that will be placed under configuration management. SP 1.1-1

Establish and maintain a configuration management and change management system for controlling work products. SP 1.2-1

Create or release baselines for internal use and for delivery to the customer. SP 1.3-1

Changes to the work products under configuration management are tracked and controlled. SG 2

Track change requests for the configuration items. SP 2.1-1

Control changes to the content of configuration items. SP 2.2-1

Integrity of baselines is established and maintained. SG 3

Establish and maintain records describing configuration items. SP 3.1-1

Perform configuration audits to maintain integrity of the configuration baselines. SP 3.2-1

PROCESS AND PRODUCT QUALITY ASSURANCE

Provide staff and management with objective insight into the processes and associated work products.

Adherence of the performed process and associated work products and services to applicable process descriptions, standards and procedures is objectively evaluated. SG 1

Objectively evaluate the designated performed processes against the applicable process descriptions, standards and procedures. SP 1.1-1

Objectively evaluate the designated work products and services against the applicable process descriptions, standards, and procedures. SP 1.2-1

Noncompliance issues are objectively tracked and communicated, and resolution is ensured. SG 2

Communicate quality issues and ensure resolution of noncompliance issues with the staff and managers. SP 2.1-1

Establish and maintain records of the quality assurance activities. SP 2.2-1

MEASUREMENT AND ANALYSIS

Develop and sustain a measurement capability that is used to support management information needs.

Measurement objectives and practices are aligned with identified information needs and objectives. SG 1

Establish and maintain measurement objectives that are derived from identified information needs and objectives. SP 1.1-1

Specify measures to address the measurement objectives. SP 1.2-1

Specify how measurement data will be obtained and stored. SP 1.3-1

Specify how measurement data will be analyzed and reported. SP 1.4-1

Measurement results that address identified information needs and objectives are provided. SG 2

Obtain specified measurement data. SP 2.1-1

Analyze and interpret measurement data. SP 2.2-1

Manage and store measurement data, measurement specifications, and analysis results. SP 2.3-1

Report results of measurement and analysis activities to all affected stakeholders. SP 2.4-1

DECISION ANALYSIS AND RESOLUTION

Make decisions using a structured approach that evaluates identified alternatives against established criteria.

Decisions are based on an evaluation of alternatives using established criteria. SG 1

Establish and use guidelines to determine which issues are subject to a structured decision analysis and resolution process. SP 1.1-1

Select the decision-making techniques. SP 1.2-1

Establish the evaluation criteria and their relative ranking. SP 1.3-1

Identify alternative solutions to issues. SP 1.4-1

Evaluate alternative solutions using the documented criteria. SP 1.5-1

Select solutions from the alternatives based on the evaluation criteria. SP 1.6-1

ORGANIZATIONAL ENVIRONMENT FOR INTEGRATION

Provide an IPPD infrastructure and manage people for integration.

An infrastructure that maximizes the productivity of people and effects the collaboration necessary for integration is provided. SG 1

Establish and maintain a shared vision for the organization. SP 1.1-1

Establish and maintain an integrated work environment that supports IPPD by enabling collaboration and concurrent development. SP 1.2-1

Identify the unique skills needed to support the IPPD environment. SP 1.3-1

People are managed to nurture the integrative and collaborative behaviors of an IPPD environment. SG 2

Establish and maintain leadership mechanisms to enable timely collaboration. SP 2.1-1

Establish and maintain incentives for adopting and demonstrating integrative and collaborative behaviors at all levels of the organization. SP 2.2-1

Establish and maintain organizational guidelines to balance team and home organization responsibilities. SP 2.3-1

CAUSAL ANALYSIS AND RESOLUTION

Identify causes of defects and other problems and take action to prevent them from occurring in the future.

Root causes of defects and other problems are systematically determined. SG 1

Select the defects and other problems for analysis. SP 1.1-1

Perform causal analysis of selected defects and other problems and propose actions to address them. SP 1.2-1

Root causes of defects and other problems are systematically addressed to prevent their future occurrence. SG 2

Implement the selected action proposals that were developed in causal analysis. SP 2.1-1

Evaluate the effect of changes on process performance. SP 2.2-1

Record causal analysis and resolution data for use across the project and organization. SP 2.3-1

Generic Goals and Generic Practices

The process supports and enables achievement of the specific goals of the process area by transforming identifiable input work products to produce identifiable output work products. GG 1

Identify the scope of the work to be performed and work products or services to be produced, and communicate this information to those performing the work. GP 1.1

Perform the base practices of the process to develop work products and provide services to achieve the specific goals of the process area. GP 1.2

The process is institutionalized as a managed process. GG 2

Establish and maintain an organizational policy for planning and performing the process. GP 2.1

Establish and maintain the requirements and objectives, and plan for performing the process. GP 2.2

Provide adequate resources for performing the process, developing the work products, and providing the services of the process. GP 2.3

Assign responsibility and authority for performing the process, developing the work products, and providing the services of the process. GP 2.4

Train the people performing or supporting the process as needed. GP 2.5

Place designated work products of the process under appropriate levels of configuration management. GP 2.6

Identify and involve the relevant stakeholders as planned. GP 2.7

Monitor and control the process against the plan and take appropriate corrective action. GP 2.8

Objectively evaluate adherence of the process and the work products and services of the process to the applicable requirements, objectives, and standards, and address noncompliance. GP 2.9

Review the activities, status, and results of the process with higher-level management and resolve issues. GP 2.10

The process is institutionalized as a defined process. GG 3

Establish and maintain the description of a defined process. GP 3.1

Collect work products, measures, measurement results, and improvement information derived from planning and performing the process to support the future use and improvement of the organization's processes and process assets. GP 3.2

The process is institutionalized as a quantitatively managed process.
GG 4

Establish and maintain quantitative objectives for the process about quality and process performance based on customer needs and business objectives. GP 4.1

Stabilize the performance of one or more subprocesses of the process to determine its ability to achieve the established quantitative quality and process performance objectives. GP 4.2

The process is institutionalized as an optimizing process. GG 5

Ensure continuous improvement of the process in fulfilling the relevant business goals of the organization. GP 5.1

Identify and correct the root causes of defects and other problems in the process. GP 5.2

Appendix B

Summary of CMMI-SE/SW/IPPD Models

Summary of Staged Representation

Note: **Specific practices that are included in the staged model for information only are not included in the following summaries.**

Maturity Level: 2

REQUIREMENTS MANAGEMENT
Manage the requirements of the project's products and product components and to identify inconsistencies between those requirements and the project's plans and work products.

Requirements are managed and inconsistencies with project plans and work products are identified. SG 1

Develop an understanding with the requirements providers on the meaning of the requirements. SP 1.1

Obtain commitment to the requirements from the project participants. SP 1.2

Manage changes to the requirements as they evolve during the project. SP 1.3

Maintain bi-directional traceability among the requirements and the project plans and work products. SP 1.4

Identify inconsistencies between the project plans and work products and the requirements. SP 1.5

The process is institutionalized as a managed process. GG 2

Commitment to Perform

Establish and maintain an organizational policy for planning and performing the requirements management process. GP 2.1 (CO 1)

Ability to Perform

Establish and maintain the requirements and objectives, and plans for performing the requirements management process. GP 2.2 (AB 1)

Provide adequate resources for performing the requirements management process, developing the work products and providing the services of the process. GP 2.3 (AB 2)

Assign responsibility and authority for performing the process, developing the work products, and providing the services of the requirements management process. GP 2.4 (AB 3)

Train the people performing or supporting the requirements management process as needed. GP 2.5 (AB 4)

Directing Implementation

Place designated work products of the requirements management process under appropriate levels of configuration management. GP 2.6 (DI 1)

Identify and involve the relevant stakeholders of the requirements management process as planned. GP 2.7 (DI 2)

Monitor and control the requirements management process against the plan and take appropriate corrective action. GP 2.8 (DI 3)

Verifying Implementation

Objectively evaluate adherence of the requirements management process and the work products and services of the process to the applicable requirements, objectives, and standards, and address noncompliance. GP 2.9 (VE 1)

Review the activities, status, and results of the requirements management process with higher-level management and resolve issues. GP 2.10 (VE 2)

PROJECT PLANNING

Establish and maintain plans that define project activities.

Estimates of project planning parameters are established and maintained. SG 1

Establish and maintain a top-level work breakdown structure (WBS) to estimate of the scope of the project. SP 1.1

Establish and document estimates of the attributes of the work products and tasks. SP 1.2

Define the project life-cycle phases upon which to scope the planning effort. SP 1.3

Estimate the project effort and cost for the attributes of the work products and tasks based on estimation rationale. SP 1.4

A project plan is established and maintained as the basis for managing the project. SG 2

Establish and maintain the project's budget and schedule. SP 2.1

Identify and analyze project risks. SP 2.2

Plan for the management of project data. SP 2.3

Plan for necessary resources to perform the project. SP 2.4

Plan for knowledge and skills needed to perform the project. SP 2.5

Plan the involvement with identified stakeholders. SP 2.6

Establish and maintain the overall project plan content. SP 2.7

Commitments to the project plan are established and maintained. SG 3

Review subordinate plans to understand project commitments. SP 3.1

Reconcile the project plan to reflect available and projected resources. SP 3.2

Obtain commitment from relevant stakeholders responsible for performing and supporting plan execution. SP 3.3

The process is institutionalized as a managed process. GG 2

Commitment to Perform

Establish and maintain an organizational policy for planning and performing the project planning process. GP 2.1 (CO 1)

Ability to Perform

Establish and maintain the requirements and objectives, and plans for performing the project planning process. GP 2.2 (AB 1)

Provide adequate resources for performing the project planning process, developing the work products and providing the services of the process. GP 2.3 (AB 2)

Assign responsibility and authority for performing the process, developing the work products, and providing the services of the project planning process. GP 2.4 (AB 3)

Train the people performing or supporting the project planning process as needed. GP 2.5 (AB 4)

Directing Implementation

Place designated work products of the project planning process under appropriate levels of configuration management. GP 2.6 (DI 1)

Identify and involve the relevant stakeholders of the project planning process as planned. GP 2.7 (DI 2)

Monitor and control the project planning process against the plan and take appropriate corrective action. GP 2.8 (DI 3)

Verifying Implementation

Objectively evaluate adherence of the project planning process and the work products and services of the process to the applicable requirements, objectives, and standards, and address noncompliance. GP 2.9 (VE 1)

Review the activities, status, and results of the project planning process with higher-level management and resolve issues. GP 2.10 (VE 2)

PROJECT MONITORING AND CONTROL

Provide understanding into the project's progress so that appropriate corrective actions can be taken when the project's performance deviates significantly from the plan.

Actual performance and progress of the project is monitored against the project plan. SG 1

Monitor the actual values of the project planning parameters against the project plan. SP 1.1

Monitor commitments against those identified in the project plan. SP 1.2

Monitor risks against those identified in the project plan. SP 1.3

Monitor the management of project data. SP 1.4

Monitor stakeholder involvement against the project plan. SP 1.5

Periodically review the project's progress, performance, and issues. SP 1.6

Review the accomplishments and results of the project at selected project milestones. SP 1.7

Corrective actions are managed to closure when the project's performance or results deviate significantly from the plan. SG 2

Collect and analyze the issues and determine the corrective actions necessary to address the issues. SP 2.1

Take corrective action on identified issues. SP 2.2

Manage corrective actions to closure. SP 2.3

The process is institutionalized as a managed process. GG 2

Commitment to Perform

Establish and maintain an organizational policy for planning and performing the requirements management process. GP 2.1 (CO 1)

Ability to Perform

Establish and maintain the requirements and objectives, and plans for performing the requirements management process. GP 2.2 (AB 1)

Provide adequate resources for performing the requirements management process, developing the work products and providing the services of the process. GP 2.3 (AB 2)

Assign responsibility and authority for performing the process, developing the work products, and providing the services of the requirements management process. GP 2.4 (AB 3)

Train the people performing or supporting the requirements management process as needed. GP 2.5 (AB 4)

Directing Implementation

Place designated work products of the requirements management process under appropriate levels of configuration management. GP 2.6 (DI 1)

Identify and involve the relevant stakeholders of the requirements management process as planned. GP 2.7 (DI 2)

Monitor and control the requirements management process against the plan and take appropriate corrective action. GP 2.8 (DI 3)

Verifying Implementation

Objectively evaluate adherence of the requirements management process and the work products and services of the process to the applicable requirements, objectives, and standards, and address noncompliance. GP 2.9 (VE 1)

Review the activities, status, and results of the requirements management process with higher-level management and resolve issues. GP 2.10 (VE 2)

SUPPLIER AGREEMENT MANAGEMENT

Manage the acquisition of products and services from suppliers external to the project for which there exists a formal agreement.

Agreements with the suppliers are established and maintained. SG 1

Analyze the project's needs and requirements that will be fulfilled by sources outside the project to determine how the needs and requirements will be satisfied. SP 1.1

Select suppliers based on an evaluation of their ability to meet the specified requirements and established criteria. SP 1.2

Establish and maintain formal agreements with the supplier. SP 1.3

Agreements with the suppliers are satisfied by both the project and the supplier. SG 2

Acquire COTS products to satisfy the specified requirements that are covered under a supplier agreement. SP 2.1

Perform activities with the supplier as specified in the supplier agreement. SP 2.2

Ensure that the supplier agreement is satisfied before accepting the acquired product. SP 2.3

Transition the acquired products from the supplier to the project. SP 2.4

The process is institutionalized as a managed process. GG 2

Commitment to Perform

Establish and maintain an organizational policy for planning and performing the requirements management process. GP 2.1 (CO 1)

Ability to Perform

Establish and maintain the requirements and objectives, and plans for performing the requirements management process. GP 2.2 (AB 1)

Provide adequate resources for performing the requirements management process, developing the work products and providing the services of the process. GP 2.3 (AB 2)

Assign responsibility and authority for performing the process, developing the work products, and providing the services of the requirements management process. GP 2.4 (AB 3)

Train the people performing or supporting the requirements management process as needed. GP 2.5 (AB 4)

Directing Implementation

Place designated work products of the requirements management process under appropriate levels of configuration management. GP 2.6 (DI 1)

Identify and involve the relevant stakeholders of the requirements management process as planned. GP 2.7 (DI 2)

Monitor and control the requirements management process against the plan and take appropriate corrective action. GP 2.8 (DI 3)

Verifying Implementation

Objectively evaluate adherence of the requirements management process and the work products and services of the process to the applicable requirements, objectives, and standards, and address noncompliance. GP 2.9 (VE 1)

Review the activities, status, and results of the requirements management process with higher-level management and resolve issues. GP 2.10 (VE 2)

MEASUREMENT AND ANALYSIS

Develop and sustain a measurement capability that is used to support management information needs.

Measurement objectives and practices are aligned with identified information needs and objectives. SG 1

Establish and maintain measurement objectives that are derived from identified information needs and objectives. SP 1.1

Specify measures to address the measurement objectives. SP 1.2

Specify how measurement data will be obtained and stored. SP 1.3

Specify how measurement data will be analyzed and reported. SP 1.4

Measurement results that address identified information needs and objectives are provided. SG 2

Obtain specified measurement data. SP 2.1

Analyze and interpret measurement data. SP 2.2

Manage and store measurement data, measurement specifications, and analysis results. SP 2.3

Report results of measurement and analysis activities to all affected stakeholders. SP 2.4

The process is institutionalized as a managed process. GG 2

Commitment to Perform

Establish and maintain an organizational policy for planning and performing the requirements management process. GP 2.1 (CO 1)

Ability to Perform

Establish and maintain the requirements and objectives, and plans for performing the requirements management process. GP 2.2 (AB 1)

Provide adequate resources for performing the requirements management process, developing the work products and providing the services of the process. GP 2.3 (AB 2)

Assign responsibility and authority for performing the process, developing the work products, and providing the services of the requirements management process. GP 2.4 (AB 3)

Train the people performing or supporting the requirements management process as needed. GP 2.5 (AB 4)

Directing Implementation

Place designated work products of the requirements management process under appropriate levels of configuration management. GP 2.6 (DI 1)

Identify and involve the relevant stakeholders of the requirements management process as planned. GP 2.7 (DI 2)

Monitor and control the requirements management process against the plan and take appropriate corrective action. GP 2.8 (DI 3)

Verifying Implementation

Objectively evaluate adherence of the requirements management process and the work products and services of the process to the applicable requirements, objectives, and standards, and address noncompliance. GP 2.9 (VE 1)

Review the activities, status, and results of the requirements management process with higher-level management and resolve issues. GP 2.10 (VE 2)

PROCESS AND PRODUCT QUALITY ASSURANCE

Provide staff and management with objective insight into the processes and associated work products.

Adherence of the performed process and associated work products and services to applicable process descriptions, standards and procedures is objectively evaluated. SG 1

Objectively evaluate the designated performed processes against the applicable process descriptions, standards and procedures. SP 1.1

Objectively evaluate the designated work products and services against the applicable process descriptions, standards, and procedures. SP 1.2

Noncompliance issues are objectively tracked and communicated, and resolution is ensured. SG 2

Communicate quality issues and ensure resolution of noncompliance issues with the staff and managers. SP 2.1

Establish and maintain records of the quality assurance activities. SP 2.2

The process is institutionalized as a managed process. GG 2

Commitment to Perform

Establish and maintain an organizational policy for planning and performing the requirements management process. GP 2.1 (CO 1)

Ability to Perform

Establish and maintain the requirements and objectives, and plans for performing the requirements management process. GP 2.2 (AB 1)

Provide adequate resources for performing the requirements management process, developing the work products and providing the services of the process. GP 2.3 (AB 2)

Assign responsibility and authority for performing the process, developing the work products, and providing the services of the requirements management process. GP 2.4 (AB 3)

Train the people performing or supporting the requirements management process as needed. GP 2.5 (AB 4)

Directing Implementation

Place designated work products of the requirements management process under appropriate levels of configuration management. GP 2.6 (DI 1)

Identify and involve the relevant stakeholders of the requirements management process as planned. GP 2.7 (DI 2)

Monitor and control the requirements management process against the plan and take appropriate corrective action. GP 2.8 (DI 3)

Verifying Implementation

Objectively evaluate adherence of the requirements management process and the work products and services of the process to the applicable requirements, objectives, and standards, and address noncompliance. GP 2.9 (VE 1)

Review the activities, status, and results of the requirements management process with higher-level management and resolve issues. GP 2.10 (VE 2)

CONFIGURATION MANAGEMENT

Establish and maintain the integrity of work products using configuration identification, configuration control, configuration status accounting, and configuration audits.

Baselines of identified work products are established and maintained. SG 1

Identify the configuration items, components, and related work products that will be placed under configuration management. SP 1.1

Establish and maintain a configuration management and change management system for controlling work products. SP 1.2

Create or release baselines for internal use and for delivery to the customer. SP 1.3

Changes to the work products under configuration management are tracked and controlled. SG 2

Track change requests for the configuration items. SP 2.1

Control changes to the content of configuration items. SP 2.2

Integrity of baselines is established and maintained. SG 3

Establish and maintain records describing configuration items. SP 3.1

Perform configuration audits to maintain integrity of the configuration baselines. SP 3.2

The process is institutionalized as a managed process. GG 2

Commitment to Perform

Establish and maintain an organizational policy for planning and performing the requirements management process. GP 2.1 (CO 1)

Ability to Perform

Establish and maintain the requirements and objectives, and plans for performing the requirements management process. GP 2.2 (AB 1)

Provide adequate resources for performing the requirements management process, developing the work products and providing the services of the process. GP 2.3 (AB 2)

Assign responsibility and authority for performing the process, developing the work products, and providing the services of the requirements management process. GP 2.4 (AB 3)

Train the people performing or supporting the requirements management process as needed. GP 2.5 (AB 4)

Directing Implementation

Place designated work products of the requirements management process under appropriate levels of configuration management. GP 2.6 (DI 1)

Identify and involve the relevant stakeholders of the requirements management process as planned. GP 2.7 (DI 2)

Monitor and control the requirements management process against the plan and take appropriate corrective action. GP 2.8 (DI 3)

Verifying Implementation

Objectively evaluate adherence of the requirements management process and the work products and services of the process to the applicable requirements, objectives, and standards, and address noncompliance. GP 2.9 (VE 1)

Review the activities, status, and results of the requirements management process with higher-level management and resolve issues. GP 2.10 (VE 2)

Maturity Level: 3

REQUIREMENTS DEVELOPMENT

Produce and analyze customer, product, and product component requirements.

Stakeholder needs, expectations, constraints, and interfaces are collected and translated into customer requirements. SG 1

Elicit stakeholder needs, expectations, constraints, and interfaces for all phases of the product's life cycle. SP 1.1

Transform stakeholder needs, expectations, constraints, and interfaces into customer requirements. SP 1.2

Customer requirements are refined and elaborated to develop product and product component requirements for the product life cycle. SG 2

Establish and maintain, from the customer requirements, product and product component requirements essential to product and product component effectiveness and affordability. SP 2.1

Allocate the requirements for each product component. SP 2.2

Identify interface requirements. SP 2.3

The requirements are analyzed and validated, and a definition of required functionality is developed. SG 3

Establish and maintain operational concepts and scenarios. SP 3.1

Establish and maintain a definition of required functionality. SP 3.2

Analyze derived requirements to ensure that they are necessary and sufficient. SP 3.3

Analyze requirements with the purpose of reducing the life-cycle cost, schedule and risk of product development. SP 3.4

Validate requirements to ensure the resulting product will perform as intended in the user's environment using multiple techniques as appropriate. SP 3.5

The process is institutionalized as a defined process. GG 3

Commitment to Perform

Establish and maintain an organizational policy for planning and performing the requirements development process. GP 2.1 (CO 1)

Ability to Perform

Establish and maintain the description of a defined requirements development process. GP 3.1 (AB 1)

Establish and maintain the requirements and objectives, and plans for performing the requirements development process. GP 2.2 (AB 2)

Provide adequate resources for performing the requirements development process, developing the work products and providing the services of the process. GP 2.3 (AB 3)

Assign responsibility and authority for performing the process, developing the work products, and providing the services of the requirements development process. GP 2.4 (AB 4)

Train the people performing or supporting the requirements development process as needed. GP 2.5 (AB 5)

Directing Implementation

Place designated work products of the requirements development process under appropriate levels of configuration management. GP 2.6 (DI 1)

Identify and involve the relevant stakeholders of the requirements development process as planned. GP 2.7 (DI 2)

Monitor and control the requirements development process against the plan and take appropriate corrective action. GP 2.8 (DI 3)

Collect work products, measures, measurement results, and improvement information derived from planning and performing the requirements development process to support the future use and improvement of the organization's processes and process assets. GP 3.2 (DI 4)

Verifying Implementation

Objectively evaluate adherence of the requirements development process and the work products and services of the process to the applicable requirements, objectives, and standards, and address noncompliance. GP 2.9 (VE 1)

Review the activities, status, and results of the requirements development process with higher-level management and resolve issues. GP 2.10 (VE 2)

TECHNICAL SOLUTION

Develop, design, and implement solutions to requirements. Solutions, designs and implementations encompass products, product components, and product related processes either singly or in combinations as appropriate.

Product or product component solutions, including applicable product related processes, are selected from alternative solutions. SG 1

Develop detailed alternative solutions and selection criteria. SP 1.1

Evolve the operational concept, scenarios, and environments to describe the conditions, operating modes, and operating states specific to each product component. SP 1.2

Select the product component solutions that best satisfy the criteria established. SP 1.3

Product or product component designs are developed. SG 2

Establish and use effective design methods. SP 2.1

Establish and maintain a complete technical data package. SP 2.2

Design product component interfaces in terms of established and maintained criteria. SP 2.3

Evaluate whether the product components should be developed, purchased, or reused based on established criteria. SP 2.4

Product components, and associated support documentation, are implemented from their designs. SG 3

Implement the designs of the product components. SP 3.1

Establish and maintain the end-use documentation. SP 3.2

The process is institutionalized as a defined process. GG 3

Commitment to Perform

Establish and maintain an organizational policy for planning and performing the requirements development process. GP 2.1 (CO 1)

Ability to Perform

Establish and maintain the description of a defined requirements development process. GP 3.1 (AB 1)

Establish and maintain the requirements and objectives, and plans for performing the requirements development process. GP 2.2 (AB 2)

Provide adequate resources for performing the requirements development process, developing the work products and providing the services of the process. GP 2.3 (AB 3)

Assign responsibility and authority for performing the process, developing the work products, and providing the services of the requirements development process. GP 2.4 (AB 4)

Train the people performing or supporting the requirements development process as needed. GP 2.5 (AB 5)

Directing Implementation

Place designated work products of the requirements development process under appropriate levels of configuration management. GP 2.6 (DI 1)

Identify and involve the relevant stakeholders of the requirements development process as planned. GP 2.7 (DI 2)

Monitor and control the requirements development process against the plan and take appropriate corrective action. GP 2.8 (DI 3)

Collect work products, measures, measurement results, and improvement information derived from planning and performing the requirements development process to support the future use and improvement of the organization's processes and process assets. GP 3.2 (DI 4)

Verifying Implementation

Objectively evaluate adherence of the requirements development process and the work products and services of the process to the applicable requirements, objectives, and standards, and address noncompliance. GP 2.9 (VE 1)

Review the activities, status, and results of the requirements development process with higher-level management and resolve issues. GP 2.10 (VE 2)

PRODUCT INTEGRATION

Assemble the product from the product components, ensure that the product, as integrated, functions properly, and deliver the product.

The strategy for conducting product integration is established and maintained. SG 1

Establish and maintain a strategy for integration of the product components. SP 1.1

Establish and maintain the environment needed to support the integration of the product components. SP 1.2

Define detailed procedures and criteria for integration of the product components. SP 1.3

The product component interfaces, both internal and external, are compatible. SG 2

Review interface descriptions for coverage and completeness. SP 2.1

Manage internal and external interface definitions, designs, and changes for products and product components. SP 2.2

Verified product components are assembled and the integrated, verified, and validated product is delivered. SG 3

Confirm, prior to assembly, that each product component required to assemble the product has been properly identified, functions according to its description, and that the product component interfaces comply with the interface descriptions. SP 3.1

Assemble product components according to the product integration strategy. SP 3.2

Checkout an assembly of product components. SP 3.3

Package the assembled product or product component and deliver it to the appropriate customer. SP 3.4

The process is institutionalized as a defined process. GG 3

Commitment to Perform

Establish and maintain an organizational policy for planning and performing the requirements development process. GP 2.1 (CO 1)

Ability to Perform

Establish and maintain the description of a defined requirements development process. GP 3.1 (AB 1)

Establish and maintain the requirements and objectives, and plans for performing the requirements development process. GP 2.2 (AB 2)

Provide adequate resources for performing the requirements development process, developing the work products and providing the services of the process. GP 2.3 (AB 3)

Assign responsibility and authority for performing the process, developing the work products, and providing the services of the requirements development process. GP 2.4 (AB 4)

Train the people performing or supporting the requirements development process as needed. GP 2.5 (AB 5)

Directing Implementation

Place designated work products of the requirements development process under appropriate levels of configuration management. GP 2.6 (DI 1)

Identify and involve the relevant stakeholders of the requirements development process as planned. GP 2.7 (DI 2)

Monitor and control the requirements development process against the plan and take appropriate corrective action. GP 2.8 (DI 3)

Collect work products, measures, measurement results, and improvement information derived from planning and performing the requirements development process to support the future use and improvement of the organization's processes and process assets. GP 3.2 (DI 4)

Verifying Implementation

Objectively evaluate adherence of the requirements development process and the work products and services of the process to the applicable requirements, objectives, and standards, and address noncompliance. GP 2.9 (VE 1)

Review the activities, status, and results of the requirements development process with higher-level management and resolve issues. GP 2.10 (VE 2)

VERIFICATION

Assure that selected work products meet their specified requirements.

Preparation for verification is conducted. SG 1

Establish and maintain a verification strategy for selected work products. SP 1.1

Establish and maintain the environment needed to support verification. SP 1.2

Establish and maintain detailed verification plans for selected work products. SP 1.3

Peer reviews are performed on selected work products. SG 2

Prepare for peer reviews of selected work products. SP 2.1

Conduct peer reviews on selected work products and identify issues resulting from the peer review. SP 2.2

Analyze data about preparation, conduct, and results of the peer reviews. SP 2.3

Selected work products are verified against their specified requirements. SG 3

Perform verification according to the verification strategy. SP 3.1

Analyze the results of all verification activities and identify corrective action. SP 3.2

Perform re-verification of corrected work products and ensure that work products have not been negatively impacted. SP 3.3

The process is institutionalized as a defined process. GG 3

Commitment to Perform

Establish and maintain an organizational policy for planning and performing the requirements development process. GP 2.1 (CO 1)

Ability to Perform

Establish and maintain the description of a defined requirements development process. GP 3.1 (AB 1)

Establish and maintain the requirements and objectives, and plans for performing the requirements development process. GP 2.2 (AB 2)

Provide adequate resources for performing the requirements development process, developing the work products and providing the services of the process. GP 2.3 (AB 3)

Assign responsibility and authority for performing the process, developing the work products, and providing the services of the requirements development process. GP 2.4 (AB 4)

Train the people performing or supporting the requirements development process as needed. GP 2.5 (AB 5)

Directing Implementation

Place designated work products of the requirements development process under appropriate levels of configuration management. GP 2.6 (DI 1)

Identify and involve the relevant stakeholders of the requirements development process as planned. GP 2.7 (DI 2)

Monitor and control the requirements development process against the plan and take appropriate corrective action. GP 2.8 (DI 3)

Collect work products, measures, measurement results, and improvement information derived from planning and performing the requirements development process to support the future use and improvement of the organization's processes and process assets. GP 3.2 (DI 4)

Verifying Implementation

Objectively evaluate adherence of the requirements development process and the work products and services of the process to the applicable requirements, objectives, and standards, and address noncompliance. GP 2.9 (VE 1)

Review the activities, status, and results of the requirements development process with higher-level management and resolve issues. GP 2.10 (VE 2)

VALIDATION

Demonstrate that a product or product component fulfills its intended use when placed in its intended environment.

Preparation for validation is conducted. SG 1

Establish and maintain a validation strategy. SP 1.1

Establish and maintain the environment needed to support validation. SP 1.2

Define detailed procedures and criteria for validation. SP 1.3

The product or product components are validated to ensure that they are suitable for use in their intended operating environment. SG 2

Perform validation according to the validation strategy. SP 2.1

Capture and analyze the results of the validation activities and identify issues. SP 2.2

The process is institutionalized as a defined process. GG 3

Commitment to Perform

Establish and maintain an organizational policy for planning and performing the requirements development process. GP 2.1 (CO 1)

Ability to Perform

Establish and maintain the description of a defined requirements development process. GP 3.1 (AB 1)

Establish and maintain the requirements and objectives, and plans for performing the requirements development process. GP 2.2 (AB 2)

Provide adequate resources for performing the requirements development process, developing the work products and providing the services of the process. GP 2.3 (AB 3)

Assign responsibility and authority for performing the process, developing the work products, and providing the services of the requirements development process. GP 2.4 (AB 4)

Train the people performing or supporting the requirements development process as needed. GP 2.5 (AB 5)

Directing Implementation

Place designated work products of the requirements development process under appropriate levels of configuration management. GP 2.6 (DI 1)

Identify and involve the relevant stakeholders of the requirements development process as planned. GP 2.7 (DI 2)

Monitor and control the requirements development process against the plan and take appropriate corrective action. GP 2.8 (DI 3)

Collect work products, measures, measurement results, and improvement information derived from planning and performing the requirements development process to support the future use and improvement of the organization's processes and process assets. GP 3.2 (DI 4)

Verifying Implementation

Objectively evaluate adherence of the requirements development process and the work products and services of the process to the applicable requirements, objectives, and standards, and address noncompliance. GP 2.9 (VE 1)

Review the activities, status, and results of the requirements development process with higher-level management and resolve issues. GP 2.10 (VE 2)

ORGANIZATIONAL PROCESS FOCUS

Establish and maintain an understanding of the organization's processes and process assets, and to identify, plan, and implement the organization's process improvement activities.

Strengths, weaknesses, and improvement opportunities for the organization's processes are identified periodically and as needed. SG 1

Establish and maintain the description of the process needs and objectives for the organization. SP 1.1

Assess the processes of the organization periodically and as needed to maintain an understanding of their strengths and weaknesses. SP 1.2

Identify improvements to the organization's processes and related process assets. SP 1.3

Improvements are planned and implemented, process assets are deployed, and process-related experiences are incorporated into the organization's process assets. SG 2

Establish and maintain process action plans to address improvements to the organization's processes and related process assets. SP 2.1

Implement process action plans across the organization. SP 2.2

Deploy the process and related process assets across the organization. SP 2.3

Incorporate process-related work products, measures, and improvement information derived from planning and performing the process into the organization's process assets. SP 2.4

The process is institutionalized as a defined process. GG 3

Commitment to Perform

Establish and maintain an organizational policy for planning and performing the requirements development process. GP 2.1 (CO 1)

Ability to Perform

Establish and maintain the description of a defined requirements development process. GP 3.1 (AB 1)

Establish and maintain the requirements and objectives, and plans for performing the requirements development process. GP 2.2 (AB 2)

Provide adequate resources for performing the requirements development process, developing the work products and providing the services of the process. GP 2.3 (AB 3)

Assign responsibility and authority for performing the process, developing the work products, and providing the services of the requirements development process. GP 2.4 (AB 4)

Train the people performing or supporting the requirements development process as needed. GP 2.5 (AB 5)

Directing Implementation

Place designated work products of the requirements development process under appropriate levels of configuration management. GP 2.6 (DI 1)

Identify and involve the relevant stakeholders of the requirements development process as planned. GP 2.7 (DI 2)

Monitor and control the requirements development process against the plan and take appropriate corrective action. GP 2.8 (DI 3)

Collect work products, measures, measurement results, and improvement information derived from planning and performing the requirements development process to support the future use and improvement of the organization's processes and process assets. GP 3.2 (DI 4)

Verifying Implementation

Objectively evaluate adherence of the requirements development process and the work products and services of the process to the applicable requirements, objectives, and standards, and address noncompliance. GP 2.9 (VE 1)

Review the activities, status, and results of the requirements development process with higher-level management and resolve issues. GP 2.10 (VE 2)

ORGANIZATIONAL PROCESS DEFINITION

Establish and maintain a usable set of organizational process assets.

A set of organizational process assets is available. SG 1

Establish and maintain the organization's set of standard processes. SP 1.1

Establish and maintain descriptions of the life-cycle process models approved for use in the organization. SP 1.2

Establish and maintain the tailoring criteria and guidelines for the organization's set of standard processes. SP 1.3

Process assets that support the use of the organization's set of standard processes are available. SG 2

Establish and maintain an organizational measurement repository. SP 2.1

Establish and maintain the organization's library of process-related assets. SP 2.2

The process is institutionalized as a defined process. GG 3

Commitment to Perform

Establish and maintain an organizational policy for planning and performing the requirements development process. GP 2.1 (CO 1)

Ability to Perform

Establish and maintain the description of a defined requirements development process. GP 3.1 (AB 1)

Establish and maintain the requirements and objectives, and plans for performing the requirements development process. GP 2.2 (AB 2)

Provide adequate resources for performing the requirements development process, developing the work products and providing the services of the process. GP 2.3 (AB 3)

Assign responsibility and authority for performing the process, developing the work products, and providing the services of the requirements development process. GP 2.4 (AB 4)

Train the people performing or supporting the requirements development process as needed. GP 2.5 (AB 5)

Directing Implementation

Place designated work products of the requirements development process under appropriate levels of configuration management. GP 2.6 (DI 1)

Identify and involve the relevant stakeholders of the requirements development process as planned. GP 2.7 (DI 2)

Monitor and control the requirements development process against the plan and take appropriate corrective action. GP 2.8 (DI 3)

Collect work products, measures, measurement results, and improvement information derived from planning and performing the requirements development process to support the future use and improvement of the organization's processes and process assets. GP 3.2 (DI 4)

Verifying Implementation

Objectively evaluate adherence of the requirements development process and the work products and services of the process to the applicable requirements, objectives, and standards, and address noncompliance. GP 2.9 (VE 1)

Review the activities, status, and results of the requirements development process with higher-level management and resolve issues. GP 2.10 (VE 2)

ORGANIZATIONAL TRAINING

Develop the skills and knowledge of people so they can perform their roles effectively and efficiently.

Training to support the organization's management and technical roles is identified and made available. SG 1

Establish and maintain the strategic training needs of the organization. SP 1.1

Determine which training needs are the responsibility of the organization and which will be left to the individual project or support group. SP 1.2

Establish and maintain an organizational training tactical plan. SP 1.3

Establish and maintain training capability to address organizational training needs. SP 1.4

Training necessary for individuals to perform their roles effectively is provided. SG 2

Deliver the training following an organizational training plan. SP 2.1

Establish and maintain records of the organizational training. SP 2.2

Assess the effectiveness of the organization's training program. SP 2.3

The process is institutionalized as a defined process. GG 3

Commitment to Perform

Establish and maintain an organizational policy for planning and performing the requirements development process. GP 2.1 (CO 1)

Ability to Perform

Establish and maintain the description of a defined requirements development process. GP 3.1 (AB 1)

Establish and maintain the requirements and objectives, and plans for performing the requirements development process. GP 2.2 (AB 2)

Provide adequate resources for performing the requirements development process, developing the work products and providing the services of the process. GP 2.3 (AB 3)

Assign responsibility and authority for performing the process, developing the work products, and providing the services of the requirements development process. GP 2.4 (AB 4)

Train the people performing or supporting the requirements development process as needed. GP 2.5 (AB 5)

Directing Implementation

Place designated work products of the requirements development process under appropriate levels of configuration management. GP 2.6 (DI 1)

Identify and involve the relevant stakeholders of the requirements development process as planned. GP 2.7 (DI 2)

Monitor and control the requirements development process against the plan and take appropriate corrective action. GP 2.8 (DI 3)

Collect work products, measures, measurement results, and improvement information derived from planning and performing the requirements development process to support the future use and improvement of the organization's processes and process assets. GP 3.2 (DI 4)

Verifying Implementation

Objectively evaluate adherence of the requirements development process and the work products and services of the process to the applicable requirements, objectives, and standards, and address noncompliance. GP 2.9 (VE 1)

Review the activities, status, and results of the requirements development process with higher-level management and resolve issues. GP 2.10 (VE 2)

INTEGRATED PROJECT MANAGEMENT (IPPD)

Establish and manage the project and the involvement of the relevant stakeholders according to an integrated and defined process that is tailored from the organization's set of standard processes. It also covers the establishment of a shared vision for the project and a team structure for integrated teams that will carry out the objectives of the project.

The project is conducted using a defined process that is tailored from the organization's set of standard processes. SG 1

Establish and maintain the project's defined process. SP 1.1

Use the organization's process assets and measurement repository for estimating and planning the project's activities. SP 1.2

Integrate the project plan and the subordinate plans to describe the project's defined process. SP 1.3

Manage the project using the project plan, the subordinate plans, and the project's defined process. SP 1.4

Contribute work products, measures, and documented experiences to the organization's process assets. SP 1.5

Coordination and collaboration of the project with relevant stakeholders is conducted. SG 2

Manage the involvement of the relevant stakeholders in the project. SP 2.1

Participate with relevant stakeholders to identify, negotiate, and track critical dependencies. SP 2.2

Resolve issues with relevant stakeholders. SP 2.3

The project is conducted using the project's shared vision. SG 3

Identify expectations, constraints, interfaces, and operational conditions applicable to the project's shared vision. SP 3.1

Establish and maintain a shared vision for the project. SP 3.2

The integrated teams needed to execute the project are identified, defined, structured, and tasked. SG 4

Determine the integrated team structure that will best meet the project objectives and constraints. SP 4.1

Develop a preliminary distribution of requirements, responsibilities, authorities, tasks, and interfaces to teams in the selected integrated team structure. SP 4.2

Establish and maintain teams in the integrated team structure. SP 4.3

The process is institutionalized as a defined process. GG 3

Commitment to Perform

Establish and maintain an organizational policy for planning and performing the requirements development process. GP 2.1 (CO 1)

Ability to Perform

Establish and maintain the description of a defined requirements development process. GP 3.1 (AB 1)

Establish and maintain the requirements and objectives, and plans for performing the requirements development process. GP 2.2 (AB 2)

Provide adequate resources for performing the requirements development process, developing the work products and providing the services of the process. GP 2.3 (AB 3)

Assign responsibility and authority for performing the process, developing the work products, and providing the services of the requirements development process. GP 2.4 (AB 4)

Train the people performing or supporting the requirements development process as needed. GP 2.5 (AB 5)

Directing Implementation

Place designated work products of the requirements development process under appropriate levels of configuration management. GP 2.6 (DI 1)

Identify and involve the relevant stakeholders of the requirements development process as planned. GP 2.7 (DI 2)

Monitor and control the requirements development process against the plan and take appropriate corrective action. GP 2.8 (DI 3)

Collect work products, measures, measurement results, and improvement information derived from planning and performing the requirements development process to support the future use and improvement of the organization's processes and process assets. GP 3.2 (DI 4)

Verifying Implementation

Objectively evaluate adherence of the requirements development process and the work products and services of the process to the applicable requirements, objectives, and standards, and address noncompliance. GP 2.9 (VE 1)

Review the activities, status, and results of the requirements development process with higher-level management and resolve issues. GP 2.10 (VE 2)

RISK MANAGEMENT

Identify potential problems before they occur, so that risk-handling activities may be planned and invoked as needed across the life cycle to mitigate adverse impacts on achieving objectives.

Preparation for risk management is conducted. SG 1

Determine risk sources and categories. SP 1.1

Define the parameters used to analyze and classify risks, and the parameters used to control the risk management effort. SP 1.2

Establish and maintain the strategy and methods to be used for risk management. SP 1.3

Risks are identified and analyzed to determine their relative importance. SG 2

Identify and document the risks. SP 2.1

Evaluate and classify each identified risk using the defined risk categories and parameters, and determine its relative priority. SP 2.2

Risks are handled and mitigated, where appropriate, to reduce adverse impacts on achieving objectives. SG 3

Develop a risk mitigation plan for the most important risks to the project, as defined by the risk management strategy. SP 3.1

Monitor the status of each risk periodically and implement the risk mitigation plan as appropriate. SP 3.2

The process is institutionalized as a defined process. GG 3

Commitment to Perform

Establish and maintain an organizational policy for planning and performing the requirements development process. GP 2.1 (CO 1)

Ability to Perform

Establish and maintain the description of a defined requirements development process. GP 3.1 (AB 1)

Establish and maintain the requirements and objectives, and plans for performing the requirements development process. GP 2.2 (AB 2)

Provide adequate resources for performing the requirements development process, developing the work products and providing the services of the process. GP 2.3 (AB 3)

Assign responsibility and authority for performing the process, developing the work products, and providing the services of the requirements development process. GP 2.4 (AB 4)

Train the people performing or supporting the requirements development process as needed. GP 2.5 (AB 5)

Directing Implementation

Place designated work products of the requirements development process under appropriate levels of configuration management. GP 2.6 (DI 1)

Identify and involve the relevant stakeholders of the requirements development process as planned. GP 2.7 (DI 2)

Monitor and control the requirements development process against the plan and take appropriate corrective action. GP 2.8 (DI 3)

Collect work products, measures, measurement results, and improvement information derived from planning and performing the requirements development process to support the future use and improvement of the organization's processes and process assets. GP 3.2 (DI 4)

Verifying Implementation

Objectively evaluate adherence of the requirements development process and the work products and services of the process to the applicable requirements, objectives, and standards, and address noncompliance. GP 2.9 (VE 1)

Review the activities, status, and results of the requirements development process with higher-level management and resolve issues. GP 2.10 (VE 2)

INTEGRATED TEAMING

Form and sustain an integrated team for the development of work products.

Team composition that provides the knowledge and skills required to deliver the team's product is established and maintained. SG 1

Identify and define the team's specific internal tasks to generate the team's expected output. SP 1.1

Identify the knowledge, skills, and functional expertise needed to perform team tasks. SP 1.2

Assign the appropriate personnel to be team members based on required knowledge and skills. SP 1.3

Operation of the integrated team is governed according to established principles. SG 2

Establish and maintain a shared vision for the integrated team that is aligned with any overarching or higher-level vision. SP 2.1

Establish and maintain a team charter based on the integrated team's shared vision and overall team objectives. SP 2.2

Clearly define and maintain each team member's roles and responsibilities. SP 2.3

Establish and maintain integrated team operating procedures. SP 2.4

Establish and maintain collaboration among interfacing teams. SP 2.5

The process is institutionalized as a defined process. GG 3

Commitment to Perform

Establish and maintain an organizational policy for planning and performing the requirements development process. GP 2.1 (CO 1)

Ability to Perform

Establish and maintain the description of a defined requirements development process. GP 3.1 (AB 1)

Establish and maintain the requirements and objectives, and plans for performing the requirements development process. GP 2.2 (AB 2)

Provide adequate resources for performing the requirements development process, developing the work products and providing the services of the process. GP 2.3 (AB 3)

Assign responsibility and authority for performing the process, developing the work products, and providing the services of the requirements development process. GP 2.4 (AB 4)

Train the people performing or supporting the requirements development process as needed. GP 2.5 (AB 5)

Directing Implementation

Place designated work products of the requirements development process under appropriate levels of configuration management. GP 2.6 (DI 1)

Identify and involve the relevant stakeholders of the requirements development process as planned. GP 2.7 (DI 2)

Monitor and control the requirements development process against the plan and take appropriate corrective action. GP 2.8 (DI 3)

Collect work products, measures, measurement results, and improvement information derived from planning and performing the requirements development process to support the future use and improvement of the organization's processes and process assets. GP 3.2 (DI 4)

Verifying Implementation

Objectively evaluate adherence of the requirements development process and the work products and services of the process to the applicable requirements, objectives, and standards, and address noncompliance. GP 2.9 (VE 1)

Review the activities, status, and results of the requirements development process with higher-level management and resolve issues. GP 2.10 (VE 2)

DECISION ANALYSIS AND RESOLUTION

Make decisions using a structured approach that evaluates identified alternatives against established criteria.

Decisions are based on an evaluation of alternatives using established criteria. SG 1

Establish and use guidelines to determine which issues are subject to a structured decision analysis and resolution process. SP 1.1

Select the decision-making techniques. SP 1.2

Establish the evaluation criteria and their relative ranking. SP 1.3

Identify alternative solutions to issues. SP 1.4

Evaluate alternative solutions using the documented criteria. SP 1.5

Select solutions from the alternatives based on the evaluation criteria. SP 1.6

The process is institutionalized as a defined process. GG 3

Commitment to Perform

Establish and maintain an organizational policy for planning and performing the requirements development process. GP 2.1 (CO 1)

Ability to Perform

Establish and maintain the description of a defined requirements development process. GP 3.1 (AB 1)

Establish and maintain the requirements and objectives, and plans for performing the requirements development process. GP 2.2 (AB 2)

Provide adequate resources for performing the requirements development process, developing the work products and providing the services of the process. GP 2.3 (AB 3)

Assign responsibility and authority for performing the process, developing the work products, and providing the services of the requirements development process. GP 2.4 (AB 4)

Train the people performing or supporting the requirements development process as needed. GP 2.5 (AB 5)

Directing Implementation

Place designated work products of the requirements development process under appropriate levels of configuration management. GP 2.6 (DI 1)

Identify and involve the relevant stakeholders of the requirements development process as planned. GP 2.7 (DI 2)

Monitor and control the requirements development process against the plan and take appropriate corrective action. GP 2.8 (DI 3)

Collect work products, measures, measurement results, and improvement information derived from planning and performing the requirements development process to support the future use and improvement of the organization's processes and process assets. GP 3.2 (DI 4)

Verifying Implementation

Objectively evaluate adherence of the requirements development process and the work products and services of the process to the applicable requirements, objectives, and standards, and address noncompliance. GP 2.9 (VE 1)

Review the activities, status, and results of the requirements development process with higher-level management and resolve issues. GP 2.10 (VE 2)

ORGANIZATIONAL ENVIRONMENT FOR INTEGRATION

Provide an IPPD infrastructure and manage people for integration.

An infrastructure that maximizes the productivity of people and effects the collaboration necessary for integration is provided. SG 1

Establish and maintain a shared vision for the organization. SP 1.1

Establish and maintain an integrated work environment that supports IPPD by enabling collaboration and concurrent development. SP 1.2

Identify the unique skills needed to support the IPPD environment. SP 1.3

People are managed to nurture the integrative and collaborative behaviors of an IPPD environment. SG 2

Establish and maintain leadership mechanisms to enable timely collaboration. SP 2.1

Establish and maintain incentives for adopting and demonstrating integrative and collaborative behaviors at all levels of the organization. SP 2.2

Establish and maintain organizational guidelines to balance team and home organization responsibilities. SP 2.3

The process is institutionalized as a defined process. GG 3

Commitment to Perform

Establish and maintain an organizational policy for planning and performing the requirements development process. GP 2.1 (CO 1)

Ability to Perform

Establish and maintain the description of a defined requirements development process. GP 3.1 (AB 1)

Establish and maintain the requirements and objectives, and plans for performing the requirements development process. GP 2.2 (AB 2)

Provide adequate resources for performing the requirements development process, developing the work products and providing the services of the process. GP 2.3 (AB 3)

Assign responsibility and authority for performing the process, developing the work products, and providing the services of the requirements development process. GP 2.4 (AB 4)

Train the people performing or supporting the requirements development process as needed. GP 2.5 (AB 5)

Directing Implementation

Place designated work products of the requirements development process under appropriate levels of configuration management. GP 2.6 (DI 1)

Identify and involve the relevant stakeholders of the requirements development process as planned. GP 2.7 (DI 2)

Monitor and control the requirements development process against the plan and take appropriate corrective action. GP 2.8 (DI 3)

Collect work products, measures, measurement results, and improvement information derived from planning and performing the requirements development process to support the future use and improvement of the organization's processes and process assets. GP 3.2 (DI 4)

Verifying Implementation

Objectively evaluate adherence of the requirements development process and the work products and services of the process to the applicable requirements, objectives, and standards, and address noncompliance. GP 2.9 (VE 1)

Review the activities, status, and results of the requirements development process with higher-level management and resolve issues. GP 2.10 (VE 2)

Maturity Level: 4

ORGANIZATIONAL PROCESS PERFORMANCE

Establish and maintain a quantitative understanding of the performance of the organization's set of standard processes, and to provide the process performance data, baselines, and models to quantitatively manage the organization's projects.

Baselines and models that characterize the expected process performance of the organization's set of standard processes are established and maintained. SG 1

Select the processes or process elements in the organization's set of standard processes that are to be included in the organization's process performance analyses. SP 1.1

Establish and maintain definitions of the measures that are to be included in the organization's process performance analyses. SP 1.2

Establish and maintain quantitative objectives for quality and process performance for the organization. SP 1.3

Establish and maintain the organization's process performance baselines. SP 1.4

Establish and maintain the process performance models for the organization's set of standard processes. SP 1.5

The process is institutionalized as a defined process. GG 3

Commitment to Perform

Establish and maintain an organizational policy for planning and performing the organizational process performance process. GP 2.1 (CO 1)

Ability to Perform

Establish and maintain the description of a defined organizational process performance process. GP 3.1 (AB 1)

Establish and maintain the requirements and objectives, and plans for performing the organizational process performance process. GP 2.2 (AB 2)

Provide adequate resources for performing the organizational process performance process, developing the work products and providing the services of the process. GP 2.3 (AB 3)

Assign responsibility and authority for performing the process, developing the work products, and providing the services of the organizational process performance process. GP 2.4 (AB 4)

Train the people performing or supporting the organizational process performance process as needed. GP 2.5 (AB 5)

Directing Implementation

Place designated work products of the organizational process performance process under appropriate levels of configuration management. GP 2.6 (DI 1)

Identify and involve the relevant stakeholders of the organizational process performance process as planned. GP 2.7 (DI 2)

Monitor and control the organizational process performance process against the plan and take appropriate corrective action. GP 2.8 (DI 3)

Collect work products, measures, measurement results, and improvement information derived from planning and performing the organizational process performance process to support the future use and improvement of the organization's processes and process assets. GP 3.2 (DI 4)

Verifying Implementation

Objectively evaluate adherence of the organizational process performance process and the work products and services of the process to the applicable requirements, objectives, and standards, and address noncompliance. GP 2.9 (VE 1)

Review the activities, status, and results of the organizational process performance process with higher-level management and resolve issues. GP 2.10 (VE 2)

Quantitative Project Management

Quantitatively manage the project's defined process to achieve the project's established quality and process performance objectives.

The project is quantitatively managed using quality and process performance objectives. SG 1

Establish and maintain the project's quality and process performance objectives. SP 1.1

Select the processes and process elements that comprise the project's defined process based on historical stability and capability data. SP 1.2

Select the subprocesses of the project's defined process that will be statistically managed. SP 1.3

Monitor the project to determine whether the project's objectives for quality and process performance will be satisfied, and take corrective action as appropriate. SP 1.4

The performance of selected subprocesses within the project's defined process is statistically managed. SG 2

Select the measures and analytic techniques to be used in statistically managing the selected subprocesses. SP 2.1

Establish and maintain an understanding of the variance of the selected subprocesses using the selected measures and analytic techniques. SP 2.2

Monitor the performance of the selected subprocesses to determine their capability to satisfy their quality and process performance objectives, and take corrective action as necessary. SP 2.3

Record statistical and quality management data in the organization's measurement repository. SP 2.4

The process is institutionalized as a defined process. GG 3

Commitment to Perform

Establish and maintain an organizational policy for planning and performing the organizational process performance process. GP 2.1 (CO 1)

Ability to Perform

Establish and maintain the description of a defined organizational process performance process. GP 3.1 (AB 1)

Establish and maintain the requirements and objectives, and plans for performing the organizational process performance process. GP 2.2 (AB 2)

Provide adequate resources for performing the organizational process performance process, developing the work products and providing the services of the process. GP 2.3 (AB 3)

Assign responsibility and authority for performing the process, developing the work products, and providing the services of the organizational process performance process. GP 2.4 (AB 4)

Train the people performing or supporting the organizational process performance process as needed. GP 2.5 (AB 5)

Directing Implementation

Place designated work products of the organizational process performance process under appropriate levels of configuration management. GP 2.6 (DI 1)

Identify and involve the relevant stakeholders of the organizational process performance process as planned. GP 2.7 (DI 2)

Monitor and control the organizational process performance process against the plan and take appropriate corrective action. GP 2.8 (DI 3)

Collect work products, measures, measurement results, and improvement information derived from planning and performing the organizational process performance process to support the future use and improvement of the organization's processes and process assets. GP 3.2 (DI 4)

Verifying Implementation

Objectively evaluate adherence of the organizational process performance process and the work products and services of the process to the applicable requirements, objectives, and standards, and address noncompliance. GP 2.9 (VE 1)

Review the activities, status, and results of the organizational process performance process with higher-level management and resolve issues. GP 2.10 (VE 2)

Maturity Level: 5

ORGANIZATIONAL INNOVATION AND DEPLOYMENT

Select and deploy incremental and innovative improvements that measurably improve the organization's processes and technologies. The improvements support the organization's quality and process performance objectives as derived from the organization's business objectives.

Process and technology improvements that contribute to meeting quality and process performance objectives are selected. SG 1

Collect and analyze process and technology improvement proposals. SP 1.1

Identify innovative improvements that would increase the organization's quality and process performance. SP 1.2

Pilot process and technology improvements to select which ones to implement. SP 1.3

Select process and technology improvement proposals for deployment across the organization. SP 1.4

Measurable improvements to the organization's processes and technologies are continually and systematically deployed. SG 2

Establish and maintain the plans for deploying the selected process and technology improvements. SP 2.1

Manage the deployment of the selected process and technology improvements. SP 2.2

Measure the effects of the deployed process and technology improvements. SP 2.3

The process is institutionalized as a defined process. GG 3

Commitment to Perform

Establish and maintain an organizational policy for planning and performing the organizational innovation and deployment process. GP 2.1 (CO 1)

Ability to Perform

Establish and maintain the description of a defined organizational innovation and deployment process. GP 3.1 (AB 1)

Establish and maintain the requirements and objectives, and plans for performing the organizational innovation and deployment process. GP 2.2 (AB 2)

Provide adequate resources for performing the organizational innovation and deployment process, developing the work products and providing the services of the process. GP 2.3 (AB 3)

Assign responsibility and authority for performing the process, developing the work products, and providing the services of the organizational innovation and deployment process. GP 2.4 (AB 4)

Train the people performing or supporting the organizational innovation and deployment process as needed. GP 2.5 (AB 5)

Directing Implementation

Place designated work products of the organizational innovation and deployment process under appropriate levels of configuration management. GP 2.6 (DI 1)

Identify and involve the relevant stakeholders of the organizational innovation and deployment process as planned. GP 2.7 (DI 2)

Monitor and control the organizational innovation and deployment process against the plan and take appropriate corrective action. GP 2.8 (DI 3)

Collect work products, measures, measurement results, and improvement information derived from planning and performing the organizational innovation and deployment process to support the future use and improvement of the organization's processes and process assets. GP 3.2 (DI 4)

Verifying Implementation

Objectively evaluate adherence of the organizational innovation and deployment process and the work products and services of the process to the applicable requirements, objectives, and standards, and address noncompliance. GP 2.9 (VE 1)

Review the activities, status, and results of the organizational innovation and deployment process with higher-level management and resolve issues. GP 2.10 (VE 2)

CAUSAL ANALYSIS AND RESOLUTION

Identify causes of defects and other problems and take action to prevent them from occurring in the future.

Root causes of defects and other problems are systematically determined. SG 1

Select the defects and other problems for analysis. SP 1.1

Perform causal analysis of selected defects and other problems and propose actions to address them. SP 1.2

Root causes of defects and other problems are systematically addressed to prevent their future occurrence. SG 2

Implement the selected action proposals that were developed in causal analysis. SP 2.1

Evaluate the effect of changes on process performance. SP 2.2

Record causal analysis and resolution data for use across the project and organization. SP 2.3

The process is institutionalized as a defined process. GG 3

Commitment to Perform

Establish and maintain an organizational policy for planning and performing the organizational innovation and deployment process. GP 2.1 (CO 1)

Ability to Perform

Establish and maintain the description of a defined organizational innovation and deployment process. GP 3.1 (AB 1)

Establish and maintain the requirements and objectives, and plans for performing the organizational innovation and deployment process. GP 2.2 (AB 2)

Provide adequate resources for performing the organizational innovation and deployment process, developing the work products and providing the services of the process. GP 2.3 (AB 3)

Assign responsibility and authority for performing the process, developing the work products, and providing the services of the organizational innovation and deployment process. GP 2.4 (AB 4)

Train the people performing or supporting the organizational innovation and deployment process as needed. GP 2.5 (AB 5)

Directing Implementation

Place designated work products of the organizational innovation and deployment process under appropriate levels of configuration management. GP 2.6 (DI 1)

Identify and involve the relevant stakeholders of the organizational innovation and deployment process as planned. GP 2.7 (DI 2)

Monitor and control the organizational innovation and deployment process against the plan and take appropriate corrective action. GP 2.8 (DI 3)

Collect work products, measures, measurement results, and improvement information derived from planning and performing the organizational innovation and deployment process to support the future use and improvement of the organization's processes and process assets. GP 3.2 (DI 4)

Verifying Implementation

Objectively evaluate adherence of the organizational innovation and deployment process and the work products and services of the process to the applicable requirements, objectives, and standards, and address noncompliance. GP 2.9 (VE 1)

Review the activities, status, and results of the organizational innovation and deployment process with higher-level management and resolve issues. GP 2.10 (VE 2)

Appendix C

References

Bate, Roger, et al. *Systems Engineering Capability Maturity Model, Version 1.1.* Pittsburgh, PA: Enterprise Process Improvement Collaboration and Software Engineering Institute, Carnegie Mellon University, November 1995.

Britcher, Robert. *The Limits of Software.* Reading, MA: Addison-Wesley, 1999.

Carr, M., and W. N. Crowder. *Continuous Appraisal Method (CAM): A New Paradigm for Benchmarking Process Maturity.* Proceedings of the Tenth Annual International Symposium of the International Council on Systems Engineering (INCOSE), Minneapolis, MN, July 2000.

Clouse, Aaron, and R. Shaw. *An Integrated Product Development Process Case Study.* Proceedings of the Sixth Annual International Symposium of the International Council on Systems Engineering (INCOSE), Boston, MA, July 7–11, 1996, vol. I, pp. 541–546.

CMMI Product Development Team. *Standard CMMI Assessment Method for Process Improvement: Method Description (SCAMPI), Version 1.0.* CMU/SEI-2000-TR-009.

CMMI Product Development Team. *Assessment Requirements for CMMI (ARC), Version 1.0.* CMU/SEI-2000-TR-011, Aug. 2000.

Crosby, P. B. *Quality Is Free: The Art of Making Quality Certain.* New York: McGraw-Hill, 1979.

Curtis, Bill, William E. Hefley, and Sally Miller. *People Capability Maturity Model (CMU/SEI-95-MM-002).* Pittsburgh, PA: Software Engineering Institute, Carnegie Mellon University, Sept. 1995.

Deming, W. Edwards. *Out of the Crisis.* Cambridge, MA: MIT Center for Advanced Engineering, 1986.

Department of Defense. *DoD Directive 5000.1: Defense Acquisition.* Washington, DC: Department of Defense, 1991.

Department of Defense. *DoD Regulation 5000.2: Mandatory Procedures for Major Defense Acquisition Programs and Major Automated Information Systems.* Washington, DC: Department of Defense, 1996.

Department of Defense. *DoD Guide to Integrated Product and Process Development (Version 1.0).* Washington, DC: Office of the Under Secretary of Defense (Acquisition and Technology), Feb. 5, 1996. http://www.acq.osd.mil/te/survey/table_of_contents.html.

Department of Defense. *Defense Acquisition Deskbook, Version 3.2.* http://web2.deskbook.osd.mil/default.asp. (This Web site is continually updated.)

Dunaway, D., and S. Masters. *CMM-Based Appraisal for Internal Process Improvement (CBA IPI): Method Description (CMU/SEI-96-TR-007).* Pittsburgh, PA: Software Engineering Institute, Carnegie Mellon University, April 1996.

EIA Interim Standard, Systems Engineering Capability. EIA/IS 731 (Part 1: Model, EIA/IS 731-1, V 1.0; Part 2: Appraisal Method, EIA/IS 731-2, V 1.0), 1999.

Eisner, H. *Essentials of Project and Systems Engineering Management.* New York: Wiley Interscience, 1997.

Federal Aviation Administration—Integrated Capability Maturity Model, Version 1.0. November 1997. http://www.faa.gov/aio/iCMM/FAA.htm.

Ferguson, Jack, Jack Cooper, Michael Falat, Matthew Fisher, Anthony Guido, Jack Marciniak, J. Matejceck, and R. Webster. *Software Acquisition Capability Maturity Model Version 1.01 (CMU/SEI-96-TR-020).* Pittsburgh, PA: Software Engineering Institute, Carnegie Mellon University, Dec. 1996.

Freeman, D., M. Hinkey, and J. Martak. *Integrated Engineering Process Covering All Engineering Disciplines,* SEPG99.

Goldenson, D., and J. Herbsleb. *After the Appraisal: A Systematic Survey of Process Improvement, Its Benefits, and Factors That Influence Success.* CMU/SEI-95-TR-009. Pittsburgh, PA: Software Engineering Institute, Carnegie Mellon University, 1995.

Hayes, W., and D. Zubrow. *Moving On Up: Data and Experience Doing CMM-Based Process Improvement.* CMU/SEI-95-TR-008. Pittsburgh, PA: Software Engineering Institute, Carnegie Mellon University, 1995.

Herbsleb, James, David Zubrow, Dennis Goldenson, Will Hayes, and Mark Paulk. "Software Quality and the Capability Maturity Model." *Communications of the ACM,* 40, June 1977, 30–40.

Humphrey, Watts S. *Managing the Software Process.* Reading, MA: Addison-Wesley, 1989.

Ibrahim, Linda. *Using an Integrated Capability Maturity Model—The FAA Experience.* Proceedings of the Tenth Annual International Symposium of the International Council on Systems Engineering (INCOSE), Minneapolis, MN, July 2000, pp. 643–648.

Ibrahim, Rosalind, and I. Hirmanpour. *The Subject Matter of Process Improvement: A Topic and Reference Source for Software Engineering Educators and Trainers.* CMU/SEI-95-TR-003. May 1995.

IEEE Standard Glossary of Software Engineering Terminology. IEEE Standard 610.12-1990. New York: Institute of Electrical and Electronics Engineers, 1990.

International Organization for Standardization. *ISO 9000: International Standard.* New York: International Organization for Standardization, 1987.

International Organization for Standardization and International Electrotechnical Commission. *Information Technology: Software Life Cycle Processes (ISO 12207).* Geneva, Switzerland: International Organization for Standardization/International Electrotechnical Commission, 1995.

Juran, J. M. *Juran on Planning for Quality.* New York: MacMillan, 1988.

Masters, S., and C. Bothwell. *CMM Appraisal Framework (CMU/SEI-95-TR-001).* Pittsburgh, PA: Software Engineering Institute, Carnegie Mellon University, Feb. 1995.

Paulk, Mark. *Software Capability Maturity Model (SW-CMM) Case Study Bibliography [online]*. 1998. http://www.sei.cmu.edu/activities/cmm/docs/roi.html.

Paulk, Mark C., "The Evolution of the SEI's Capability Maturity Model for Software." *Software Process—Improvement and Practice*, 1995, pp. 3–15.

Paulk, Mark C., et al. *Capability Maturity Model for Software, Version 1.1.* CMU/SEI-93-TR-24; also ESC-TR-93-177. Pittsburgh, PA: Software Engineering Institute, Carnegie Mellon University, Feb. 1993.

Radice, R. A., J. T. Harding, P. E. Munnis, and R. W. Philips. "A Programming Process Study." *IBM System Journals*, 2/3, 1999.

Radice, R. A., and R. W. Phillips. *Software Engineering, an Industrial Approach, vol. 1.* Englewood Cliffs, NJ: Prentice Hall, 1988.

Software Engineering Institute. *CMMI A—Specification, Version 1.3.* July 15, 1998. http://www.sei. cmu.edu/cmm/cmmi/cmmi.spec.html.

Software Program Managers Network. *Program Managers Guide to Software Acquisition Best Practices, Version V.2.* April 1997. http://www.spmn.com/products_guidebooks.html.

Systems Engineering Capability Assessment Model, Version 1.50. International Council on Systems Engineering, June 1996.

Womack, James P., and Daniel Jones. *Lean Thinking.* New York: Simon and Schuster, 1996.

Appendix D

Resources

This appendix lists some other places where readers can look for information and support. While certainly not complete, this list should provide a springboard for further research. If you know of other resources that you would like to share, please contact us at cmmi-distilled@ awl.com. We will be maintaining an updated list of resources and contacts at **http//www.awl.com/cseng/titles/0-201-73500-8.**

Electronic Industries Alliance

The Electronic Industries Alliance (EIA) is a partnership of electronic and high-tech associations and companies committed to shared knowledge and shared influence. EIA includes the Consumer Electronics Association (CEA); Electronic Components, Assemblies, Equipment, and Supplies Association (ECA); Electronic Industries Foundation (EIF); Government Information Technology Association (GEIA); JEDEC—Solid State Technology Association; and Telecommunications Industry Association (TIA). Accredited by the American National Standards Institute (ANSI), EIA provides a forum for industry to develop standards and publications in the major technical areas of electronic components, consumer electronics, electronic information, and telecommunications.

In addition, EIA publishes standards and technical publications to serve the public interest by minimizing misunderstandings between manufacturers and purchasers, facilitating interchangeability and improvement of products, and assisting purchasers in quickly selecting and obtaining the proper product for a particular need. The EIA Interim Standard, Systems Engineering Capability, EIA/IS 731, was one of the three source models for CMMI. More on EIA may be found at www.eia.org.

European Software Process Improvement Foundation

The European Software Process Improvement Foundation (ESPI) promotes good software practice in Europe through the adoption of software process improvement. It provides information and training to assist those starting out on the process improvement journey, and it facilitates the exchange of knowledge and experience between practicing organizations. ESPI and the Software Engineering Institute (SEI) cosponsor the European Software Engineering Process Group (E-SEPG) Conference every spring. ESPI's Web site is www.espi.co.uk/.

Federal Aviation Administration

The Federal Aviation Administration (FAA) has been involved with integrated process improvement since 1995 and released the first integrated CMM, the FAA-iCMM, in 1997. The agency has provided a steering group member and a developer to the CMMI project, and it has publicly expressed a desire to migrate from the FAA-iCMM to the CMMI at an appropriate time in the near future. For information on the FAA-iCMM and FAA's experience with integrated process improvement, visit its Web site at www.faa.gov/aio/iCMM/.

Institute of Electrical and Electronic Engineers

The Institute of Electrical and Electronic Engineers (IEEE) is a nonprofit, technical professional association with more than 350,000 members in 150 countries. Thanks to the expertise of its members, the IEEE is a leading authority in technical areas ranging from computer engineering, biomedical technology, and telecommunications, to electric power, aerospace, and consumer electronics, among others. Through its technical publishing, conferences, and consensus-based standards activities, the IEEE

- Produces 30% of the world's published literature on electrical engineering, computers, and control technology,
- Holds more than 300 major conferences annually, and
- Has more than 800 active standards and 700 standards under development.

Of particular interest to CMMI users are the IEEE Computer Society (www.computer.org/) and the IEEE Engineering Management Society (www.ewh.ieee.org/sox/ems/). IEEE can support your integrated process improvement activities through conferences, collections of best practices, standards, cutting-edge engineering articles, and networking with its international members. You can reach the IEEE at www.ieee.org.

International Council on Systems Engineering

The International Council on Systems Engineering (INCOSE) is an international nonprofit organization formed to develop, nurture, and enhance the systems engineering approach to multidisciplinary system product development. It was established in 1990 and has grown to serve a membership of more than 3900 systems engineering professionals. INCOSE was the primary force behind the development of EIA/IS 731, and it has provided systems engineering expertise throughout the CMMI project.

INCOSE offers several categories of systems engineering resources to its members and the public:

- INCOSE hotlist: links to items of interest to systems engineers on the Internet
- INCOSE Web site library index
- INCOSE's Yellow Pages: vendors of interest to systems engineers
- List of INCOSE publications
- Standards references: a detailed standards reference
- Technical Committee, Working Groups, and Interest Groups: resources such as the Capability Assessment Working Group

See INCOSE's Web site at www.incose.org.

National Defense Industrial Association

As the "Voice of the Industrial Base," the National Defense Industrial Association (NDIA) educates and provides a link for its members to defense officials and leaders of industry. Located in Arlington, Virginia, it stands in a key position to share issues and influence defense policies related to acquisition and procurement. NDIA, a nonpartisan, non-profit international association founded in 1997, leads the way in communicating industrial perspectives to Congress, the Pentagon, and the American people.

NDIA provides steering committee support and product development team members to CMMI through representatives of its member companies. More about NDIA and its activities may be found at its Web site at www.ndia.org.

Practical Software and Systems Measurement

The Practical Software and Systems Measurement (PSM) project is sponsored by the Department of Defense and the U.S. Army. Its goal is to provide project managers with the objective information needed to successfully meet the cost, schedule, and technical objectives of programs. The measurement methodologies developed by PSM have wide applicability across disciplines and support the measurement aspects of the CMMI products. PSM activities and capabilities are described at the Web site at www.psmsc.com.

Software Engineering Australia

Software Engineering Australia (SEA) is a national organization whose aim is to improve the quality and reliability of software in Australia. SEA works collaboratively, forming domestic and global alliances with government departments, organizations, and professional bodies to drive its mission. Of primary interest to process improvement practitioners is the organization's provision of services for both developers and acquirers of software and software systems support for the continuous but rapid improvement of productivity, timeliness, and quality levels. Training software practitioners and acquirers in best-practice techniques is a priority for SEA, and it continues to add new courses and workshops to its offerings. More on SEA may be found at www.seanational.com. au/index.html.

Software Engineering Institute at Carnegie Mellon University

The Software Engineering Institute at Carnegie Mellon University is a federally funded research and development center (FFRDC) and the world leader in software process improvement technology. Established in 1984, the SEI has as its long-range goal making the acquisition, development, and sustainment of software-intensive systems predictably better, faster, and cheaper for the U.S. Department of Defense. For the SEI, the hallmark of the engineering discipline is predictability: predictable cost, predictable schedule, predictable quality, and predictable functionality. The Institute is committed to the evolution of software engineering away from an ad hoc, labor-intensive, heroic activity. It seeks to facilitate the development of a managed, technology-supported engineering discipline, focused on technical and management practices that yield high-quality systems delivered on time and within expected cost every time. In short, it seeks predictable acquisition, development, and evolution of systems that depend on software.

To this end, the SEI provides a variety of resources for improving management practices. At the center of this effort is its role as the Steward for the CMMI product suite, and its efforts in developing, expanding, or maintaining other Capability Maturity Models (CMMs). The SEI has developed CMMs for software, people, and software acquisition, and it has assisted in the development of CMMs for systems engineering and integrated product development. The SEI's goals in developing CMMs include the following:

- Addressing software and disciplines that affect software
- Providing integrated process improvement reference models
- Building broad community consensus
- Harmonizing with standards
- Enabling efficient improvement across disciplines

Currently, the highest priority of the management practices work at the SEI is CMM Integration. For information on CMMI and the many other resources available to support process improvement, see the SEI's Web site at www.sei.cmu.edu.

Software Engineers Association of Japan

Software Engineers Association of Japan (SEA Japan) was established in December 1985 to create a vehicle for technical exchange between software engineers in a wide variety of fields. Its goal is to provide a mechanism for technology transfer that does not naturally exist within Japanese society. SEA Japan's major activities include publication of a monthly newsletter (*SEAMAIL*); support of local chapters and special-interest groups; and seminars, workshops, and symposia, held in cooperation with related academic/professional societies in and outside Japan.

At present, SEA Japan has approximately 500 individual members and more than 20 institutional members. Seven local chapters and a number of special-interest groups, including one on software process, are currently in operation. SEA Japan can be found on the Web at www. iijnet.or.jp/sea/index-e.html.

Software Productivity Consortium

The Software Productivity Consortium (SPC) is a nonprofit partnership of industry, government, and academia. For its more than ninety member companies, SPC provides technologies and expertise needed to improve the quality, reliability, and time-to-market performance of systems and software. The Consortium's technical program serves to integrate the essential process-based activities of integrated systems and software development. SPC offers courses in a variety of improvement models and methods, including CMM for Software and CMMI, measurement and software engineering techniques, and integrated system and software process development. The Consortium provides appraisal and consulting services, and it publishes a quarterly newsletter and other technical articles concerning systems engineering, software engineering, system and software integration, and process improvement. For more information, see www.software.org.

Software Technology Support Center

The Air Force Software Technology Support Center (STSC) at Hill Air Force Base in Ogden, Utah, was established to help Air Force organizations identify, evaluate and adopt technologies that improve software product quality, production efficiency, and predictability. Using the term technology in its broadest sense to include processes, methods, techniques, and tools that enhance human capability, STSC focuses on field-proven technologies that will benefit the DoD mission. Along with its support and consulting roles, STSC publishes *CrossTalk, The Journal of Defense Software Engineering* and maintains an extensive web site at www.stsc.hill.af.mil. It also co-hosts the annual Defense Software Technology Conference in Salt Lake City. A strong proponent of CMMI, STSC has been a leader in piloting CMMI training and assessment activities and so can provide a wealth of practical experience for help in using CMMI.

SEI figure list *(continued from page iv)*

Index

The SEI Series in Software Engineering

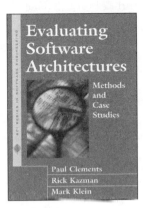

Evaluating Software Architectures
Methods and Case Studies
Paul Clements, Rick Kazman, and Mark Klein

This book is a comprehensive, step-by-step guide to software architecture evaluation, describing specific methods that can quickly and inexpensively mitigate enormous risk in software projects. The methods are illustrated both by case studies and by sample artifacts put into play during an evaluation: viewgraphs, scenarios, final reports —everything you need to evaluate an architecture in your own organization.

0-201-70482-X • Hardcover • 304 Pages • ©2002

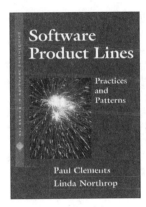

Software Product Lines
Practices and Patterns
Paul Clements and Linda Northrop

Building product lines from common assets can yield remarkable improvements in productivity, time to market, product quality, and customer satisfaction. This book provides a framework of specific practices, with detailed case studies, to guide the implementation of product lines in your own organization.

0-201-70332-7 • Hardcover • 576 Pages • ©2002

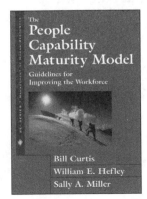

The People Capability Maturity Model
Guidelines for Improving the Workforce
Bill Curtis, William E. Hefley, and Sally A. Miller

Employing the process maturity framework of the Software CMM, the People Capability Maturity Model (People CMM) describes best practices for managing and developing an organization's workforce. This book describes the People CMM and the key practices that comprise each of its maturity levels, and shows how to apply the model in guiding organizational improvements. Includes case studies.

0-201-60445-0 • Hardback • 448 Pages • ©2002

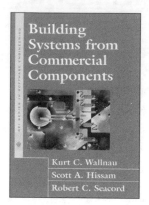

Building Systems from Commercial Components

Kurt C. Wallnau, Scott A. Hissam, and Robert C. Seacord

Commercial components are increasingly seen as an effective means to save time and money in building large software systems. However, integrating pre-existing components, with pre-existing specifications, is a delicate and difficult task. This book describes specific engineering practices needed to accomplish that task successfully, illustrating the techniques described with case studies and examples.

0-201-70064-6 • Hardcover • 416 pages • ©2002

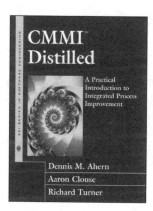

CMMI Distilled

A Practical Introduction to Integrated Process Improvement
Dennis M. Ahern, Aaron Clouse, and Richard Turner

The Capability Maturity Model Integration (CMMI) is the latest version of the popular CMM framework, designed specifically to integrate an organization's process improvement activities across disciplines. This book provides a concise introduction to the CMMI, highlighting the benefits of integrated process improvement, explaining key features of the new framework, and suggesting how to choose appropriate models and representations for your organization.

0-201-73500-8 • Paperback • 240 pages • ©2001

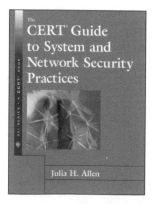

The CERT Guide to System and Network Security Practices

By Julia H. Allen

The CERT Coordination Center helps systems administrators secure systems connected to public networks, develops key security practices, and provides timely security implementations. This book makes CERT practices and implementations available in book form, and offers step-by-step guidance for protecting your systems and networks against malicious and inadvertent compromise.

0-201-73723-X • Paperback • 480 pages • ©2001

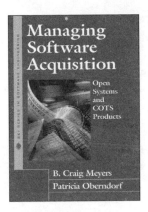

Managing Software Acquisition
Open Systems and COTS Products
B. Craig Meyers and Patricia Oberndorf

The acquisition of open systems and commercial off-the-shelf (COTS) products is an increasingly vital part of large-scale software development, offering significant savings in time and money. This book presents fundamental principles and best practices for successful acquisition and utilization of open systems and COTS products.

0-201-70454-4 • Hardcover • 288 pages • ©2001

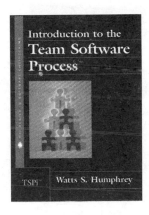

Introduction to the Team Software Process
Watts S. Humphrey

The Team Software Process (TSP) provides software engineers with a framework designed to build and maintain more effective teams. This book, particularly useful for engineers and students trained in the Personal Software Process (PSP), introduces TSP and the concrete steps needed to improve software teamwork.

0-201-47719-X • Hardcover • 496 pages • ©2000

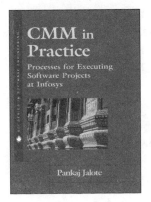

CMM in Practice
Processes for Executing Software Projects at Infosys
Pankaj Jalote

This book describes the implementation of CMM at Infosys Technologies, and illustrates in detail how software projects are executed at this highly mature software development organization. The book examines the various stages in the life cycle of an actual Infosys project as a running example throughout the book, describing the technical and management processes used to initiate, plan, and execute it.

0-201-61626-2 • Hardcover • 400 pages • ©2000

Measuring the Software Process

Statistical Process Control for Software Process Improvement
William A. Florac and Anita D. Carleton

This book shows how to use measurements to manage and improve software processes within your organization. It explains specifically how quality characteristics of software products and processes can be quantified, plotted, and analyzed, so that the performance of software development activities can be predicted, controlled, and guided to achieve both business and technical goals.

0-201-60444-2 • Hardcover • 272 pages • ©1999

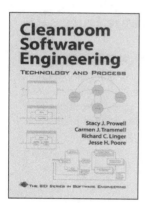

Cleanroom Software Engineering

Technology and Process
Stacy Prowell, Carmen J. Trammell, Richard C. Linger, and Jesse H. Poore

This book provides an introduction and in-depth description of the Cleanroom approach to high-quality software development. Following an explanation of basic Cleanroom theory and practice, the authors draw on their extensive experience in industry to elaborate the Cleanroom development and certification process and show how this process is compatible with the Capability Maturity Model (CMM).

0-201-85480-5 • Hardcover • 400 pages • ©1999

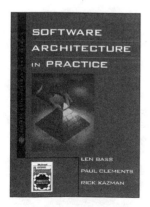

Software Architecture in Practice

Len Bass, Paul Clements, and Rick Kazman

This book introduces the concepts and practice of software architecture, not only covering essential technical topics for specifying and validating a system, but also emphasizing the importance of the business context in which large systems are designed. Enhancing both technical and organizational discussions, key points are illuminated by substantial case studies.

0-201-19930-0 • Hardcover • 480 pages • ©1998

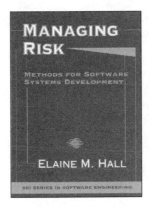

Managing Risk
Methods for Software Systems Development
By Elaine M. Hall

Written for busy professionals charged with delivering high-quality products on time and within budget, this comprehensive guide describes a success formula for managing software risk. The book follows a five-part risk management road map designed to take you from crisis to control of your software project.

0-201-25592-8 • Hardcover • 400 pages • ©1998

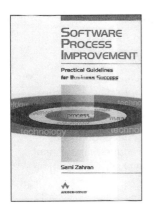

Software Process Improvement
Practical Guidelines for Business Success
By Sami Zahran

This book will help you manage and control the quality of your organization's software products by showing you how to develop a preventive culture of disciplined and continuous process improvement.

0-201-17782-X • Hardcover • 480 pages • ©1998

Introduction to the Personal Software Process
By Watts S. Humphrey

This workbook provides a hands-on introduction to the basic discipline of software engineering, as expressed in the author's well-known Personal Software Process (PSP). By applying the forms and methods of PSP described in the book, you can learn to manage your time effectively and to monitor the quality of your work, with enormous benefits in both regards.

0-201-54809-7 • Paperback • 304 pages • ©1997

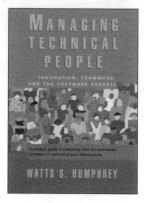

Managing Technical People
Innovation, Teamwork, and the Software Process
By Watts S. Humphrey

Drawing on the author's extensive experience as a senior manager of software development at IBM, this book describes proven techniques for managing technical professionals. The author shows specifically how to identify, motivate, and organize innovative people, while tying leadership practices to improvements in the software process.

0-201-54597-7 • Paperback • 352 pages • ©1997

The Capability Maturity Model
Guidelines for Improving the Software Process
By Carnegie Mellon University/Software Engineering Institute

This book provides the authoritative description and technical overview of the Capability Maturity Model (CMM), with guidelines for improving software process management. The CMM provides software professionals in government and industry with the ability to identify, adopt, and use sound management and technical practices for delivering quality software on time and within budget.

0-201-54664-7 • Hardcover • 464 pages • ©1995

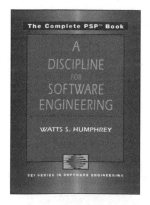

A Discipline for Software Engineering
The Complete PSP Book
By Watts S. Humphrey

This book scales down to a personal level the successful methods developed by the author to help managers and organizations evaluate and improve their software capabilities—methods comprising the Personal Software Process (PSP). The author's aim with PSP is to help individual software practitioners develop the skills and habits needed to plan, track, and analyze large and complex projects, and to develop high-quality products.

0-201-54610-8 • Hardcover • 816 pages • ©1995

Software Design Methods for Concurrent and Real-Time Systems
By Hassan Gomaa

This book provides a basic understanding of concepts and issues in concurrent system design, while surveying and comparing a range of applicable object-oriented design methods. The book describes a practical approach for applying real-time scheduling theory to analyze the performance of real-time designs.

0-201-52577-1 • Hardcover • 464 pages • ©1993

Managing the Software Process
By Watts S. Humphrey

This landmark book introduces the author's methods, now commonly practiced in industry, for improving software development and maintenance processes. Emphasizing the basic principles and priorities of the software process, the book's sections are organized in a natural way to guide organizations through needed improvement activities.

0-201-18095-2 • Hardcover • 512 pages • ©1989

Other titles of interest from Addison-Wesley

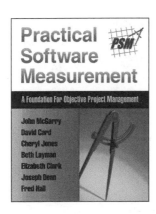

Practical Software Measurement
A Foundation for Objective Project Management
By John McGarry, David Card, Cheryl Jones, Beth Layman, Elizabeth Clark, Joseph Dean, and Fred Hall

A critical task in developing and maintaining software-intensive systems is to meet project cost, schedule, and technical objectives. This official guide to Practical Software Measurement (PSM) shows how to accomplish that task through sound measurement techniques and the development of a software measurement process. It provides a comprehensive description of PSM's techniques and practical guidance based on PSM's actual application in large-scale software projects.

0-201-71516-3 • Hardcover • 512 pages • ©2002

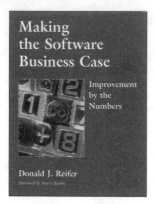

Making the Software Business Case
Improvement by the Numbers
By Donald J. Reifer

This book shows software engineers and managers how to prepare the *business* case for change and improvement. It presents the tricks of the trade developed by this well-known author over many years, tricks that have repeatedly helped his clients win the battle of the budget. The first part of the book addresses the fundamentals associated with creating a business case; the second part uses case studies to illustrate cases made for different types of software improvement initiatives.

0-201-72887-7 • Paperback • 224 pages • ©2002

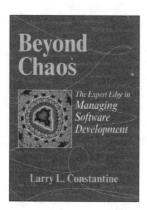

Beyond Chaos
The Expert Edge in Managing Software Development
Larry L. Constantine

The essays in this book, drawn from among the best contributions to Software Development magazine's Management Forum, reveal best practices in managing software projects and organizations. Written by many top names in the field—including Larry Constantine, Karl Wiegers, Capers Jones, Ed Yourdon, Dave Thomas, Meilir Page-Jones, Jim Highsmith, and Steve McConnell—each piece has been selected and edited to provide ideas and suggestions that can be translated into immediate practice.

0-201-71960-6 • Paperback • 400 pages • ©2001

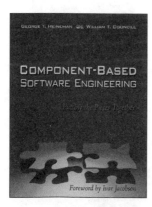

Component-Based Software Engineering
Putting the Pieces Together
By George T. Heineman and William T. Councill

This book provides a comprehensive overview of, and current perspectives on, component-based software engineering (CBSE). With contributions from well-known luminaries in the field, it defines what CBSE really is, details CBSE's benefits and pitfalls, describes CBSE experiences from around the world, and ultimately reveals CBSE's considerable potential for engineering reliable and cost-effective software.

0-201-70485-4 • Hardcover • 880 pages • ©2001

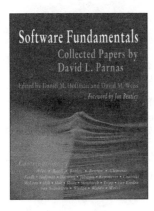

Software Fundamentals

Collected Papers by David L. Parnas
By Daniel M. Hoffman and David M. Weiss

David Parnas's groundbreaking writings capture the essence of the innovations, controversies, challenges, and solutions of the software industry. This book is a collection of his most influential papers in various areas of software engineering, with historical context provided by leading thinkers in the field.

0-201-70369-6 • Hardcover • 688 pages • ©2001

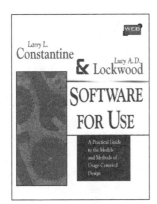

Software for Use

A Practical Guide to the Models and Methods of Usage-Centered Design
by Larry L. Constantine and Lucy A. D. Lockwood

This book describes models and methods that help you deliver more usable software-software that allows users to accomplish tasks with greater ease and efficiency. Aided by concrete techniques, experience-tested examples, and practical tools, it guides you through a systematic software development process called usage-centered design, a process that weaves together two major threads in software development: use cases and essential modeling.

0-201-92478-1 • Hardcover • 608 pages • ©1999

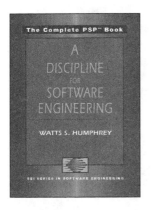

CMM Implementation Guide

Choreographing Software Process Improvement
by Kim Caputo

This book provides detailed instruction on how to put the Capability Maturity Model (CMM) into practice and, thereby, on how to raise an organization to the next higher level of maturity. Drawing on her first-hand experience leading software process improvement groups in a large corporation, the author provides invaluable advice and information for anyone charged specifically with implementing the CMM.

0-201-37938-4 • Hardcover • 336 pages • ©1998

The Mythical Man-Month, Anniversary Edition
Essays on Software Engineering
By Frederick P. Brooks, Jr.

Fred Brooks blends software engineering facts with thought-provoking opinions to offer insight for anyone managing complex projects. Twenty years after the publication of this influential and timeless classic, the author revisited his original ideas and added new thoughts and advice, both for readers already familiar with his work and for those discovering it for the first time.

0-201-83595-9 • Paperback • 336 pages • ©1995
